A HISTORY OF BROOKLYN BRIDGE PARK

Aerial view of Brooklyn
Bridge Park site, ca. 1980.
© MICHAEL VAN VALKENBURGH
ASSOCIATES, INC.

A HISTORY OF

BROOKLYN

Aerial view of future Brooklyn
Bridge Park, ca. 1980.
© MICHAEL VAN VALKENBURGH
ASSOCIATES, INC.

NANCY WEBSTER + DAVID SHIRLEY

BRIDGE PARK

HOW A COMMUNITY RECLAIMED AND TRANSFORMED NEW YORK CITY'S WATERFRONT

COLUMBIA UNIVERSITY PRESS | NEW YORK

COLUMBIA UNIVERSITY PRESS
Publishers Since 1893
New York   Chichester, West Sussex
cup.columbia.edu

Library of Congress Cataloging-in-Publication Data

Names: Webster, Nancy, 1960– author. | Shirley, David, 1955– author.
Title: A history of Brooklyn Bridge Park : how a community reclaimed and transformed New
    York City's waterfront / Nancy Webster and David Shirley.
Description: New York : Columbia University Press, 2016. | Includes bibliographical
    references and index.
Identifiers: LCCN 2016009008 (print) | LCCN 2016019804 (ebook) | ISBN 9780231171229
    (cloth : alk. paper) | ISBN 9780231542944 (ebook)
Subjects: LCSH: Brooklyn Bridge Park (New York, N.Y.)—History. | Parks—New York
    (State)—New York—History.
Classification: LCC F129.B7 W24 2016 (print) | LCC F129.B7 (ebook) | DDC 974.7—dc23
LC record available at https://lccn.loc.gov/2016009008

Columbia University Press books are printed on permanent and durable acid-free paper.
Printed in the United States of America

c 10 9 8 7 6 5 4 3 2 1

COVER AND BOOK DESIGN: VIN DANG
COVER PHOTO: JORGE QUINTEROS © STOCKSY

CONTENTS

ACKNOWLEDGMENTS

W E WOULD LIKE TO EXPRESS OUR THANKS to the following individuals whose memories, advice, and perseverance were essential to completing this history of Brooklyn Bridge Park.

First, thank you to Otis Pearsall and Scott Hand, whose monograph on the early 1980s provided such a valuable stepping off point for our research of the Brooklyn Bridge Park movement.

Thank you to the staff members of the Brooklyn Collection at the Brooklyn Public Library and the Othmer Library at the Brooklyn Historical Society (particularly Deborah Schwartz, president of the Brooklyn Historical Society) for providing us with access to their extensive archives of photographs, reports, institutional records, personal correspondence, and media articles on the history of the west Brooklyn waterfront.

Our interview subjects provided the substance of this narrative and allowed the history of the social movement that gave birth to the park to come alive on the page. As we hope to have successfully demonstrated, many hundreds of people made meaningful contributions to the park. We wish there had been the time and resources to interview more of them.

Thank you to JillEllyn Riley, Nina Collins, Howard Morhaim, and Johnny Temple, all literary sages, who steered us from proposal to publisher. And thank you to Philip Leventhal at Columbia University Press who took the book in hand, shaped it, and made it better.

Marianna Koval, Tensie Whelan, and Regina Myer provided particular assistance in helping us identify key dates, players, and events in the life of the park.

This book could not have been written without the support of the Brooklyn Bridge Park Conservancy, whose board and staff supported the extensive research effort into the origins of the park. A particular thank you goes to former board chairwoman Nancy Bowe and current chairman Mark Baker, who believe deeply and passionately in Brooklyn Bridge Park and the Conservancy and have devoted untold hours to help create this special park on the Brooklyn waterfront.

Finally, every project of worth and import has an overseer who pushes it forward and provides encouragement—as well as the occasional upbraid—to ensure that deadlines are met and quality remains high. We owe our deepest gratitude to Kara Gilmour for her luminous spirit, insight, patience, and steady hand. She got us here.

A HISTORY OF BROOKLYN BRIDGE PARK

THE EVOLUTION OF THE WATERFRONT

Flow on, river! Flow with the flood-tide and ebb with the
   ebb-tide!
Frolic on, crested and scallop-edged waves!
Gorgeous clouds of the sunset! drench with your splendor me,
Or the men and women generations after me!
Cross from shore to shore, countless crowds of passengers!
Stand up, tall masts of Mannahatta! Stand up, beautiful hills of
   Brooklyn!

WALT WHITMAN, "CROSSING BROOKLYN FERRY"

 N A RAINY MONDAY MORNING in late March 2010, a large and illustrious group of New Yorkers crowded together on a granite staircase on a landscaped hillside above the west Brooklyn shoreline, with the spectacular views of New York Harbor, the Brooklyn Bridge, and the lower Manhattan skyline sprawling out beneath them. The occasion for the gathering was the highly anticipated ribbon cutting for Pier 1, the first official section of Brooklyn Bridge Park to be opened to the public. The nine-acre site featured vast green lawns, a playground, and a spacious promenade along the river. New York City mayor Michael Bloomberg and New York governor David Paterson were on hand to voice their appreciation of the achievement, along with an impressive collection of state legislators, city officials, and community leaders and a soggy but enthusiastic group of teenage twirlers from nearby Fort Hamilton High School.

   In the six years since the public celebration at Pier 1, Brooklyn Bridge Park has expanded to include 1.3 miles and close to 85 acres of public space on and adjacent to Piers 1–6, along with the Fulton Ferry Landing area just north of the piers between the Brooklyn and Manhattan Bridges. In addition to the green lawns and playground on Pier 1, the park now includes numerous athletic fields and recreational facilities, a sandy beach for strolling and nonmotorized boating, a row of "sound-attenuating" hills that insulate the park grounds from the noise of the roadways and busy neighborhoods above it, and a continuous "greenway" along the waterfront. Since its opening in 2010, the park has attracted millions of visitors, with thousands of people arriving each day to enjoy the beauty of the landscape and the scenic views of the East River and the lower Manhattan skyline; to use the park's playgrounds and recreational facilities; and to participate in the hundreds of volunteer programs and cultural, educational, and recreational events conducted at the park each year.

ALTHOUGH BROOKLYN BRIDGE PARK STANDS as the crown jewel of the East River waterfront and one of New York City's most popular destinations for both tourists and local residents, it almost never came to be. The realization of the park was the result of a long and challenging process for the committed group of citizens who first envisioned a public space along the west Brooklyn shoreline. The park represents the culmination of a three-decade-long campaign on the part of local residents and community leaders to restore the once-bustling Brooklyn waterfront to public access and control.

The campaign to create a park on the piers began in the early 1980s, when employees of the Port Authority of New York and New Jersey (the independent public agency that owned the vast majority of the property) contacted the leaders of the neighborhood associations that represented the communities adjacent to the waterfront regarding the agency's intentions to dispose of Piers 1–6 on the Brooklyn shoreline of the East River. Changes in the global-shipping industry had recently resulted in the increasing disuse of the property, and state and local political leaders and public authorities, eager to revitalize the city's economy following the recession of the previous decade, viewed the development of the once-thriving but by then mostly abandoned piers as a potential source of revenue and job creation. The Brooklyn community leaders' initial concerns centered on the potential impact of the proposed disposition of the piers on the neighborhoods they represented. Many local residents were particularly worried that high-rise condominiums and other commercial developments would disturb the extraordinary views of the East

River, the Brooklyn Bridge, and the Manhattan skyline that had long been a hallmark of Brooklyn Heights, an affluent neighborhood situated on a high bluff above the East River.

In 1985, the Port Authority joined with the administration of New York City mayor Edward Koch to announce the public authorities' intention to lease the waterfront property for commercial development, confirming the worst fears of a growing number of local residents and inspiring community leaders to replace their initial emphasis on view protection and neighborhood preservation with a proposal for the creation of a public park along the waterfront. What began as a strategic decision (providing local residents with a constructive proposal around which they could rally, rather than a list of concerns and complaints) soon became an abiding passion for a growing number of local residents. The community's newfound commitment to a waterfront park empowered the members of Brooklyn's Community Board 2 to block the public authorities' plans for the commercial development of the piers and inspired the members of the Brooklyn Bridge Park Coalition (an outgrowth of the Piers Committee of the Brooklyn Heights Association [BHA]) to pursue a decade-long campaign to mobilize public support for a park along the piers; enlist the endorsement and financial commitment of local, city, and state officials to the park concept; and develop the guiding principles for the park's design, construction, and ongoing maintenance.

In the early years of the park movement, the general idea of a public space along the piers served as a unifying vision for the residents of the neighborhoods that shared the waterfront and the growing number of local, city, and state officials who lent their support to the project. Disagreements arose, however, as guidelines and plans for the park actually began to take shape in the late 1980s and early 1990s. How were the construction and maintenance of the park to be funded? Which routes should visitors from outside the adjacent neighborhoods use to gain access to the waterfront? Should the park property be devoted to passive or active recreational use? Should portions of the piers be retained for maritime and industrial use? What types of residential or commercial structures, if any, should be included in the park's design? Who should ultimately be in charge of the planning, construction, and maintenance of the park?

Throughout most of the 1990s, the Brooklyn Bridge Park Coalition represented the organizing force behind the park movement and the center for discussion and debate about the major issues involved in the realization of a park along the Brooklyn piers. During this period, the organization's reputation and its ability to work with city government and other stakeholders was marked by both achievement and conflict, and the competing interests of local residents, public authorities, and state and municipal governments at times resulted in controversy, stalled negotiations, and public dissent. Although a number of the Coalition's early leaders and active members left the movement over the years, the organization continued to endure and to maintain its original focus on the realization of the park. Near the end of the decade, following the creation of a pubic entity in charge of the planning of the park, the Coalition renewed its relevance in the park movement by calling for an expansion of the park to include the area between the Brooklyn and Manhattan Bridges, north of the piers, and by advocating for a vital role for the park in the recreational, educational, and cultural life of the city through an ambitious public-programming component.

Since formal planning for the park began in 1998, park advocates successfully overcame a variety of setbacks and hurdles: the terrorist attacks on September 11, 2001; the global financial crisis; the destructive flooding and punishing winds of Hurricane Sandy on October 29, 2012; confusions and delays resulting from the competitive leadership of state and city governments; and the ongoing public controversy about the inclusion of residential housing in the park's design. Today Brooklyn Bridge Park is widely recognized as a world-class waterfront park and a model of financially sustainable and environmentally responsible urban-park development. The park rivals its celebrated counterparts—Central Park and Prospect Park—in its scale, beauty, and popularity, and it ranks as one of the great physical accomplishments in the city's proud history.

In the pages that follow, we describe the conflicts, the compromises, and the achievements that resulted in the creation of Brooklyn Bridge Park. The story of Brooklyn Bridge Park provides insight into the inner workings of city and state planning and the various commercial, political, and community interests that come into play in pursuit of a common goal. The park's history recounts the surprising story of the remarkable things that can happen when a group of concerned citizens rally their community around a common cause and are prepared to stay the course until their vision is realized, even in the face of resistance and controversy. Finally, the creation of Brooklyn Bridge Park reflects the changing nature—understood both literally and metaphorically—of New York City since the mid-1980s. The Brooklyn piers, which had by the 1970s fallen into disrepair and disuse, have now been transformed into a stunning park widely celebrated for its innovative and award-winning design. Along with the recently constructed High Line in Manhattan, Brooklyn Bridge Park stands as a majestic symbol of the gradual rehabilitation and rejuvenation of New York City's waterfront and the cooperative efforts of the city's residents and leaders to transform once-forgotten industrial spaces into beautiful, environmentally sustainable postindustrial parks.

AS THIS BRIEF SUMMARY of the park's history suggests, a wide variety of individuals and institutions have contributed over the years to the realization of Brooklyn Bridge Park. The park in its present form would not exist without the public authorities who released the property for conversion to a park; the community leaders who advocated year after year and built public support for the park; the journalists who openly promoted the park concept; the borough, city, and state officials who agreed on the guidelines for the park's development and provided the funding for its construction; the architects and urban planners who designed the park; and the public entity in charge of its construction and maintenance.

While fully recognizing the important contributions of all the individuals and institutions involved in the park's realization, this book focuses primarily on the experiences and contributions of the local residents of Brooklyn. Behind the activities and contributions of all these groups at every stage of the park's evolution, the citizens of Brooklyn's residential communities immediately adjacent to the waterfront continued to believe in and campaign for the park. More than any other group, the residents of Brooklyn provided the vision, the enthusiasm, and the outspoken commitment that ensured the eventual realization of the park.

At the center of the story of the local park movement is the Brooklyn Bridge Park Coalition. For the past three decades, the Coalition (known today as the Brooklyn Bridge Park Conservancy) has played a leading role in representing the aspirations of the people of Brooklyn for a public park along the piers—from the early negotiations between the Waterfront Subcommittee of the Brooklyn Heights Association (the Coalition's earliest incarnation) and the Port Authority over the appropriate use of the waterfront property to the open conflicts between the Coalition and the public authorities over the commercial development of the piers to the role currently played by the Brooklyn Bridge Park Conservancy in providing programmed activities for and promoting the use of the park.

In telling the story of the activities, controversies, and achievements described in the book, we have relied heavily on the personal testimonies of the people who were most closely involved in the park's realization. Research for the book included in-depth interviews with most of the key persons involved in the park movement, including leaders of the public entities in charge of the waterfront property; elected officials and their staff members who were instrumental in achieving public and financial support for the park; the architects and urban designers who gave visual form to the park concept; and the brownstone Brooklyn community leaders and other neighborhood residents who spearheaded the park movement over the course of three decades. Each of the major events described in the book (from the initial resistance to the commercial development of the Brooklyn piers to the conflicts and compromises between city and state government to the design and construction of the park) has been brought to life through the perspectives and observations of those individuals who were involved in the process. Consistent with the book's focus on the aspirations, frustrations, and achievements of the local community, the majority of these interviews were conducted with the residents of Brooklyn themselves. It is through their voices—and the voices of the public authorities, elected officials, and designers with whom they debated, compromised, and cooperated over the course of thirty years—that the story of Brooklyn Bridge Park will be told.

"Nobody was viewing the site the way we were," recalls early Coalition leader Anthony Manheim regarding the Brooklyn community's original vision of a majestic waterfront park. "We saw the potential for something grand, whereas we were being offered something small and uninspiring by the Port Authority. We saw this as a tremendous planning opportunity to create an enormous public benefit in the center of the city and to take advantage of an opportunity that would never present itself again."[1]

"When it came to development as it was usually conducted, all of us knew our parts," explains former City Council member Ken Fisher, who played an instrumental role in securing the initial city funding for the park. "A developer would come in and put a model on the table, and then the community would react. And everyone at the table knew what role they were supposed to play. But Brooklyn Bridge Park was different. This was a community initiative. Government and other stakeholders and opinion leaders didn't know how to react to it, because it was a reversal of the ordinary roles. While a number of groups played an important role, the sustainment of the effort over time was a function of the Coalition. Had the Coalition not existed, inertia would have eventually claimed the piers."[2]

"This never would have happened without the involvement of the Brooklyn community," agrees Adrian Benepe, the New York City parks commissioner during the early years of the park's planning and construction, "both in the community's willingness to fight against the commercial development of the piers and also in the very patient involvement of the community in the lengthy process that resulted in the Brooklyn Bridge Park Development Corporation [the public entity entrusted with the park's construction] and the realization of the park. The history of the park demonstrates how effective the community can be both in staking out elected officials and in staking out the moral high ground to which the elected officials should respond."[3]

THE EARLY HISTORY OF
THE BROOKLYN WATERFRONT

Throughout its history, the west Brooklyn waterfront has been characterized by competition, controversy, and the need to adapt in the face of change. The area's first settlers were the people of the Lenape Nation. The Lenape—who lived in small villages along the shorelines and riverbanks of western Long Island, the Delaware River watershed, and the lower Hudson Valley—were drawn to the East River's eastern banks by both the beauty and the utility of the landscape. The steep bluff to the east sheltered the shore-level villages from the threat of outsiders, while the river's smooth, deep waters provided a convenient source of transportation up and down the coastline and a rich supply of seafood (salmon, sturgeon, oysters, clams, scallops, and shad) and wildlife (turtles, frogs, deer, geese, herons, and cranes). An early European settler, inspired to hyperbole by the unprecedented abundance he encountered along the shore, described a paradise of "twelve-inch oysters" and "monster lobsters" (some up to six feet in length), with fish so plentiful that "they could be caught by hand."[4]

The Lenape practiced an early form of sustainable fishing, seasonally alternating the sections of water in which they speared their prey and periodically rotating the harvesting grounds for the rich supplies of oysters and freshwater mussels. The river was also the source of commerce, art, and religion for the community. The prized whelk and clamshells that were gathered from the riverbeds were converted into multicolored wampum beads, which were both admired for their beauty and used for currency. Stones and water from the river were also used in religious rituals, in which cold water sprinkled onto heated stones that had been gathered from the riverbed provided worshippers assembled in steam houses with a source of spiritual elation and release.[5]

THE FIRST EUROPEANS entered the region in 1609, when Dutch explorer Henry Hudson navigated his ship, the *Halve Maen* (*Half Moon*), through the narrow tidal strait separating the Atlantic Ocean from what is now known as Upper New York Bay. Although Hudson failed to find the Northwest Passage to the Pacific Ocean, which he was seeking, he did return to Holland with a bounty of lucrative beaver pelts that led to the issuance of a patent to the territory of New Netherland in 1614, the founding of the Dutch West India Company in 1621, and the construction of Fort Amsterdam (or New Amsterdam, as the surrounding settlement was known) at the mouth of the Hudson River in 1625.

A decade later, in 1636, settlers from New Amsterdam gradually began to migrate across the East River to farm the western shore of what would later be called Long Island. The tiny settlement, which occupied approximately the same territory as the neighborhood now known as Brooklyn Heights, was called Breuckelen (or Brooklyn), after a prosperous riverside town in the Vechtstreek area of the Netherlands. In less than a decade, a ferry service had been established to promote regular commerce between the southern tip of New Amsterdam and a slightly upriver landing on the eastern shore owned by "the Ferryman," Cornelis Dircksen Hooglandt.[6]

The Dutch rule of Brooklyn and New Amsterdam ended suddenly in August 1664, when a small fleet of English frigates surprised the undermanned Dutch forces on the islands, resulting in an unconditional surrender. With Director-General Peter Stuyvesant sailing back to the Netherlands in disgrace, the colony, which would be reincorporated as New York City the following year, was ceded to the English. Under English rule, the farms that had been cultivated beside the old Lenape trails along the East River grew into great plantations, eventually forcing the original inhabitants, who had managed to remain on the land under Dutch rule, from the region. The plantation owners erected enormous mansions along the heights above the riverbank, providing their owners with magnificent views of the East River and the island of New York City beyond it.

WHILE THE ORIGINAL VILLAGE at the southern tip of New York City grew into a thriving center of trade and commerce, the economy and social life of Brooklyn continued to be dominated by agriculture throughout the American Revolution and the early years of U.S. governance (figure 1). The great change came in 1814, when steamboat inventor Robert Fulton leased the ferry landing just north of the farmland from wealthy Brooklyn merchant and real-estate developer Hezekiah Beers Pierrepont and began taxiing passengers across the East River in his steam-driven ferry, the *Nassau*, in twelve minutes flat.

Credited with the creation of the nation's first "suburban community," Pierrepont divided the vast estate that he owned at the top of the bluff into street-lined lots for residential development, which he sold to

FIGURE 1 (OPPOSITE)
Bernard Ratzer, "Plan of the City of New York in North America," ca. 1770.
COURTESY OF BROOKLYN HISTORICAL SOCIETY

prosperous bankers, merchants, and shippers who made their fortunes in the city on the western shore but longed for a peaceful home life away from the hustle and bustle of the waterfront. Thanks to Pierrepont and the surveyor he hired to design the layout for the property, the neighborhood's streets bore (and still bear) the names of the wealthy merchants and plantation owners (Pierrepont, Montague, Joralemon, Clark, Clinton, Henry, Hicks, Remsen, and Middagh) whose huge estates had earlier dominated the bluff.

With the opposite banks of the East River now quickly and cheaply accessible (with early fares ranging from 1 cent to 4 cents), thousands of prosperous residents of New York City migrated across the river to build stately homes along the heights of Brooklyn. By 1820, just six years after the introduction of Fulton's steam-driven ferry, the population of Brooklyn was 5,210, more than three times what it had been just two decades earlier, and in 1854, more than 186,000 of Brooklyn's 300,000 residents were commuting back and forth to Manhattan by ferry each day.[7]

In 1856, former Brooklyn Heights resident Walt Whitman captured the visceral thrill experienced by mid-century passengers during the ferry ride across the East River in the poem "Crossing Fulton Ferry," included in his great poetic collection, *Leaves of Grass*. The following lines from the poem are inscribed on one of the rails that guard the foot of Fulton Ferry Landing:

> Others will enter the gates of the ferry and cross from shore to shore,
> Others will watch the run of the flood-tide,
> Others will see the shipping of Manhattan north and west, and the heights of Brooklyn to the south and east,
> Others will see the islands large and small;
> Fifty years hence, other will see them as they cross, the sun half an hour high,
> A hundred years hence, or ever so many hundred years hence, others will see them,
> Will enjoy the sunset, the pouring-in of the flood-tide, the falling-back to the sea of the ebb-tide.[8]

While Brooklyn Heights was becoming a popular residential destination, the lowlands sprawling north along the East River gradually developed into a thriving commercial center, the waterfront lined with loading docks and ferry landings. By 1880, Brooklyn had become the fourth largest manufacturing center in the nation, with the Fulton Ferry district serving as a bustling center of commerce, storage, and shipping for both the borough and the city at large. While the affluent residents of the Heights strolled the neighborhood's tranquil, tree-lined streets with

FIGURE 2

Empire Stores, ca. 1880.

GEORGE J. BISCHOF PAPERS AND
PHOTOGRAPHS, BROOKLYN
HISTORICAL SOCIETY

their top hats and parasols, the landing just below them to the north was teeming with traders, stevedores, and Long Island farmers, who used the connecting railroad lines to transport their livestock and crops to the docks, warehouses, and trade markets of the landing.

During the late nineteenth century, the district's cobblestone streets became crowded with commercial warehouses, as Brooklyn's newly established merchants and manufacturers constructed massive brick structures to store the raw materials and finished goods that would eventually be shipped across the nation and around the world. Among the most durable and impressive of these structures were the five-story Tobacco Warehouse at 26 Dock Street, erected as a tobacco-inspection center by the Lorillard Tobacco Company in the 1860s on the upland section just above the original ferry landing, and the nearby Empire Stores at 53–55 Water Street, constructed in an impressive Romanesque Revival style in 1869, with additional structures added in 1885 (figure 2).[9] A century and a half later, these two impressive structures would play a pivotal role in the formation of a waterfront park in the landing area.

THE BROOKLYN BRIDGE

With the opening of the Brooklyn Bridge on May 24, 1883, the dominance of the ferry in the lives of the people of Brooklyn began to decline. The bridge was designed by celebrated German American architect John Augustus Roebling (who died as a result of an accident shortly after construction began), with construction supervised by his son, Washington Roebling. After he was also immobilized by an accident, the younger Roebling continued to supervise construction for a time from an apartment at 110 Columbia Heights, the windows of which provided a panoramic view of the East River, the Manhattan skyline, and the massive construction site. When the younger Roebling's injuries and illnesses eventually prevented him from continuing with the supervision, his wife, Emily Warren Roebling, took charge of the construction of the bridge. At the time of its completion, the neo-Gothic masterpiece was one of the world's largest, most innovative, and most visually compelling engineering achievements.

With the Brooklyn Bridge spanning the shores of Brooklyn and Manhattan, bankers and merchants from the Heights could now ride to work by horse-drawn carriage or, if time allowed, take a leisurely stroll along the wide, boarded promenade at the center of the bridge (with more than 150,000 pedestrians and 1,800 vehicles crossing the bridge on its opening day alone), enjoying an elevated perspective of the river and the shoreline that surpassed the sea-level views from the weathered bows of a steamboat. While the Union Ferry would continue operation until 1924, the bridge, with its bustling traffic and lofty vistas, had become a center for the economic, social, and imaginative life of Brooklyn.

In addition to its role in the decline of the ferry business, the Brooklyn Bridge took a punishing toll on the economy and population of Brooklyn Heights. With more and more people commuting back and forth across the East River each day, the once-tranquil neighborhood became increasingly accessible to new businesses and industrial development, and many of the wealthy bankers and merchants who had been lured by the promise of serenity and solitude migrated back across the river to Greenwich Village and the other fashionable neighborhoods that were thriving throughout lower Manhattan, with property values in the Heights plummeting on their departure. By the early decades of the twentieth century, many of the once-fashionable residences of Brooklyn Heights had been abandoned and boarded up by their owners, with other buildings divided into rooming houses for the poor.

WHILE THE EAST RIVER FERRIES were slowly grinding to a halt, the commercial-shipping industry was booming, with tall ships and steamboats continually loading and unloading cargo all along Brooklyn's western and southern waterfronts. In 1902, the newly formed New York Dock Company, which already owned forty piers; miles of railroad tracks; and hundreds of stores, warehouses, and loft buildings along the city's shorelines, announced its plans to extend its piers southward along the two-mile stretch of Brooklyn waterfront from Fulton Ferry Landing, near the Brooklyn Bridge, to the Hamilton Avenue Ferry House in Red Hook.

The New York State Legislature had authorized the commercial appropriation of the Brooklyn shoreline the previous year, over the objections of Governor Theodore Roosevelt, who claimed that the action violated the city's founding document, the Dongan Charter. Granted by colonial governor Thomas Dongan on April 27, 1686, the Dongan Charter provided for public ownership of "waste, vacant, unpatented and other un-appropriated lands," which were to be maintained under the jurisdiction of a "Common Council."[10] The lands protected by the charter included the outdoor marketplaces, public commons, and other open spaces that would later become the first urban parks.[11] Although the Dongan Charter itself would not continue to play a role in future conflicts between local residents and commercial developers, the principle of "public ownership" that it introduced would be critical in the formation of the demands and expectations of local community leaders in the movement for a park on the waterfront later in the century.

Brooklyn's status as a leading industrial center was paralleled by the continuing growth and dominance of its shipping trade. During the early decades of the twentieth century, the borough established itself as one of the world's busiest commercial harbors, handling one-quarter of the United States' foreign trade (figures 3 and 4). The city's terminals and warehouses were packed with cocoa, paint, paper bags, preserves, varnish, drugs, coffee, chemicals, lamps, wire, molasses, bed springs, hair-waving equipment, straw hats, glucose, and soda fountain supplies, either arriving from distant ports or waiting to be shipped around the world. "It can be said without fear of reprisal," boasted the *Brooklyn Eagle* in 1936, "that no industry or product exists in the country that does not touch, at some time, on one of Brooklyn's piers or rest, at some point along its way, in one of the terminals."[12]

THE INCREASED ACCESSIBILITY and decline in property values that had driven wealthy professionals across the East River from Brooklyn Heights to Manhattan precipitated a reverse migration of the city's young writers, composers, and visual artists. During the early decades of the twentieth century, a steady stream of young bohemians abandoned the brownstones of Greenwich Village for the cheaper and less distracting accommodations on the highlands across the river. In the late 1930s and early 1940s, an impressive collection of gifted artists and entertainers that included the poet W. H. Auden, the composer Benjamin Britten, the novelist Carson McCullers, the burlesque dancer Gypsy Rose Lee, and the literary couple Paul and Jane Bowles crowded into a single building on 7 Middagh Street in the Heights, known as the February House,

AUG 27.1924

with writer and friend Truman Capote living in a nearby basement apartment on 70 Willow Street.[13] Brooklyn Heights, wrote Capote at the time, "stands atop a cliff that secures a sea-gull's view of the Manhattan and Brooklyn bridges, of lower Manhattan's tall dazzle and the ship-lane waters, breeding river to bay to ocean, that encircle and seethe past posturing Miss Liberty."[14]

Earlier, in the 1920s, a brilliant young poet named Hart Crane was living in an apartment belonging to the father of a friend at 110 Columbia Heights in Brooklyn Heights (the same apartment from the windows of which Washington Roebling supervised the construction of the Brooklyn Bridge) while working on a long narrative poem about the bridge. In a letter written to his mother and grandmother in Cleveland, Ohio, in 1928, Crane described the spectacular view from the window of his apartment on the bluff above the shoreline: "Just imagine looking out your window directly on the East River with nothing intervening between your view of the Statue of Liberty, way down the harbour, and the marvelous beauty of the Brooklyn Bridge close above on your right! All of the great new skyscrapers of lower Manhattan are marshaled directly across from you, and there is a constant stream of tugs, liners, sail boats, etc. in procession before you on the river! It's really a magnificent place to live!"[15]

In the "Proem" to his great epic poem *The Bridge,* Crane converted his passion for the river, the bridge and the shorelines that it connected into myth:

> O sleepless as the river under thee,
> Vaulting the sea, the prairies dreaming sod,
> Unto us lowliest sometime sweep, descend
> And of thy curveship lend a myth to God.[16]

ROBERT MOSES

In 1941, New York City's powerful parks commissioner, Robert Moses, announced his plans to construct a four-lane highway (to be known as the Brooklyn–Queens Expressway) right through the middle of Brooklyn Heights along Hicks Street. The proposed construction was part of Moses's ambitious plans to rezone and rebuild extensive sections of the city's infrastructure. Moses's proposal, if enacted as planned, would have transformed Hezekiah's Pierrepont's tranquil, suburban neighborhood into a busy, modern commercial thoroughfare. The planned construction was vigorously opposed by local residents, however, many of them young professionals who had recently followed the first wave of bohemians into

Brooklyn Heights and were now busy renovating the neighborhood's affordable brownstones.

Leading the opposition was the powerful Brooklyn Heights Association, a community group that had been formed in 1910 to register the neighborhood's complaints about its transit facilities to the New York City Public Service Commission. At the time of its formation, the BHA was already feared by public authorities for "the might" and "the wrath" of its illustrious membership.[17] The organization had grown even stronger and better organized in the three decades since its formation, and the normally indomitable Moses compromised with the community. After years of negotiations and debate, the city agreed to build the expressway along the far western border of Brooklyn Heights, with two levels of roadway above Furman Street, which runs parallel to the waterfront near the water's edge, and an expansive esplanade (which would later be known as the Brooklyn Heights Promenade) cantilevered above the traffic.

ALONG WITH MOSES'S AMBITIOUS PLANS for remaking New York City, Brooklyn Heights and the waterfront would be affected by changes in the global maritime industry, which would transform the west Brooklyn waterfront. In 1956, the Port Authority of New York and New Jersey assumed control of the planning and maintenance of the west Brooklyn piers. The twenty-five "five-finger" piers that had lined the waterfront for decades and that had been built to accommodate the tall sailing vessels and small and moderate-size steam ships of the past were demolished to make way for landings large enough to accommodate the huge, slow-moving steam freighters of the modern era (figure 5). In addition to the finger piers, 130 warehouses and storage facilities were also destroyed at the time. Between 1956 and 1964, the New York Dock Company constructed thirteen piers along the 2.5-mile stretch of shoreline between the Brooklyn Bridge to the north and Red Hook to the south (figure 6).[18]

On April 25, 1956, the same year that construction began on the new west Brooklyn piers, businessman Malcolm McLean introduced the practice of "containerization" to the worldwide maritime industry, arranging for the transport of fifty-eight rigging containers on a converted World War II tanker from Port Newark, New Jersey, to a shipping facility in Houston, Texas. Prior to McLean's innovation, commercial shipping had been an exclusively "break-bulk" operation, in which products were transported and stored in individual pieces or small lots. Through "containerization," vast quantities of products could be packaged snugly together in large containers and loaded directly from and onto semitrailers

FIGURE 5

The narrow piers and slips of the Brooklyn piers, shown here around 1960, were later reconstructed by the Port Authority.

GIFT OF B. McTIERNAN.
BROOKLYN BRIDGE PARK
CONSERVANCY COLLECTION

for highway transport, allowing for more efficient storage, reduced costs, and expedited delivery.[19]

The shift from break bulk to containerized cargo would soon result in dramatic changes to the look and the economy of the west Brooklyn waterfront, with more and more commercial freighters loading and unloading their containerized cargo at the shipping facilities at Port Newark and nearby Port Elizabeth, New Jersey, leading to the neglect and decline of the once-dominant west Brooklyn piers. By the mid-1970s, most of the piers were completely inactive, and the warehouses and storage sheds that once bustled with activity along the Brooklyn waterfront were either underused or abandoned (figure 7).

DURING THE SAME PERIOD, Fulton Ferry Landing, the backwater area flanking the Brooklyn Bridge, and the current neighborhood of Dumbo (Down Under the Manhattan Bridge Overpass), to the north, had also fallen into disuse and disrepair. The gradual decline of the ferry service, which ceased operation completely in 1924, had precipitated the collapse of the borough's once-bustling center of storage, shipping, and trade.[20] The landing area was further isolated by the opening in 1909 of the Manhattan Bridge, which completely bypassed the area, and the

FIGURE 6
Austin J. Tobin,
executive director of the
Port Authority (*far right*),
explaining to Port Authority
commissioners the $85
million project to rebuild the
piers along 2.5 miles of the
Brooklyn waterfront, 1955.
GIFT OF B. McTIERNAN.
BROOKLYN BRIDGE PARK
CONSERVANCY COLLECTION

opening in 1951 of the Brooklyn–Queens Expressway, whose enormous concrete supports formed an imposing barrier between the district and the rest of the borough.[21]

In 1963, Consolidated Edison purchased a nine-acre parcel at the center of the property, surrounding and including the abandoned and dilapidated Empire Stores, inaugurating what would become a five-decade-long struggle among Brooklyn residents, commercial developers, and public authorities over the appropriate use of the Fulton Ferry area. In 1967, hoping to capitalize on its investment, Con Edison proposed the conversion of the Empire Stores site into a wholesale meat market. The proposal was successfully opposed by the BHA, whose members complained about the proximity of the market to their own neighborhood and worried that the proposed development would threaten the structural integrity of the Empire Stores and other adjacent structures.[22] A similar proposal in 1971 to convert the property into a "festival marketplace" was also shelved in response to opposition from the Brooklyn Heights community.[23]

ACHIEVING LANDMARK STATUS AND THE BEGINNING OF THE PARK CONCEPT

In 1974, the BHA, with the active support of the Landmarks Preservation Commission, successfully campaigned to have Fulton Ferry Landing, excluding the property owned by Con Edison, listed on the National Register of Historic Places, a status reserved for local property with "limited historical value." The neighborhood's campaign to secure landmark status for the area was not without opposition, as both Con Edison and the Board of Estimate expressed concern about the impact of the decision on the commercial potential of the property. In a letter dated December 12,

1975, to Brooklyn Borough President Sebastian Leone, Commissioner E. C. Farber of the New York City Department of Ports and Terminals expressed concern that the action would restrict the "creative re-use" of the Empire Stores and "would hinder if not prevent revitalization of the Fulton Ferry area."[24]

In 1976, the New York State Office of Parks, Recreation and Historic Preservation purchased the nine-acre parcel for $750,000 as part of a land-swap agreement with Con Edison, clearing the way for the inclusion of the Empire Stores as part of the designated property. On June 28, 1977, through the active support of the BHA, the Fulton Ferry Landing area (including the Empire Stores and Tobacco Warehouse) was officially designated as the Fulton Ferry Historic District, a status reserved for sites or structures with "an outstanding degree of historical significance," by the Landmarks Preservation Commission. The creation of the new historic district required the Landmarks Preservation Commission to review and issue permits for any future construction or renovation within the site.[25]

In June 1977, restaurateur Michael "Buzzy" O'Keefe opened the River Café on a platform barge on the East River just under the Brooklyn Bridge. Despite the warnings of local business leaders and government

FIGURE 7
By the mid-1970s, with the majority of container shipping having moved to Port Newark and Port Elizabeth, New Jersey, the Brooklyn Heights waterfront was no longer an active shipping site.
COURTESY OF TOM FOX

FIGURE 8 (TOP)
**Main Street parking lot,
ca. 1998.**
COURTESY OF BROOKLYN BRIDGE PARK CONSERVANCY

FIGURE 9 (BOTTOM)
Main Street Park, 2008.
© ETIENNE FROSSARD, NEW YORK, N.Y.

officials that the floating restaurant was doomed to failure, the River Café soon enjoyed both commercial and critical success, winning the Parks Council Award in 1978 and the Municipal Art Society Award in 1979 and being selected for induction into the Restaurant Hall of Fame in 1980.[26]

The same year, the west Brooklyn waterfront also became the home of Bargemusic, a classical music hall located on a converted coffee barge moored on the East River shoreline near the Brooklyn Bridge near the River Café. Founder Olga Bloom had discovered the 102-foot barge that housed the venue harbored near the Statue of Liberty and had it towed to its present site. Like the nearby River Café, Bargemusic quickly gained a devoted following, drawing capacity crowds of 130 to 140 people to its Thursday evening, Friday evening, and Sunday afternoon classical-music performances.[27]

In 1979, the Department of Ports and Terminals created the first public park on the abandoned west Brooklyn waterfront. The modest public space, known as Empire–Fulton Ferry State Park, was built on the site of a 4.5-acre parking lot near Fulton Street just under the Brooklyn Bridge (figure 8). The parking lot had been used by local longshoremen working on the nearby Port Authority piers, who had agreed to relocate the parking lot based on assurances by the city that a new job-creating container port would soon be created at another site along the waterfront. As mentioned, the floating restaurant known as the River Café was built on a platform barge adjacent to the landing. The Department of Ports and Terminals contributed landfills, bulkhead repairs, and landscaping for the park project.[28]

As the 1980s began, the idea of a park along the piers immediately south of Fulton Ferry had not yet captured the imagination of local residents, and the public authorities in charge of the waterfront were only beginning to consider the financial benefits that could be reaped from the dispossession and commercial development of the property. However, with the decline of the piers, the acquisition of the Fulton Ferry district by the New York State Office of Parks, Recreation and Historic Preservation, and the creation of Empire–Fulton Ferry State Park, the stage had been set for the negotiations, the controversies, and, ultimately, the achievements of the decades to follow (figure 9). Over the next few years, competing ambitions for the public use versus the commercial development of the piers would become important priorities for their respective champions, and the conflict over the appropriate use of the west Brooklyn waterfront would emerge as a major theme for both the borough of Brooklyn and the city at large.

ONE
WHAT SHALL WE DO WITH THE PIERS?

> The waterfront is there, lying fallow as it has for so many years.
> It cries out for development.
>
> **LARRY A. SILVERSTEIN**

Y THE END OF THE 1970S, the private and public development of abandoned and underused waterfronts had become a major emphasis for city governments and urban planners across the United States. Inspired by a number of recent high-profile development projects—including Harbor Place in Baltimore, Fanueil Hall in Boston, and Fisherman's Wharf in San Francisco—city governments were increasingly looking to waterfront conversion as a viable way to create jobs, provide housing, attract investors, and restore the visual appeal of urban areas that had been ravaged by the impact of the global recession of 1973 to 1975 on state and municipal economies nationwide.[1]

From the earliest days of his tenure, Mayor Edward Koch, elected in 1977, made the transformation of New York City's vast waterfront from traditional maritime operations to private uses a priority of his administration, devoting $4 million in capital funds to develop South Street Seaport, resuscitating stalled waterfront construction projects at Battery Park in lower Manhattan and Westway on the Hudson River, and soliciting proposals for a number of office and residential projects along the East River in Manhattan and Brooklyn.[2]

Koch's commitment to the private development of the city's abandoned piers included the proposed reconfiguration of the bureaucracy responsible for the maintenance of the city's waterfront. In 1980, he privately encouraged and publicly endorsed the initial efforts of Susan M. Heilbron, the Commissioner of Ports and Terminals, to dissolve the agency, which had traditionally been entrusted with construction, lease management, and security on the city's ports and piers, and place the waterfront property under the Office of Economic Development, the powerful agency responsible for facilitating the sale and lease of public property in New York City. "Everything done by Ports and Terminals could be done more rapidly and efficiently by the Office of Economic Development or the Department of General Services [which handled land transactions]," Heilbron explained at the time, echoing Koch's attitude toward the piers and their appropriate role in the life and economy of the city.[3]

Immediately encountering serious and highly vocal opposition from local political leaders in Brooklyn (including Brooklyn Borough President Howard Golden and City Council Majority Leader Thomas J. Cuite), Congressmen Leo C. Zeferetti and Frederick W. Richmond, and the International Longshoremen's Association, Koch temporarily altered his plans for the Department of Ports and Terminals, calling instead for the modification, not the abolishment, of the agency and its responsibilities. Speaking on behalf of the administration in 1981, Deputy Mayor Robert F. Wagner maintained that the routine responsibilities of Ports and Terminals ("the maintenance tasks, including the markets, lease management and dock building") should be consolidated and transferred to other available agencies, transforming Ports and Terminals into "a traditional water development agency."[4] Under the revised plan, Ports and Terminals would assume the responsibility of incrementally disposing of the very properties it had been created to maintain and service. Predictably, the opponents of the mayor's plans to eliminate Ports and Terminals were equally unimpressed with his alternative proposal to convert the maritime agency into a makeshift real-estate agency, and, at least for the time being, Ports and Terminals continued in its traditional responsibilities for New York City's waterfront.

In addition to the opposition of local politicians in Brooklyn, congressional leaders, and the International Longshoremen's Association, Koch's plans for the private development of the city's piers encountered resistance from the Port Authority of New York and New Jersey, the independent, state-funded corporation that actually owned and controlled much of the available waterfront property along the Hudson and East Rivers and New York Harbor.

Formed in 1921 through a joint action of the governments of New York and New Jersey, the Port Authority was created to function as an independent corporation, free from the red tape, partisanship, and potential corruption of government bureaucracies, with the states' citizens as its sole stakeholders. In this capacity, it occasionally found itself at cross purposes with state and metropolitan officials over the most effective strategies for constructing, maintaining, and financing major bridges, tunnels, airports, and port operations in the region. Decisions regarding the dispossession of public properties represented particular points of contention between the Port Authority and state and municipal governments, for which the prospects of short-term windfalls from the sale or lease of public properties held the potential to override longer-term public interests.

In 1982, Linda W. Searle, the newly appointed Commissioner of Ports and Terminals, the Port Authority department responsible for the oversight of waterfront and maritime properties, announced the agency's commitment to preserving the city's piers for traditional shipping and storage purposes. "We are helping to support and strengthen maritime in New York City," she explained in a statement to the *New York Times*, "because it is still important to the city's economic base."[5]

In the same *New York Times* article, the Port Authority's executive director, Peter C. Goldmark, reaffirmed Searle's commitment to traditional maritime uses for the city's waterfront, describing the agency's failure to convert the Brooklyn waterfront to containerization during the previous two decades as "the real missed opportunity." "What was needed," Goldmark maintained, "was not the abandonment of the waterfront, but the creative transformation of waterfront facilities to appropriate and productive maritime uses, converting existing piers to containerization wherever possible and consolidating and, if containerization was not a possibility, adapting abandoned or under-used waterfront property to address other maritime needs."[6]

In addition to its mandated responsibility for protecting the long-term interests of its citizen stakeholders, the Port Authority's reluctance to dispose of the Brooklyn piers was fueled by recent charges by local politicians and community leaders of favoritism on its part toward the New Jersey waterfront. Since the early 1960s, when the neighboring New Jersey ports of Newark and Elizabeth were originally equipped for containerization, the prominence of the New Jersey piers had steadily risen while the volume, work hours, efficiency, and profitability of maritime activities along the Brooklyn shoreline (which had once boasted some of the world's most active piers) had steadily declined.

By the early 1980s, the Newark–Elizabeth ports were known as "America's Container Capital,"[7] ranking as the world's busiest containerization facility by the middle of the decade,[8] while the majority of the

Brooklyn piers were either underused or abandoned and deteriorating along the shore.

In response to the growing disparity in volume, profitability, and job creation between the New York and New Jersey piers, the Port Authority was desperately looking for innovative ways to revitalize the once-proud Brooklyn waterfront and reverse the recent decline of the borough's piers. By 1983, the construction of a large containerization facility was already under way at the abandoned Erie Basin Terminal in Red Hook, along with plans for a massive fish-processing center to be constructed nearby.[9] Although both of these projects failed, throughout the early years of the decade, the Port Authority publicly entertained the hope that some type of profitable maritime use could still be found for all the borough's remaining piers along the East River and that some level of equity could be reestablished between the New York and New Jersey waterfronts.

By the end of 1983, however, the Port Authority had finally given up on the possibility of continuing traditional maritime operations on the vast waterfront property immediately north of the Red Hook pier, stretching from Pier 6 near Atlantic Avenue at its southernmost point to Pier 1 just south of the Brooklyn Bridge to the north. The limited cargo operations being conducted on the piers were scheduled to end the following year, and the dual constraints imposed by the elevated lanes of the Brooklyn–Queens Expressway and the steep cliffs of Brooklyn Heights effectively blocked the piers from the substantial upland areas required for containerization and land transport.

TOWARD THE END OF 1983, Anthony Manheim, the president of the Brooklyn Heights Association (BHA), received a telephone call from a representative of the Port Authority's Commission on Ports and Terminals, informing him of the Port Authority's plans to dispose of the piers. Consistent with its corporate mandate to protect the public interest, dispossession of public property by the Port Authority has traditionally been a lengthy and complicated process, requiring the agency in charge of the property to consult with local leaders to solicit the concerns and recommendations of the affected communities.

"He called me in my capacity as president of the Brooklyn Heights Association," Manheim recalls, "and explained that the decision had been made that the Port Authority was going to begin disposing of these piers. He explained that they were required to do so because the piers were no longer germane to any of the Port Authority charter-mandated activities."[10] The Port Authority representative quickly brought Manheim up to speed on the reasons for the impending disposal of the waterfront property (the recent shift from break-bulk shipping to containerization, restricted access to the upland area above the piers). The decision had also been made, he explained, to dispose of similar pier properties in Hoboken, New Jersey, and at Hunter's Point in Queens. Near the end of the conversation, the representative asked Manheim the question that would haunt officials at the Port Authority, along with their counterparts in city government, for the next three decades and that would ultimately result in the complete transformation of the west Brooklyn waterfront.

"What do you think we should do?" he asked, pausing briefly to repeat his question, as Manheim listened in disbelief. "What do you think we should do with the piers?"

"They made what I'm sure many people would later consider to be a mistake," remembers Manheim, chuckling at his own understatement. "It was an open invitation to have input into their disposition process, and I took this very seriously. Very seriously."

A former investment banker with a lifelong passion for community activism, Manheim had been living in a spacious apartment above the Brooklyn Heights Promenade since 1960, his rear windows affording a spectacular, panoramic view of the East River and the Manhattan skyline. As he gazed at the vast stretch of waterfront property beneath him, he quickly assessed both the serious threat and the once-in-a-lifetime opportunity represented by the proposed dispossession of the piers. "I looked out my window," he continues, "at the view that I had been seeing at that point for twenty-three years, and I could see it all spread out in front me, from Pier 1 just south of the Brooklyn Bridge all the way to Pier 6 just north of Atlantic Avenue. And I thought to myself, 'What an unbelievable opportunity!'"[11]

In spite of his initial visions for the property and his concerns about the impending dispossession of Piers 1–6, Manheim was not surprised to learn that his enthusiasm to become actively involved in the future of the Brooklyn waterfront was not immediately shared by his associates at the BHA.

"The biggest issues confronting Brooklyn Heights at the time were development pressures," he continues. "And the particular development pressure that tended to dominate the serious thinkers of the Brooklyn Heights Association was the inexorable-seeming expansion of the Jehovah's Witnesses, who had had their world headquarters at the bottom of the hill since 1909 and had recently been going through a worldwide expansion to the extent that they were buying up every multiple dwelling that came on the market."[12]

During the 1970s and early 1980s, the Watchtower Bible and Tract Society, the not-for-profit legal entity through which the leaders of Jehovah's Witnesses conducted their business, had purchased sixteen prime properties in and around Brooklyn Heights for office space, printing facilities, and housing for their rapidly increasing membership, including then-current plans to build a thirty-four-story residential tower at Columbia Heights and Furman Street, just outside the scenic-view protection zone of the Brooklyn Heights Historic District.[13]

In addition to their controversial real-estate and high-rise construction ventures, Jehovah's Witnesses were a conspicuous presence in Brooklyn Heights in the early 1980s, including their daily activities to, from, and along the Brooklyn waterfront. The Watchtower Society had recently purchased a large warehouse facility at 360 Furman Street, on the future park site, which was used for carpentry and maintenance operations, as well as storage and loading of the society's semimonthly magazine, the *Watchtower*, and other religious materials that were shipped to members of Jehovah's Witnesses around the world, and each day thousands of cars owned by Watchtower residents and employees streamed into and out of an enormous parking lot on the uplands at Pier 5. The familiar sight of Watchtower employees walking up and down Joralemon Street between the Court Street area and the piers below was a constant reminder to other Brooklyn Heights residents of the society's growing presence and impact on the neighborhood.

"It was not as easy in retrospect as you might suppose to get the interest of my fellow board members to focus on the incredible opportunity that, in effect, presented itself by this phone call from and later meeting with this relatively junior official of the Port Authority in charge of the Brooklyn piers," says Manheim of the neighborhood association's initial reluctance to become involved in the proposed dispossession of the waterfront.

Following a lukewarm response from his colleagues on the board of governors of the Brooklyn Heights Association regarding plans for the piers, Manheim decided to reach out to two friends, Otis Pearsall and Scott Hand, in Brooklyn Heights with extensive experience in community activism and neighborhood preservation.

Whatever Piers 1–6 might become over time, Manheim reasoned, the most immediate concern was the protection of the Brooklyn Heights neighborhood and the views it provided, for both its residents and the thousands of visitors who enjoyed the Promenade each year, of the East River and the Manhattan skyline. An attorney for the prestigious Manhattan law firm of Hughes Hubbard & Reed, Otis Pearsall was, in the estimation of both his supporters in the neighborhood and his adversaries in city government and real-estate development, the neighborhood's, if not the city's, leading figure in neighborhood preservation and view protection.

In 1965, Pearsall had led the campaign for the enactment of the New York Landmarks Preservation Law and the subsequent designation of Brooklyn Heights as the city's first Historic District. Two years later, he led the effort to protect Brooklyn's view of the East River and the Manhattan skyline through the enactment of LH-1, limiting all construction along and above the waterfront to fifty feet.

"Otis was the progenitor of the whole historical preservation movement, both in Brooklyn and citywide," Manheim explains. "As a governor and then president of the Brooklyn Heights Association board, he was the first person I consulted on any preservation issue, and the protection of the waterfront and the preservation of the magnificent views were certainly major concerns at the time."[14]

The second person that Manheim contacted, former BHA president and Inco executive Scott Hand, also had an impressive record in civic activism and neighborhood preservation. In the late 1970s, Hand had successfully advocated with the state for the purchase and preservation of the Empire Stores and Tobacco Warehouse property along the waterfront between the Brooklyn and Manhattan Bridges.

IN THE MONTHS THAT FOLLOWED, Manheim continued in his capacity as president of the BHA, devoting as much time as possible to the newly formed ad hoc Waterfront Committee, which included both Pearsall and Hand, along with several other members he had managed to recruit from the BHA membership. He continued to speak regularly by phone with representatives of the Port Authority, and in April 1984, he and his fellow Waterfront Committee members Earl Weiner, Joyce Curll, and Pat Coady attended their first formal meeting with officials of the Port Authority's Commission on Ports and Terminals at the organization's headquarters on the sixty-seventh floor of 1 World Trade Center in lower Manhattan.[15] "They could literally look out their conference room windows and see the piers below," Manheim remembers. "That may have something to do with why they took the site, which was such a tiny part of the overall properties they were responsible for, so seriously."[16]

Brooklyn Heights residents had been invited across the river to share their community's opinions about the proposed dispossession of Piers 1–6 and were assured that their concerns and recommendations would be included in a forthcoming feasibility study on the potential uses of the

Brooklyn waterfront. With the view of the piers and the west Brooklyn skyline clearly on display below, the committee members identified the three concerns that they would continue to emphasize in their future negotiations with the Port Authority: protection of the scenic-view plane of the river and the Manhattan skyline, the exclusion of any new pedestrian or vehicular corridor directly linking the neighborhood promenade to the shoreline, and the dedication of meaningful space for public access and use of the waterfront property.

Consistent with Manheim's earlier informal conversations with the Port Authority, the committee members' first formal meeting with the Port Authority focused primarily on the Brooklyn community's concerns about what the development should *not* involve. A general consensus had emerged among community representatives that, whatever changes were made to the waterfront and the piers, the existing environment and day-to-day experiences of the residents of Brooklyn Heights and the adjoining neighborhoods should be left undisturbed, from the spectacular scenic views of the East River and the Manhattan skyline to the tranquil, cul-de-sac layout of the Brooklyn Heights neighborhood.

"The main concerns during those early meetings were the protection of the view and the possibility of a corridor linking the promenade with the piers," remembers Fred Bland, a Beyer Blinder Belle partner, Brooklyn architect, and future BHA president, who, along with Manheim, Pearsall, and Hand, attended an early meeting with Port Authority public-relations director and Brooklyn Heights resident Rita Schwartz, shortly after the meeting at 1 World Trade Center. "We hoped the scenic-view restrictions would protect us, but it was an important concern for everyone.

"There was some talk here and there about including public space as a part of whatever was developed on the waterfront," Bland continues, "but at the time, nobody was saying 'park.' "[17]

Manheim agrees that the focus on building a park evolved over time, though he insists that it was always assumed that whatever use was made of the property, at least some of the space would be preserved for park and recreational use. "I'm not exactly sure when the park idea came up in our discussions," he says. "I think we always considered 'park' as a part of it, but not necessarily 'pure park.' A park with things in it.

"The goal," Manheim continues, "was to take this publicly owned asset, about eighty-five acres, about one-third water, about one-third piers, supported largely by deteriorating wooden pilings, and about one-third upland, and decide what to do with it."

The overriding objective was to find the most beneficial use of the property for the community residents and the rest of the city: "We looked

at it very simply the same way that you would look at a private development project intending to maximize profit, although 'profit' was not for
me measured in dollar return; it was measured in public benefit."[18]

The Port Authority officials with whom Manheim, Bland, and the
other committee members met during 1984 and most of 1985 were generally sympathetic to the concerns expressed by the community leaders.
Whatever plans the Port Authority officials may privately have been en-
tertaining for the piers, Bland recalls, "they really didn't put up a fight" in
response to the concerns expressed by the committee.[19]

At least one office at the Port Authority was taking the local community's concerns and recommendations very seriously at the time. Between
July 1984 and April 1985, Robert Parsekian was a member of the Commission on Ports and Terminals' Task Force for the Brooklyn Piers, a
three-person design team preparing multiple schemes for the use of the
west Brooklyn waterfront. "Several of the schemes we designed did have
a lot of parkland," remembers Parsekian. "We had created a model in the
office of Piers 1 to 6. It was full scale in white foam core. It was meant
to study how massing of structures and parkland could be funded at the
site. We figured out the economics of the amount of upland versus parkland use.

"We had a model scope," he continues, "a device that had a fine stain-
less-steel tube that you could place in the model and look down on
through optics as though you were a person in the model walking through
the space. There was some housing, but we weren't trying to fill the space
with housing. I remember that there was a tremendous concern for not
interrupting the view plane."[20]

THE ABILITY OF THE PORT AUTHORITY to honor its early, informal commitments to the Waterfront Committee would soon be seriously compromised by both the internal restructuring of the organization itself and
the realignment of its relationship with city government. Even before
the organization's first formal meeting with the Waterfront Committee
in April 1984, negotiations were under way at 1 World Trade Center that
would completely alter the governance of the region's piers and the Port
Authority's goals and priorities for dispossession and development.

In March 1984, the Port Authority and New York City signed a Letter of Agreement to jointly study the potential development of the piers,
including the formulation of general guidelines for the dispossession of
Piers 1–6 in Brooklyn. The Port Authority's partners in this new arrangement included the New York City Department of Ports and Terminals,
which temporarily maintained nominal authority for the maintenance

and control of the piers; Department of City Planning; and Public Development Corporation (PDC).[21] The inclusion of the PDC, a powerful, well-funded enterprise with 140 full-time workers (compared with just 14 employees in Ports and Terminals), signaled that Mayor Koch was finally on the verge of achieving his objective of converting the abandoned piers to real estate.

In little more than a year, the PDC would be formally designated as the lead agent for waterfront development, with the executive director, James Stuckey, publicly chanting the mayor's mantra that abandoned waterfronts, converted into real estate, were the future of profitable urban development. "Nowhere is this more true than in New York City," Stuckey explained in the ambitious report *New York City's Waterfront: A Plan for Development*, "where the fast pace of development in Manhattan has left little undeveloped land save the waterfront, and has increased the desirability of waterfront areas facing Manhattan."[22]

In addition to the joint planning initiative with the city, critical changes were simultaneously taking place in the Port Authority. By the end of 1984, the Port Authority's Commission on Ports and Terminals would effectively relinquish control of the piers and the dispossession and development process to the agency's Department of World Trade and Economic Development, with its mandated focus on economic growth and job creation.

As Manheim and his colleagues would soon learn, the new arrangement between the Port Authority and the city represented a determined and inflexible commitment to private development as the sole destiny of Piers 1–6. In January 1985, the Port Authority and the city jointly retained the consulting firm Halcyon Ltd., of Hartford, Connecticut, to study the alternatives for development. In place of the proposed feasibility study to which the Waterfront Committee members had been told they were contributing, Halcyon had instead been commissioned to produce a marketing study. The task at hand was to sell the Port Authority and the city's decision in favor of the private development of Piers 1–6 to potential investors and the general public—either with the support or over the objections of the communities that would be directly affected by private development.

Later that month, Philip LaRocco, the Port Authority's Director of World Trade and Economic Development and the agency's newly designated liaison with the waterfront communities, convened a meeting with Manheim, newly elected BHA president Earl Weiner, and several other members of the Waterfront Committee. The purposes of the meeting were to inform the committee that the Port Authority and its partners "had decided to go the route of private development," to introduce the committee members to the Halcyon consulting team, and to reassure the Brooklyn Heights residents that, in spite of the sudden unilateral shift in direction, the community's concerns would continue to be respected in the ongoing plans for development.[23]

"Suddenly, the attitude of the Port Authority changed," Manheim recalls. "I remember being specifically told by Philip LaRocco, who was one of six department directors of the Port Authority, who reported directly to the executive director, and his department was called Economic Development. And the disposition of the piers property, both our piers and Hoboken and Queens West, had been turned over to that department, taken out of another co-equal department that operated piers and shipping facilities.

"They had spent, I believe he said, a million bucks on a planning study for Hoboken and found it to be unproductive," continues Manheim. "And they weren't going to repeat that mistake in Brooklyn. They didn't want to hire a planning firm just to interview people to tell them about the piers' potential—or lack of potential—for break-bulk shipping. They'd just be interviewing their own employees to tell them what they already knew. And they didn't need a consultant to tell them that luxury-housing condos would sell there. Why did you need to spend a million to have somebody tell you what everybody already knew from the get-go? Instead, they had decided to conduct a marketing study for Piers 1–6. I remember that he used those words: 'marketing study.' "[24]

While Manheim expressed concern about the possible construction of high-rise buildings on the "triangles of opportunity" at the northern and southern boundaries of the site, immediately outside the protected scenic-view zones, both he and the other committee members remained guardedly optimistic with the explanations and assurances they received from LaRocco and the representatives of the Halcyon consulting team. As Manheim reported in the BHA newsletter shortly after the meeting, "We have no reason to believe that there is currently any contemplation of not respecting this constraint [the scenic-view zone]."[25] For the time being at least, most of the BHA's members were willing to give the Port Authority and the city the benefit of the doubt.

At the time, it seemed to many residents of the Brooklyn Heights community as if there were little else that they could do. With the combined financial resources and public influence of the PDC, the Port Authority's Department of World Trade and Economic Development, and the Department of City Planning, along with the enthusiastic endorsement of the mayor's office, the private development of Piers 1–6 had all the marks of a fait accompli. The Waterfront Committee's best hope of preserving the neighborhood's scenic views and tranquil streets and sidewalks was to continue working with the Port Authority behind the scenes, building trust, and, hopefully, gaining leverage by reassuring community residents of the good will and trustworthiness of those in authority.

WHATEVER GOOD WILL AND TRUST had been established during the continuing meetings and negotiations between the Port Authority and the Waterfront Committee during the spring and summer of 1985 was seriously undermined the following October when the Port Authority and its partners in city government launched a media campaign, releasing the tentative findings from the forthcoming Halcyon Report and publicly announcing its plans for the private development of Piers 1–6.

In a 1,700-word special report, "In Brooklyn Heights, a Spotlight on 87 Neglected Acres," *New York Times* journalist Richard D. Lyons made a strong case for the disposal of Piers 1–6 (which he described as having been reduced to "a parking lot for a few bulk cargo ships of the sort that have used the area since the turn of the century") while praising the potential benefits of developing the property for commercial use. The article, which read more like a public-relations announcement than an investigative report, revealed that the proposed development of the piers property would include a mix of "public housing, parkland, a resort hotel, condominiums, athletic fields, exhibition halls, marinas and manufacturing plants."[26] The unfolding development process, as described by Lyons, was complete with heroes and villains and suggested, for the discerning reader, the blame-the-critic strategy that the Port Authority and the city would use to discredit its opponents and achieve its objectives in developing the piers.

The heroes, as Lyons presented them, were the Port Authority and its partners in the Department of City Planning and the PDC, along with the commercial investors who would soon be revitalizing the abandoned piers on behalf of the borough and the city at large. An opening statement by Theodore Kleiner, the director of the Port Authority's Task Force for the Brooklyn Piers, immediately established the optimistic, civic-minded, pro-development tone of the article. "This is the most exciting project I've ever been involved with," Kleiner gushed, citing the proposed development's potential benefits for the city and region.

Wilbur Woods, the director of the Brooklyn office of the Department of City Planning, reiterated Kleiner's enthusiasm for the potential public benefits of development, explaining that, along with his partners in the Port Authority, he viewed the site as a "regional resource, not merely a local asset" whose future should not be determined exclusively by the desires of Brooklyn Heights or Wall Street (where many of the neighborhood's residents were employed).

The article's villains, as Woods's comments suggested, were the wealthy, well-connected residents of Brooklyn Heights who would resist the broader public benefit simply to protect their own privileged views of the East River and the Manhattan skyline. "My guess is that the real-estate developers will do anything to raise the height restrictions for the property," complained longtime Brooklyn Heights resident and celebrated author Norman Mailer. "Disposal of the site could be a political scam that would generate an enormous sense of outrage. But if they try to do something against the interest of the area, the opposition here will make the fight over Westway look like All Souls' Night."[27]

With his high profile, combative style of public debate, and flair for colorful hyperbole, Mailer was the perfect foil for the Port Authority's strategy to discredit public resistance to its plans for the commercial development of the west Brooklyn waterfront. Many *New York Times* readers would have still remembered Mailer's controversial positions in his unsuccessful New York City mayoral campaign in 1969, particularly his outspoken commitment to the right of each of the city's neighborhoods to make its own decisions and determine its own destiny, independent of centralized municipal rules and regulations.

At the time, Mailer's stubborn defense of neighborhood autonomy and self-determination had resonated powerfully among a wide variety of citizens dissatisfied with both the intrusions and the neglect of city government, including African American separatists in Harlem and Bedford-Stuyvesant. To many other voters, however, Mailer's comments reflected his singular commitment to the concerns of his own privileged neighborhood, where scenic views and tranquil streets were more highly valued than the interests of the city at large.

"I don't care too much about those people whose views might be obstructed because I see the issue as being much bigger than that," explained Martin Gallent, vice chairman of the City Planning Commission, openly mocking what he claimed to be the inflexible position of some residents of Brooklyn Heights that the neighborhood's historic views of the East River and the Manhattan skyline were an "untouchable" right that trumped other potential civic benefits, such as job creation and economic revitalization.

Although it had apparently not been the intention of the Port Authority in its initial overtures to Manheim and the Waterfront Committee, the concerns that the representatives of the Brooklyn Heights community had expressed about preserving the integrity of their neighborhood and protecting their view of the skyline—along with the community's past successes in neighborhood preservation and view protection—were now being turned against them. Far from ignoring the suggestions of the Waterfront Committee and other local representatives, the Port Authority's current leadership had clearly taken them to heart—not as legitimate concerns about the future development of the waterfront but as talking points for caricaturing and vilifying local resistance to commercial development. The strategy of the public authorities was to neutralize preemptively public objections to the commercial development of the piers by portraying local activists as self-interested elites, eager to sacrifice the greater public interest for their own privileged views of the East River and the Manhattan skyline.

In spite of their own private frustrations with the direction the Port Authority and the city had announced for Piers 1–6, Pearsall and Manheim were not as quick as Mailer had been to take the public authority's bait in a citywide forum. Pearsall acknowledged to the *Times* reporter that "some people are voicing disillusionment with city officials because of the Morgan Stanley building [which had recently, with the aggressive support of the PDC and the approval of the City Planning Commission, erected a seventeen-story computer-operations facility on the corner of Pierrepont and Court Streets]." He was far more restrained and diplomatic in expressing his own views, however. "I can't bring myself to believe that anything underhanded is going on," he said, affirming his continuing commitment to work cooperatively with the Port Authority.

Manheim was even more conciliatory in his comments, essentially endorsing the Port Authority's plans to use the waterfront for the commercial development of the property, as long as "some fraction" of the property was devoted to public use. "A mix of uses is what is needed," he told the *Times* reporter. "It would be unrealistic to put eighty-seven acres out as public parkland."

Even before the *New York Times* article was published, rumors regarding the findings and recommendations from the forthcoming Halcyon Report had reached the local Brooklyn media. In contrast to the enthusiasm of the *Times* piece and the guarded optimism voiced by Manheim and Pearsall, Brooklyn Heights journalists were highly critical of the Port Authority's plans for a "mammoth" recreational, residential, and commercial center on the site currently occupied by Piers 1–6.

A special edition of the *Brooklyn Heights Paper*, issued a week before the *Times* article, expressed alarm about a proposed pedestrian walkway connecting the piers to the tip of Montague Street or to Squibb Park, below Columbia Heights.[28]

A week later, the *Brooklyn Heights Press & Cobble Hill News* published multiple responses to the proposed development. A featured editorial warned local readers that the proposed construction of a luxury hotel on the waterfront would inevitably result in traffic congestion on Joralemon and Furman Streets, the only accessible routes to and along the piers.[29] A separate report in the same edition by journalist George Winslow cautioned that the Height's spectacular view of the skyline may be blocked by the impending development. "The development of the piers may offer some surprises," cautioned Winslow, citing past betrayals of the neighborhood by Robert Moses in the 1940s and the Port Authority's failed attempt to erect high-rise buildings on the piers in the mid-1950s. "Heights residents could wake up one morning and find a thirty-one-story Watchtower building blocking their views north of the Promenade and a thirty-story hotel blocking the view of the harbor at the south end." To support his concerns, Winslow cited a letter from Herbert Sturz, chairman of the City Planning Commission, explaining that the Department of City Planning could provide developers with a "zoning variance" reducing current view protections and properties that fall outside the designated scenic-view zones would not be protected from high-rise development.[30]

While Manheim and Pearsall were wisely reluctant to share their frustrations through the media, they and their colleagues on the Waterfront Committee were privately angered and discouraged by the preliminary information from the Halcyon Report. "It became clear," recall Hand and Pearsall, "that for all the pains of the Waterfront Committee members in urging their points, they might just as well have saved their breath. Pure and simple, what the agencies wanted was development with a capital 'D.'"[31]

It had also become clear that the Port Authority and the city were prepared to play hardball to get their way in privately developing Piers 1–6, publicly depicting opponents of development as privileged, self-serving elites with little concern for the public good. If Manheim, Pearsall, Hand, and the other members of the Waterfront Committee were to have any chance of success in protecting the interests of their community, they would have to adopt a much bolder and well-organized approach in their future interactions with the public authorities, the local community, and the media.

IN LIGHT OF THESE REVELATIONS, Manheim, Pearsall, Hand, and the other members of the Waterfront Committee immediately realized that they could no longer simply trust the Port Authority to incorporate their community's priorities and concerns into its development scheme for the piers. A far more aggressive, well-funded, and broad-based approach would be required for the committee to succeed in gaining leverage with the authorities and protecting the Brooklyn Heights community and the surrounding neighborhoods from the negative impact of the private development of the piers.

The first action in the committee's more aggressive waterfront campaign was to convene a public meeting to inform neighborhood residents about the details of the Halcyon Report and its potential impact on the community. Although the Port Authority would not release the complete content of the report to the public for several months, Halcyon had submitted its final report, *Development Concepts for the Brooklyn Piers*, to the Port Authority and the city in December 1985, and preliminary drafts of the document had begun to circulate informally throughout the community, increasing the anger and frustration that had been generated by the media coverage in late October.

As Philip LaRocco, Director of World Trade and Economic Development at the Port Authority, had already confided to Manheim months earlier,[32] Halcyon had indeed prepared and submitted a marketing study—recommending optimal scenarios for selling the concept of private development to potential developers—in place of the type of community-informed planning study to which the Waterfront Committee members had originally been led to believe they were contributing by voicing their concerns to Port Authority representatives.

As the *Times* article had suggested, recommendations for private development and use of the piers property dominated the report, with minimal references to public use and recreation. At the center of the Halcyon concept was the creation of "an 'international city,' which takes full advantage of the unique assembly of land and waterfront at a prime, visible location in a major metropolitan area."[33] The proposed "international city" would feature a research institute, a trade-oriented exhibition center, and a conference center, sponsoring programs on world trade. Additional private developments would include office buildings, corporate headquarters, residential buildings, retails centers, and a large boat marina and ferry terminal.

Faced with the barrage of negative local media coverage, the Port Authority and the city quickly distanced themselves from the Halcyon Report's recommendations for an international trade center to be constructed along the Brooklyn waterfront. "Their [Halcyon's recommendations] inclusion here should not be interpreted as an endorsement of any of their ideas by either the City or the Port Authority," explained the Port Authority's Philip LaRocco and Deputy Mayor Alair Townsend in a joint press release in early 1986.[34] Whatever the Port Authority and the city actually thought of Halcyon's specific recommendations, however, their commitment to private development was clear.

WITH THE PORT AUTHORITY DECLINING an invitation to defend its report at a public meeting, the Waterfront Committee decided instead to assemble a panel of distinguished experts in urban planning and development, who would be asked to assess the merits of the Halcyon Report and provide their own recommendations about what should and should not be done with the piers property. With the advice and assistance of local architect Ted Liebman (former chief architect for the New York State Urban Development Corporation), Manheim, Hand, and Pearsall quickly recruited "an all-star panel"[35] that included

- Architect David M. Childs, of the prominent architecture, urban-planning, and engineering firm Skidmore, Owings & Merrill
- Barbara J. Fife, former chair of the Waterfront Committee of the Parks Council and former Deputy Mayor for Planning and Development
- Edward J. Logue, former president of the New York State Urban Development Corporation
- Robert Campbell, architecture critic for the *Boston Globe*
- Roger Starr, former New York City Housing and Development Administrator and member of the *New York Times* editorial board
- Michael H. Zisser, president of the New York Metropolitan chapter of the American Planning Commission

The panel discussion, which was moderated by Municipal Art Society president Kent Barwick, was held at the Annual Meeting of the Brooklyn Heights Association on February 25, 1986, at St. Ann's Church in Brooklyn Heights, with "several hundred associates, members, residents and business owners" in attendance.[36]

Predictably, given their widely divergent backgrounds and experiences, the panelists differed in their views of the appropriate use of the waterfront property, with recommendations ranging from open parkland (Childs and Fife) to self-contained residential and commercial quarters (Campbell) to delaying development indefinitely in the hope that appropriate maritime uses could be identified that would restore the piers' traditional importance along the shoreline (Starr).[37]

While the speakers diverged in their recommendations for the appropriate use of the waterfront property, they were unanimous in their repudiation of the methodology, findings, and recommendations of the Halcyon Report, which was variously described as "incompetent," "inappropriate," "irresponsible," "ridiculous," "embarrassing," and completely lacking in the type of "comprehensive planning" that would give legitimacy to the Port Authority's proposal for the private development of the piers. At one point in the discussion, panelist Robert Campbell openly wondered "why the city agencies were not embarrassed to duplicate and distribute it."[38]

In addition to their rejection of the report's grand vision of an international trade center sprawling along the waterfront property, the panelists repeatedly criticized the fact that Halcyon had presented—and the Port Authority and the city had apparently commissioned—a marketing study *before* conducting sufficient research and planning to determine what precisely it was that they were trying to sell. The report, wrote local journalist Tracey Garrity in summarizing the panelists' combined critiques, "offered no foresight in planning and was in fact a marketing study—and a bad marketing study."[39]

IN ADDITION TO ITS SCATHING REBUKE of the Halcyon Report, the BHA panel discussion on February 25 also called attention to the lack of substantive research and planning for the development of the Brooklyn piers. Even as they publicly distanced themselves from Halcyon's international-trade-center concept, the Port Authority and its partners in city government were moving full speed ahead with the development process, announcing in the spring of 1986 that they intended to issue Requests for Proposals to eighteen major real-estate developers by late summer,[40] with tentative plans for infrastructure development in the fall of 1988 and site construction in the summer of 1989.[41]

To date, however, no substantive research had been conducted to determine a viable plan for the property using the traditional indicators for urban development (environmental impact, land use, technical and engineering requirements, zoning and regulatory constraints, market potential), nor (apart from Halcyon's ill-fated international city) had any specific plans been submitted for the consideration of public officials, potential investors, or the general public. The Port Authority and the city's strategy was simply to opt for private development in advance and then hope for the best, both in the results of the environmental impact and engineering reviews to follow and in the interest of potential developers.

TWO

FIGHTING BACK

> No one else was doing planning. The Port Authority wasn't, and the city wasn't. There was no such thing as a citywide waterfront plan.
>
> **ANTHONY MANHEIM**

T HE DECISION TO COMMISSION A PLANNING STUDY for the piers property and the commitment to a more aggressive public campaign inevitably involved substantial changes in the size, organization, and skill set of the Waterfront Committee of the Brooklyn Heights Association (BHA). Since its creation by Anthony Manheim in late 1983, the committee "had functioned as a small, hands-on operating unit," occasionally adding another member to provide assistance with a specific issue or concern.[1] In the face of the Port Authority and the city's rapidly evolving ambitions for the development of the piers and the increasing concern of local media and residents, the committee members soon realized that they simply lacked the financial resources, expertise, and influence throughout the broader Brooklyn community to keep pace with the challenges with which they were confronted on a day-to-day basis. If the Brooklyn Heights community was to have any hope of ensuring that its interests were protected in the current rush to development, a new committee was needed with a significantly expanded membership and clearly defined roles and responsibilities.

The Committee for the Redevelopment of the Brooklyn Piers (more commonly known as the Piers Committee) was formed and convened in August 1986, with Scott Hand as chair and Anthony Manheim and Otis

Pearsall as vice chairs. Manheim proposed the name for the new committee, the term "redevelopment" carefully chosen to counter "any possible identification of the committee as 'anti-development zealots,'" a pejorative that the *Brooklyn Paper* had used to caricature opponents of local development projects in the past.[2]

Within a few months, the small, ad hoc Waterfront Committee had been transformed into the broad-based, influential forty-eight-member Piers Committee, which included leaders in business and financial management such as John Watts and John S. Wadsworth Jr.; respected journalist Henrik Krogius; John Dozier Hasty, publisher of the *Brooklyn Heights Press & Cobble Hill News*; Carol Bellamy, president of the City Council and mayoral candidate; novelist Norman Mailer; and Martin Segal, founder of the Film Society of Lincoln Center.

"There was nobody you couldn't get to by knowing someone in Brooklyn Heights," remembers Manheim of the relative ease with which he and his colleagues were able to recruit the highly qualified membership for the committee. "If you wanted to arrange a meeting with the governor of Washington, there would be someone in the Heights whose sister's daughter had a friend who knew somebody who knew him."[3]

By the end of the year, the Piers Committee had also gained the nominal endorsement and support of the fourteen-member Advisory Committee, which included the Municipal Art Society, the Parks Council, the New York Landmarks Conservancy, the Open Space Coalition, Brooklyn Community Boards 2 and 6, and representatives of the various neighborhood associations from the other communities surrounding the piers.

Hand, Manheim, and Pearsall worked diligently during the last months of 1986 to get the Piers Committee up and running and to reassure the Brooklyn Heights community that they now had sufficient leverage with the Port Authority and its partners in city government to ensure that their community's interests were protected in the dispossession and development of the piers. During this period, however, Port Authority and city officials seemed to be going out of their way to convince the media, the general public, and local politicians that they had no intention of respecting the community's concerns in their ambitions for the private development of the piers.

In his annual report to the mayor, *New York City's Waterfront: A Plan for Development*, released in July 1986, James Stuckey, executive director of the New York City Public Development Corporation (PDC), openly acknowledged his agency's willingness to modify existing zoning restrictions in the private development of the city's abandoned waterfronts. "To this day, most waterfront property continues to be zoned in such a way as to effectively prevent development," Stuckey reported, explaining the need to take the necessary legal actions to change or suspend current restrictions. "While the implementation of new zoning will require several years, we believe it will serve to eliminate a tremendous amount of ambiguity and, in the long run, facilitate both public and private efforts to develop the city's waterfront."[4]

Public announcements of the city's intention to override existing zoning restrictions quickly attracted the attention of journalists and political leaders, both in Brooklyn Heights and throughout New York City. In August, a *New York Times* editorial by Brooklyn journalist and Piers Committee member Henrik Krogius introduced the concerns of the Brooklyn Heights community and the surrounding neighborhoods to a much broader audience. Citing both the Port Authority's right to seek exemptions from municipal zoning restrictions and the vulnerability of the unprotected properties immediately outside the scenic zone to high-rise development, Krogius openly questioned the commitment of the Port Authority and its counterparts in city government to preserve the existing views of the East River and the Manhattan skyline. "To diminish so remarkable an achievement and to spoil a public view that is nothing less than a national treasure would seem unthinkable," Krogius wrote. "However, in this age of the unthinkable there's a real danger of ill-conceived development."[5]

IN RESPONSE TO THE PORT AUTHORITY and the city's failure to provide a reasonable development plan for the piers property, the Waterfront Committee decided to commission its own planning study. As BHA president Earl Weiner explained to his membership at the time, it was imperative that the Waterfront Committee come up with a plan of its own in the early stages of the development process and "not have to react to someone else's plan well down the line when the possibilities for modifications and change are remote."[6]

In the spring of 1986, Waterfront Committee chair Scott Hand again solicited the assistance of Ted Liebman to determine the appropriate scope and rationale for an independent planning study for the development of the piers and to identify potential consulting firms with the experience and credibility to conduct the study. Hand followed up by mailing a Request for Proposals (RFP) to ten consulting firms, followed by a second round of invitations during the summer. As Hand explained in his letter to potential consultants, the proposed study was to reflect the priorities and expectations not only of Brooklyn Heights and the surrounding neighborhoods but also of the entire city.[7] In late August, the

Selection Sub-Committee (consisting of Manheim, Pearsall, Hand, and local architects Ted Liebman, Fred Bland, and Michael Zisser) selected the New York City planning and design firm Buckhurst Fish Hutton Katz (BFHK) as the consultant for the planning study.[8] Among the factors that resulted in the selection of BFHK was the firm's extensive experience conducting planning, zoning, and economic-feasibility studies for New York City, including recent projects at Snug Harbor and Bay Street Landing on Staten Island, the Battery Park City Ferry Terminal, and the Riverwalk development at East Twenty-third Street in Manhattan.

Predictably, Philip LaRocco, Director of World Trade and Economic Development at the Port Authority, and his counterparts in city government were opposed to the idea of an independent planning study commissioned by the residents of the affected community. In a meeting with the committee leaders at the Port Authority headquarters in July, LaRocco urged that the committee defer from retaining a consultant until after the Port Authority had selected its own developer for the site, "when collective attention could be focused on fleshing out and refining that developers' proposals."[9] With each new encounter with the Port Authority, it became increasingly clear that community input was to be limited to choosing among preestablished options, not actively contributing to the planning and design process.

In a letter to LaRocco announcing the selection of BFHK to conduct the piers planning study, Waterfront Committee chair Scott Hand managed to turn the table on the past attempts by the Port Authority and its Halcyon consultants to portray representatives of the waterfront movement in Brooklyn Heights as a small group of self-interested elites with little concern for the public good. Hand's measured comments instead suggested that it was the Port Authority, in its single-minded commitment to financial profit—not the Brooklyn Heights community—that was actually turning its back on the greater public good. The forthcoming planning study, Hand insisted, "may not necessarily be the one that returns the largest immediate cash return to the Port Authority but nevertheless may well earn highest public benefit over time."[10]

In spite of the public authorities' resistance, the Piers Committee continued unabated with its planning study for the piers property. A working group met regularly throughout late 1986 and early 1987 with BFHK partner Ernest Hutton to prepare a preliminary presentation of the findings and recommendations from the planning study at the Annual Meeting of the BHA in February.

On February 5, 1987, two weeks before the Annual Meeting, a special joint meeting of the BHA board of governors, the Piers Committee, and the Advisory Committee was held in the undercroft of First Unitarian Church at 50 Monroe Place in Brooklyn Heights. The purpose of the meeting was to provide the BHA governors and committee members with an advance briefing on the findings and recommendations from the BFHK study and to allow the association's leaders to prepare collectively for the open community discussion that would follow the presentation of the study at the Annual Meeting.

The meeting was notable for a passionate, impromptu presentation by Piers Committee member Benjamin Crane, a Wall Street lawyer and forty-year resident of Brooklyn Heights. Along with many other Brooklyn Heights residents, Crane was disturbed by the Port Authority's refusal to provide assurances that the neighborhood's scenic view would be protected in the forthcoming development of the piers as well as by recent rumors circulating throughout the neighborhood that much of the waterfront property would be devoted to luxury condominiums. The sudden increase in the Heights population that would inevitably be generated by the construction of multiple high-rise condominiums along the waterfront was a particularly unappealing prospect for many residents, who were originally drawn to the neighborhood by its quiet streets and sidewalks and tranquil public spaces. "I'd lived in the Heights for forty years and close to the Promenade for most of that time," Crane recalls. "So this notion of the Port Authority, that they wanted to have housing down on the piers, came as a dreadful shock."[11]

Shortly before the meeting, Crane, who had been only nominally involved in the Piers Committee up until this point, visited the local public library, where he discovered some provocative information about the availability of both parks and recreational space in the borough of Brooklyn and the statutory rights and responsibilities of the Port Authority.

"I had had absolutely no role in anything of this sort before this meeting," Crane acknowledges. "I had a couple of days off, and so I looked up a couple of things. I looked up the availability of parks in Brooklyn and found that Brooklyn was severely underparked, certainly compared to Manhattan.

"And then I looked up the statute creating the Port Authority," he continues. "I'm a lawyer and that's what you do. And I looked up the statute, which said they could do this and they could do that and they could appropriate things, but they could *not* do housing. There was a specific prohibition on the Port Authority doing housing.

"So I stood up in the meeting and gave them my report on the results into the research on the Port Authority's authority and the real need for park space in Brooklyn, and I also made the argument that you can't say, 'no,' forever, and we must have a goal. And because of the under-parked situation in Brooklyn, the perfectly logical goal for Brooklyn Heights was to go for a park. And that really spread widely in the neighborhood."[12]

Crane's unexpected presentation captured the current public mood on two important levels. In the first place, he openly challenged the Port Authority's right to dispose of the piers for private development, particularly for housing. To date, all of the committee's negotiations with the Port Authority and the city had been based on the presupposition that some type of private development of the piers was a foregone conclusion. The Brooklyn Heights community could and should work diligently to mitigate the negative impact of private development by protecting its historic view and the tranquil, cul-de-sac design of the neighborhood, the committee members had reasoned, but there was nothing that could realistically be done to stop private development altogether. For many Brooklyn Heights residents, however, the trustworthiness and the authority of the Port Authority and its partners in city government were no longer simply taken for granted.

Second, Crane expressed the growing conviction among many in the Brooklyn Heights community that the waterfront property should be devoted primarily to public, not private, interests—and that a park was the most natural and appropriate way to serve the public good. While the discussions between the BHA Waterfront and Piers Committees and the Port Authority had always included some public access and use of the site, allowances for park and recreational space had been minimal to date. What was needed, many Heights residents believed, was a park—not a massive private development with token public space here and there.

While many of those in attendance at the meeting on February 5 recognized that Crane's call for a community-owned and -sponsored public park was neither politically nor financially feasible under the current circumstances, Crane's demand that the property be devoted to the public good and that the Brooklyn Heights community should assume greater control of the development process deeply resonated with many of the community's residents—and would have a profound impact on the future development of the waterfront property.[13]

TWO WEEKS LATER, on February 24, 1987, more than 400 people crowded into St. Ann's Church to hear Ernest Hutton's presentation about what could and should be done with the piers. Recognizing that many in the crowd might be unfamiliar with the history of the Piers Committee's negotiations with the Port Authority, BHA president Earl Weiner's opening remarks emphasized the inevitability of at least some level of private development of the piers and the importance of continuing to work cooperatively with the Port Authority and its partners in city government in finalizing a plan for the waterfront. In commissioning a plan for the piers, the BHA itself was not advocating development, he explained: "We are forced, however, to consider development because of the Port Authority's stated intention to develop the piers in conjunction with the city."[14]

Hutton began his presentation by identifying six criteria that he and his partners had used to guide their plans for the waterfront:

1 Preserving and enhancing the area's unique view of the Manhattan skyline
2 Maintaining maritime use of the piers
3 Enhancing public access and use of the waterfront area
4 Ensuring environmentally sensitive development
5 Providing character, quality, and scale compatible with the surrounding historic district
6 Providing uses appropriate to the local and regional context[15]

Next Hutton introduced four "illustrative schemes" for developing the waterfront property along Piers 1–6.

Scheme A involved an enhanced working waterfront, which could provide the area with traditional maritime services that had been displaced by other local development projects. Scheme B—the one that predictably caused the greatest stir among those in attendance—proposed the dedication of the entire waterfront property, including the available upland areas, as a "Major Public Park." The proposed park would feature a balanced mix of active and passive recreational space, along with a park-length pedestrian walkway, a museum, a performing arts center, a boat basin, and public restaurants. Scheme C described a "Moderate Mixed-Use Development," preserving much of the active and passive recreational space of the second scheme, while adding a hotel/conference center. Finally, Scheme D, which called for "Intensive Mixed-Use Development," added 750 units of residential housing.

In the question-and-answer session that followed Hutton's presentation, Piers Committee chair Scott Hand explained that the committee's goal in commissioning the planning study was to fulfill a crucial responsibility that the Port Authority and the city had repeatedly neglected to take on—providing the community and potential developers with viable development models from which to choose. "Our goal is not to endorse any specific plan," he insisted, "but to suggest ideas for the responses of residents."[16]

With the public presentation and subsequent positive media coverage of the findings from the BFHK planning study, the Piers Committee had gained the upper hand from the Port Authority and the city in the public debate about the future of the Brooklyn waterfront.[17] In the wake of the public presentation by Benjamin Crane and the barrage of newspaper editorials openly questioning the reliability of the Port Authority and the city as a partner for developing the piers, it was becoming increasingly clear that the Piers Committee would have to pay far more attention to the fears and aspirations of the community itself if it was to be successful in its ongoing negotiations with the Port Authority.

DURING THE SPRING AND SUMMER OF 1987, public support for a park along Piers 1–6 was strengthened by the findings from a borough-wide study conducted by the BHA's Subcommittee for the Recreational Use of the Brooklyn Piers 1–6, chaired by Piers Committee member Irene Janner. The study, which had been completed in November 1986 and the findings of which were included in BFHK's report, *The Future of the Piers: Planning and Design Criteria for Brooklyn Piers 1–6*, surveyed the recreational requirements and available public resources of a diverse collection of primary and secondary schools, colleges, and youth organizations across the borough, including the Brooklyn Friends School, Packer Collegiate Institute, St. Charles Borromeo School, St. Francis College, St. Ann's School, Long Island University (Brooklyn Campus), the Brooklyn YMCA, the American Youth Soccer Organization, Public Schools 8 and 29, and Community School Districts 13 and 15.[18]

The findings from the study were both distressing and compelling: the collective recreational needs of the borough's youth far exceeded the resources and space that were currently available to address those needs. "We did a survey in the neighborhood of local athletic associations, schools, anyone we could think of, really," remembers Piers Committee member and survey organizer Irene Janner. "And we had a survey that ran in the *Heights Press* also for residents to comment on what they wanted to see there. That was basically it: What do you want there? And the overwhelming response was that there was a crying need for active recreational space."[19]

At the time, formal statements released by the BHA Piers Committee still endorsed the hybrid concept of extensive commercial development on Piers 1–6 with some allowances for public space. The percentage of space that the Piers Committee maintained should be reserved for open parkland and recreational use had substantially increased over the first three years of the committee's existence—from early requests that "some fraction" of the property be devoted to public use to the more recent demand for "up to a third of the park to be used for passive, and possibly active, recreation."[20] The basic assumption remained, however, that the piers would be primarily dedicated to commercial redevelopment, with minimal disruption of the views and lifestyle of the adjacent neighborhoods and with a reasonable (still-to-be-determined) amount of "supplemental" public space.

The findings of Janner's subcommittee survey reinforced a growing sentiment among the general public—as well as an emerging private conviction among many Piers Committee members—that the waterfront property should be devoted primarily (if not exclusively) to the park concept, with open and recreational space comprising the primary use of the waterfront property. Commercial constructions (such as restaurants, stores, parking facilities, and conference centers), if they were to be included at all, would be supplemental to and supportive of the park concept.

AS PUBLIC TOLERANCE of the commercial development of Piers 1–6 declined, the authorities in charge of the disposition of the property continued to make a case for the private development of the New York City waterfront, not limited to but including the west Brooklyn piers. During the spring and summer of 1987, PDC director James Stuckey was back in the spotlight, working the media to persuade political leaders and reassure real-estate developers about the public benefit and commercial viability of developing the city's extensive waterfront properties, including the abandoned west Brooklyn piers.

"From our point of view, there's a wealth of opportunity, and we want to make sure the city takes advantage of it," Stuckey told a reporter from *Round-Up*. The recent designation of the powerful PDC as the lead agency in waterfront development, Stuckey assured readers, was a clear sign of the city's commitment to do whatever was necessary to facilitate the development process and address the concerns of potential investors. "We approach development like a private developer," Stuckey insisted, echoing Mayor Ed Koch's conviction that public benefit and private investment were essentially the same. "But we represent the city."[21]

As Stuckey openly acknowledged, his aggressive promotion of the benefits of private development was driven, at least in part, by the specter of stalled waterfront-development projects across the city and a precipitous decline in confidence among potential real-estate investors. Faced with ubiquitous zoning restrictions and growing public resistance to the Koch administration's ambitions for the waterfront, corporate planners and real-estate developers—many of whom had long-standing concerns regarding crime, transportation, and the quality of public schools in the outer boroughs—were beginning to reweigh the risks versus the benefits of investing in development projects in Brooklyn and Queens, with a particularly dampening effect on proposed projects along the East River.[22] "A major problem the city has had in competing is it inability to convince tenants that it can deliver space," Stuckey explained to a *New York Times* reporter in June. "We promised to deliver and Morgan Stanley believed us, but other tenants aren't so sure."[23]

As waterfront-development projects like Westway in Manhattan and a $17 million commercial construction project at Pier 10 in Sheepshead Bay in Brooklyn encountered public opposition and the confidence of investors began to decline, Stuckey became increasingly passionate in his promotion of the virtues of the private development of the city's waterfronts, particularly the vast, abandoned waterfronts along both sides of the East River. "New York is sitting on a tremendous opportunity for expansion along the East River waterfront," Stuckey explained to a *New York Times* reporter in August, "for both the commercial space that the city, as a world financial center, needs and better housing, which the city demands."[24]

WHILE STUCKEY WAS PUBLICLY EXTOLLING the virtues of private development of the Brooklyn waterfront, the idea of a public park along Piers 1–6 continued to gain traction throughout Brooklyn Heights and the adjacent communities, as well as in the local media. The release of the final version of the full report of the findings from the BFHK study, *The Future of the Piers: Planning and Design Criteria for Brooklyn Piers 1–6*, in June 1987 added further credibility to the idea that a park along the west Brooklyn piers was a worthy and achievable goal with enormous potential benefit to the greater New York region—and not just the romantic fantasy of a small group of privileged elites.

"One hundred years from now, looking back at the decisions made," wrote BFHK partner Ernest Hutton, the report's principal author, "it will have been important to have fully examined this opportunity [for a park along the piers]: an area of this size already recognized and protected by zoning legislation because of its unsurpassed view, could provide for the long-term benefit of future New Yorkers and visitors a regional resource containing both active and passive open space, comparable to such other large waterfront open spaces as Riverside Park, the open space adjacent to the Belt Parkway, or Liberty State Park in New Jersey.

"In this development possibility, the pier area would be developed for active open space," the report continued, providing readers with an enticing vision of the types of opportunities that a waterfront park could provide, "large open play areas, tennis courts, tot lots and passive open space. The ends of each pier, looking west towards the view of Manhattan and the bay, would contain a park/plaza area for strolling, sitting or picnicking. Considerations could be given to enclosed recreation structures for year-round use. Water-related uses could include a boat basin for berthing of both work and pleasure craft along the existing piers, as well as sites for facilities such as a restaurant or floating swimming pool."[25]

IN SEPTEMBER 1987, the Piers Committee suddenly found itself in the midst of a long-standing dispute between the Port Authority and the New York State Legislature over the appropriate use of the west Brooklyn waterfront. Since the late 1950s, with the opening of the massive containerization terminals at Port Elizabeth and Port Newark, New York State legislators had repeatedly accused the Port Authority of concentrating its maritime development activities in New Jersey, to the neglect and eventual abandonment of the Brooklyn piers as viable shipping facilities. As a continuation of this ongoing and still unresolved conflict, both legislative bodies had recently convened special task forces to investigate the Port Authority's current plans for the piers in Red Hook, Brooklyn Heights, and Fulton Ferry Landing and the potential impact of these plans on the adjacent communities.[26]

As part of this bicameral investigation, State Senator Martin Connor, who represented waterfront areas in Brooklyn, Manhattan, and Staten Island, invited a representative from the BHA Piers Committee to testify before a newly formed investigative body that he chaired, the New York State Democratic Task Force on Waterfront Development. Along with his colleague in the New York State Assembly, Eileen C. Dugan, Connor suspected that the Port Authority was preparing to sell the west Brooklyn piers to the highest bidder to finance the exorbitant costs of maintaining its maritime facilities in New Jersey, including the ongoing dredging of silt required to allow the enormous containerships to dock, and he was eager to hear what local leaders felt about the proposed commercial development of the piers. "The Port Authority made a major investment twenty-five years ago in New Jersey for container-handling facilities," Connor explained to a journalist at the time, "and now they must cover that investment."[27]

"The Port Authority has made a conscious decision to move the waterfront to New Jersey," charged Dugan, who was conducting parallel hearings in the Assembly and who also represented Brooklyn Heights in the state legislature. "They want to see the Brooklyn waterfront developed as real estate. There are great views of downtown Manhattan from there, and they think there is more revenue in land than in cargo. But we say that is a misuse of Port Authority funds."[28]

In response to a request from Connor, Piers Committee vice chair Otis Pearsall appeared before the Task Force on Waterfront Development on September 23, 1987, responding to questions from the legislators while making extensive use of a comprehensive statement prepared in advance by the Piers Committee. "Brooklyn has a far lower percentage of its area devoted to parkland than other boroughs," Pearsall explained to the task force members, "and as the most populous borough, has far less parkland than the others on a per capita basis. There is a strong case to be made," he continued, "that this spectacular harborside site should be devoted 100 percent to active and passive recreation since, with its ownership already in public hands and at least morally subject to the public trust, there should be no requirement here for a private development that must pay its own way."[29]

In addition to making a compelling case for the conversion of Piers 1–6 into a public park, Pearsall complained to the legislators that the Piers Committee had been treated as an outsider in the development process by the Port Authority and its partners in city government, which seemed determined to "maximize development profit at the cost of irretrievably lost public benefit," indifferent to the concerns and suggestions of the communities affected by their actions. "While the agencies have always been willing to receive us courteously and hear our planning ideas, they never, never share theirs," Pearsall charged.[30]

While Connor and Dugan were holding their respective hearings in the state legislature, the Port Authority and the city were preparing to move ahead with the commercial development of Piers 1–6. In August, they composed a tentative RFP to be sent to potential developers for the site, and the Manhattan architectural firm Beyer Blinder Belle was retained in November to assist in the finalization of the criteria and guidelines that would be included in the request.

As the members of the Piers Committee would later learn, however, the initial RFP included a mandate for high-density commercial development totaling 2.3 million square feet of housing and an additional 700,000 square feet of commercial development, with virtually no room reserved for public space or other alternatives. According to Pearsall, the thankless task assigned to the urban designers at Beyer Blinder Belle amounted to little more than "rearranging deck chairs on the *Titanic*."[31]

JUST DAYS AFTER PEARSALL'S TESTIMONY before the New York State Democratic Task Force on Waterfront Development, the Port Authority took a further step toward the commercial development of Piers 1–6 when Public Relations Director Rita Schwartz issued a formal request at the monthly meeting of Community Board 2 (CB2) for the formation of a community board subcommittee on waterfront development "to act as a sounding board" for the Port Authority's plans for the piers.[32]

The City Charter required that the disposition of all *city-owned* property pass through the Uniform Land Use Review Procedure, through which the Board of Estimate, the City Planning Commission, and the local community board each had sixty days to review and vote on a development proposal. Only the approval of the Board of Estimate was considered binding, though a negative response by a local community board would further undermine the confidence of a real-estate market that was already wary of the risks involved in development projects in the outer boroughs.[33] Although the Port Authority was actually exempted from the three-party review process and was subject only to approval by the Board of Estimate, its formal partnership with the PDC and the New York City Department of City Planning necessitated the full standard review in this case.

While the inclusion of local community boards was a routine part of the dispossession and private development of public land in New York City, the Port Authority's stated intention of using the CB2 subcommittee as a "sounding board" for its commercial-development plans struck the BHA Piers Committee as an outright betrayal of the informal relationship that had been established between the Port Authority and the Waterfront and Piers Committees over the previous three years. Faced with continuing resistance and increasingly sophisticated counterproposals from the Piers Committee, the Port Authority and its partners in city government had apparently decided to take their case for the commercial development of Piers 1–6 to what they considered to be a more hospitable audience.

"At some point, the Port Authority just stopped cooperating with us and sought to go around us by endeavoring, with the help of City Planning, to draw up a housing plan for the piers and then to take their design to the Community Board 2 planning committee," recalls Anthony Manheim of the Port Authority's sudden shift in strategy and abrupt abandonment of the relationship that it had cultivated with the BHA committees during the previous three years. "This would allow them to say in the RFP that they already had the endorsement of the community board, whereas they knew they would probably encounter resistance from us."[34]

"We have not had a response from the Port Authority," Otis Pearsall complained to a reporter from the *Brooklyn Paper* after learning of Schwartz's announcement. "At the same time we are being greeted by a stone wall as we see the Port Authority actively seeking to pursue an apparent community participation in another forum."[35]

When questioned by the same reporter about the Port Authority's motivations in reaching out to CB2, Schwartz denied Pearsall's claims that the Port Authority was turning its back on the BHA or the Piers Committee. Given its multiple activities in redevelopment projects throughout the city, Schwartz insisted, the Port Authority simply lacked the time and resources to interact directly with every community group that had something to say about the proposed redevelopment of the piers. CB2 (which included the west Brooklyn neighborhoods of Cobble Hill, Boerum Hill, Fort Greene, Fulton Mall, Clinton Hill, Brooklyn Navy Yard, and Fulton Ferry) had been selected by the Port Authority as the most appropriate surrogate for representing the needs and concerns of the entire community. "We want the community board to develop an appropriate mechanism for community input," Schwartz insisted. "I can't continue to meet with every community group."[36]

Based strictly on CB2's recent involvement in local redevelopment schemes, the Port Authority and its partners in city government would have expected the community board to be a receptive audience for the proposed dispossession and commercial development of Piers 1–6. During the mid-1980s, CB2 had become known for its aggressive focus on economic growth and its enthusiastic support of downtown redevelopment projects (including major constructions at Cadman Plaza, Atlantic Avenue, and MetroTech), even when tenants and residents in the affected neighborhoods opposed the projects. In May 1987, for example, CB2 had voted 25 to 0 to support a development project at Livingston Plaza, over the vigorous objections of local merchants who feared that their businesses would be permanently displaced by the proposed construction. "The community feels that development is needed to keep business in New York," CB2 chairman Jerry J. Renzini explained to a *New York Times* reporter at the time of the Livingston Plaza vote.[37]

With almost three years invested in their efforts to ensure the greatest public benefit for the west Brooklyn waterfront, Scott, Pearsall, Manheim, and the other members of the BHA were not prepared to give up without a fight. "To the extent that the Port Authority thinks that by promoting CB2's involvement on the issue they are going to be able to ignore the concerns of the Brooklyn Heights community, they are wrong," Pearsall proclaimed to a local reporter at the time.[38]

Shortly after Schwartz's call for the creation of a CB2 subcommittee on waterfront development, recently elected BHA president Denise Clayton persuaded Renzini to include six BHA members on the newly formed Piers Subcommittee (including Hand, Pearsall, Fred Bland, Carol Bellamy, Irene Janner, and Mary Ellen Murphy). While the BHA and the Piers Committee could not determine the final decision that came out of the CB2 Piers Subcommittee, they could ensure that the other subcommittee members would be fully informed of the concerns of the Brooklyn Heights community and of the BHA Piers Committee's alternative plans for Piers 1–6.

THE CB2 PIERS SUBCOMMITTEE held what would be the first of ten meetings on January 11, 1988. The subcommittee members were informed by a Port Authority representative attending the meeting that they would be given a three-month time frame (one month longer than the standard community board review process) to review the criteria and guidelines for the development of Piers 1–6 submitted by Beyer Blinder Belle and to establish their own community-based supplemental criteria to be included in the forthcoming RFP that would be sent to potential developers later in the year.[39]

In contrast to the Port Authority's expectations that CB2 would be receptive to its goals for Piers 1–6, the members of the CB2 Piers Subcommittee were resistant to plans for the commercial development of the piers from the start, openly questioning the proposed scale for residential development ("the propriety of calling for three million square feet of housing prior to any community input"), the limited three-month time frame for the community review, and the exclusive focus on financial profit in determining the appropriate use for the piers property.[40]

Clearly caught off guard by the intensity of the questioning from Piers Subcommittee members, Philip LaRocco was defensive in his responses, particularly regarding the importance of financial profit in the proposed guidelines and criteria for developing Piers 1–6. "Financial return is a factor in this project," responded LaRocco to an accusation that the Port Authority and the city emphasized profit at the expense of other public benefits in their goals for the waterfront property. "The public good is determined not only by recreational space, but by the creation of jobs through the development of commercial establishments. The Port Authority will consider a 'matrix of possibilities' to balance different interests."[41]

Hand, Pearsall, and the other BHA representatives on the CB2 Piers Subcommittee were encouraged by the direct and insightful questions that their fellow subcommittee members posed to LaRocco during the initial gathering. They quickly realized, however, that simply questioning the criteria and motivations of the Port Authority and its partners in city government would not be sufficient to thwart the Port Authority's ambitions for lining the west Brooklyn waterfront with high-rise residential buildings. If the needs and interests of Brooklyn's citizens were to be protected, the BHA Piers Committee would have to assume the responsibility for presenting the subcommittee with a compelling alternative for the use of Piers 1–6. The criteria for such a plan, along with illustrative schemes for its realization, had already been clearly laid out in BFHK's study, which had been released in June. The challenge ahead was to expand BFHK's criteria and recommendations beyond the conceptual stage, into a visual model that would capture the imaginations and address the concerns of the entire Brooklyn community.

DURING 1987, Hand and Pearsall had continued to believe that the interests of the Brooklyn Heights community could be adequately protected by adopting provisions from the mixed-use "illustrative schemes" presented in the BFHK report, supplementing the "pure park" model of Scheme B with both the hotel and conference center described in Scheme C and "some portion of the 750 units of housing" provided in Scheme D. Not only would the model of an expansive park supplemented by a hotel, a conference center, and limited public housing satisfy the concerns and desires of most Brooklyn citizens, the two men reasoned, but it might also prove acceptable to the Port Authority and its counterparts in city government, now that they had begun to encounter broad public opposition to their own unilateral ambitions for commercial development. "With all the intellectual effort invested over the past year and a half in advancing the Committee's thinking this far," Pearsall would later reflect, "[we] might have been forgiven for believing that the course forward was both soundly conceived and clear."[42]

Hand and Pearsall's continuing belief in the viability of a hybrid plan for Piers 1–6, with provisions for low- and medium-rise housing, was perfectly reasonable, based on the Piers Committee's original goals in negotiating with the Port Authority (protecting the scenic view of the Manhattan skyline and preserving the cul-de-sac nature of Brooklyn Heights, while ensuring that at least some of the space was retained for public use).

During the previous year and a half, however, the concept of a public park along the west Brooklyn waterfront had taken on a life of its own among many Brooklyn citizens, both within and beyond the membership of the BHA and the Piers Committee. A number of factors—including public discussions of the recently released BFHK report, the findings from Irene Janner's study describing the critical need for recreational space throughout the borough, and growing support of the concept of a west Brooklyn waterfront park from the media—had suddenly made public aspirations for a park on the piers seem not only achievable but perhaps also inevitable for many residents, including Anthony Manheim and other members of the Piers Committee itself.

Manheim, who had nurtured private ambitions for the public use of the piers property since his initial conversation with the Port Authority four years earlier, had been alert to the shift in public sympathy all along, and the growing public enthusiasm for a park on the piers had rekindled his original dreams for a grand public space along the waterfront beneath the Brooklyn Heights Promenade.[43] "Here you had a site that was literally at the center of the city," Manheim remembers, "fifty acres of already publicly owned land that would never again be available. There was talk of park development in other places, but it all involved buying land from public owners. I think we all understood that this was a unique opportunity."[44]

On the evening of February 8, 1988, almost exactly a year after its first public hearing on the public authorities' plans for the piers, the Piers Committee met once again with local community members in the undercroft of the First Unitarian Church in Brooklyn Heights. This time, however, the concerns and aspirations of a few local residents had swollen into broad-based and outspoken community support for a public park on the waterfront. In a matter of moments—and to the utter amazement of Hand and Pearsall—the terms of the debate had been completely transformed, with the balance of opinion shifting from a "hybrid" public–private development scheme to a "pure park" concept, with minimal tolerance for supplemental commercial development and no tolerance whatsoever for a plan that emphasized housing along the piers.

"While no actual vote was taken," remembers Pearsall, "it was clear enough from the voices of those who spoke out that housing was a dead letter not only for the purposes of a Piers Committee presentation to the

CB2 Piers Subcommittee but also, unless reversed by the BHA board, as a matter of BHA strategic policy going forward."[45] At the Annual Meeting of the BHA, held the evening after the special Piers Committee meeting, Manheim enthusiastically reported to those in attendance, "The Committee strongly endorsed the concept of public benefit/public use as opposed to housing which, notwithstanding its financial benefits, is too exclusive."[46]

MEANWHILE, the CB2 Piers Subcommitee hearings continued unabated. In addition to their frustrations with the presentations at the hearings, the members' resistance to the Port Authority's plans for the commercial development of the piers was also inspired by an informal site visit arranged by the agency following the second subcommittee hearing. "The biggest mistake the Port Authority ever made," remembers subcommittee member Irene Janner, "was in January. I guess they figured it was a horrible time to be out by the water. They got a little bus and we were allowed to go where no one had gone before—we were allowed to go out on a pier. Of course, that had always been closed off because they had a working waterfront. And they had a little bus for the community board on a Saturday, on a miserable January day, and they took us out and let us walk all the way out on Pier 2.

"Well, they lost their fight right there," concludes Janner, "because none of us had ever been out on the water. And as miserable as the weather was—what an experience! Literally being out on this pier all the way out into the East River. We loved it. They lost their battle right there."[47]

At the conclusion of the Piers Subcommittee meeting on March 30, just a few days before the three-month deadline for the subcommittee's recommendations to be submitted to the public authorities in charge of the disposition of Piers 1–6, the eleven members who were present openly rebelled against the constraints that had been placed on them by the Port Authority and the insufficient time and information that they had been given for responding to the Port Authority's proposal for the piers. To ensure that their responses and recommendations were fully informed about the Port Authority's intentions and adequately represented the needs of the communities they represented, the subcommittee members demanded and voted unanimously in favor of indefinitely extending the scope and timeline for their work.

In her closing remarks at the meeting, Chairwoman Ethel Purnell acknowledged that the Port Authority retained the legal option of issuing RFPs to potential developers and authorizing the development of the site without securing the approval of the local community board. Given the anemic condition of the development market at the time, however, and the dramatic decline in investor confidence in the outer boroughs as viable sites for development, both the subcommittee members and the public authorities fully recognized that a "no" vote (or even a non-vote) from CB2 would have a dampening effect on the RFP process, frightening away private developers already wary of the possibility of public resistance or unfavorable legal rulings to delay or restrict construction.

Reluctant to begin the RFP process for Piers 1–6 without the formal endorsement of the local community board, the Port Authority reluctantly accommodated the CB2 Piers Subcommittee's request for an extension. They refused an invitation from Purnell to reconvene the subcommittee meetings in April, however. It would be late July before the Port Authority and its partners in the Department of City Planning would finally agree to meet in person with the subcommittee again.

Following the first CB2 Piers Subcommittee meeting on January 11, Scott Hand, Otis Pearsall, and Ted Liebman (the three BHA Piers Committee representatives on the Piers Subcommittee) began discussing the possibility of presenting the subcommittee with a viable alternative to the Port Authority's expansive housing-development scheme for Piers 1–6. With the support of the Piers Committee, Liebman reached out to Terry Schnadelbach, founder and principal partner of the highly respected Schnadelbach Partnership. A landscape architect with extensive experience in environmental planning and urban design, Schnadelbach was the past recipient of numerous awards in urban and landscape design. Schnadelbach, who had worked with Liebman in the past, was immediately intrigued by the challenge of countering the public authorities' plans for the private development of Piers 1–6 and of bringing the Piers Committee's vision of a west Brooklyn waterfront park to life.

Working closely with the Piers Committee, Schnadelbach completed his plan, "Harbor Park: A Maritime and Public Use Development on the Brooklyn Piers," by late May. Building on the mixed-use "illustrative schemes" in the BFHK study, the Harbor Park plan included extensive open spaces and playing fields, shaded sitting areas, interactive waterfalls, a skating rink, a conference center and hotel, an expansive marina (with a permanently docked "boatel"), and a continuous walkway providing park visitors with easy access to all the site's features (figure 10).[48] Of vital importance for the current debate with the public authorities, Schnadelbach's recommendations also featured colorful visual illustrations of the proposed park area, including an aerial view of the entire property, a view of the park from the perspective of lower Manhattan across the East River, and a view looking northward from the marina

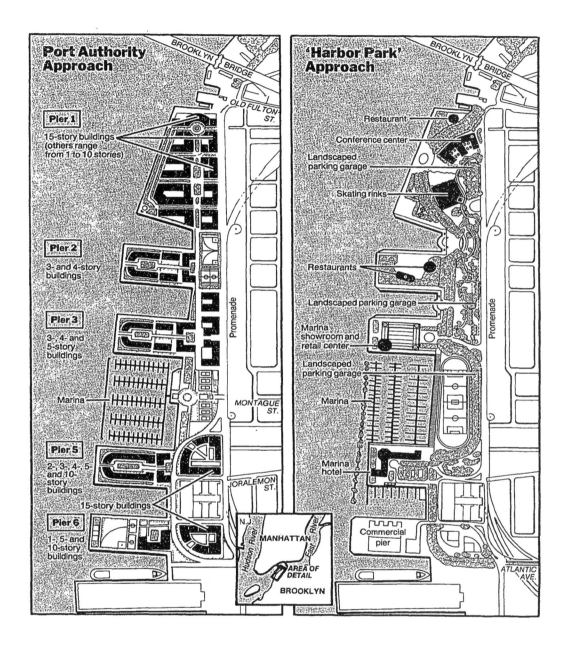

Port Authority Approach

Pier 1
15-story buildings (others range from 1 to 10 stories)

Pier 2
3- and 4-story buildings

Pier 3
3-, 4- and 5-story buildings

Marina

Pier 5
2-, 3-, 4-, 5- and 10-story buildings

15-story buildings

Pier 6
1-, 5- and 10-story buildings

BROOKLYN BRIDGE

OLD FULTON ST.

Promenade

MONTAGUE ST.

JORALEMON ST.

N.J.
MANHATTAN
Hudson River
East River
AREA OF DETAIL
BROOKLYN

'Harbor Park' Approach

Restaurant

Conference center

Landscaped parking garage

Skating rinks

Restaurants

Landscaped parking garage

Marina showroom and retail center

Landscaped parking garage

Marina

Marina hotel

Commercial pier

BROOKLYN BRIDGE

Promenade

ATLANTIC AVE.

FIGURE 10

The Port Authority approach versus the Brooklyn Heights "Harbor Park" approach to the redevelopment of the piers, as illustrated in the *New York Times*, August 19, 1988.
COURTESY OF *NEW YORK TIMES*

and upland playing fields between Piers 3 and 5, including the Brooklyn–Queens Expressway and the western boundary of Brooklyn Heights.

Aware that the Piers Committee was preparing an alternative proposal for Piers 1–6 and still not ready to present their own plans, the Port Authority and the city repeatedly delayed the next round of hearings, cancelling scheduled meetings in April and June before finally agreeing to present their plan for the piers on July 27. In addition to the Piers Subcommittee members, a roomful of reporters, consultants, BHA members, and more than forty representatives of the general public were on hand to hear Eileen Daly, from the Port Authority's Department of World Trade and Economic Development, and Bill Woods, the director of the Brooklyn office of the Department of City Planning, present the public authorities' plans for the commercial development of the Brooklyn piers. Although Beyer Blinder Belle had reportedly been commissioned to guide the Port Authority and the city's design for the waterfront, representatives from the firm were conspicuously absent from the presentation.

As the subcommittee members and others in attendance listened in disbelief, Daly and Woods presented four separate but virtually identical designs for the piers and adjacent upland areas, each one crowding more than thirty buildings representing more 3 million square feet of residential space (approximately 2,200 to 2,800 apartments) onto the fifty-five acres of waterfront property.[49] A grand total of five acres (less than 10 percent of the site) was reserved for open or recreational space, including two baseball diamonds and a rooftop tennis court. Five of the proposed structures were fifteen stories high, sufficient to obscure the view of the East River and the Brooklyn Bridge and much of the view of the Manhattan skyline, and plans were also included for a pedestrian walkway that would join the Promenade at Montague Street and essentially abolish the cul-de-sac design of Brooklyn Heights.

"The worst fears of Brooklyn Heights are realized in the planned development of the piers below the Promenade by the Port Authority and New York City," wrote Henrik Krogius, reflecting the anger and disbelief of those in attendance. "Short of openly violating the zoning view plane, which protects the major part of the view from the Promenade, and short of filling in the water between the piers, they have wrung virtually every bit of buildable space out of that limited area, even to the extent of building condominiums out on the piers themselves."[50]

On August 3, exactly a week later, representatives of the BHA Piers Committee assembled to present the CB2 Piers Subcommittee with their alternative plan for Piers 1–6.[51] The centerpiece of the Piers Committee proposal was the presentation of "Harbor Park," the report by architect Terry Schnadelbach. Linking his vision for the park to the grand urban designs of Frederick Law Olmsted and Robert Moses, Schnadelbach provided the CB2 Piers Subcommittee members with an illustrated walk through the site, carefully explaining the rationale for the positioning of each of the integrated features while making constant reference to the vivid, colored drawings included in the report. As many of those in attendance would later recall, the contrasting visual images of the park—more than any other factor—established Harbor Park as the inevitable choice for the use of Piers 1–6.

"The power of the image has been crucial throughout this process to get people on board in supporting the park concept," explains Piers Committee member David Offensend. "Over the years, each step of the way, we've always had a picture. This is what it's going to look like. It has the advantage of making it look real, and everybody looks at it and goes, 'Ah, I like that.' So, you know, it's not just a concept."[52]

In the days that followed, the Port Authority and the Department of City Planning did their best to counter the enthusiasm of the Piers Subcommittee members and other Brooklyn residents for the Harbor Park design, focusing on what they claimed to be the prohibitive cost of building and maintaining a vast public space on the piers. "To be responsible, you must propose something that's feasible," Allen Morrison, a senior information officer at the Port Authority, explained to David Dunlap of the *New York Times*. "We have yet to see any evidence that it can be built."[53]

On November 14, when the Piers Subcommittee reconvened to vote on the competing proposals for Piers 1–6, the outcome was all but certain. A few days earlier, Pearsall had provided Ethel Purnell and each of the subcommittee members with a six-page resolution, meticulously contrasting the two proposals while highlighting the benefits of the Harbor Park plan, along with letters of endorsement and support from organizations outside Brooklyn Heights that Anthony Manheim had spent the previous four months securing.[54]

After more than ten months of hearings and deliberations, the subcommittee members voted overwhelmingly (12 for, 0 against, and 1 abstaining) in favor of a motion rejecting the housing plan for the piers proposed by the Port Authority and approving the "mixed public use plan" proposed by Schnadelbach and the BHA Piers Committee.[55] Two weeks later, on November 28, the CB2 Planning and District Development Committee reaffirmed the Brooklyn community's support for a public park on Piers 1–6, with all twelve members in attendance rejecting the Port Authority's proposal for the commercial development of the piers and supporting the BHA Piers Committee's Harbor Park concept.[56]

Although the vote was nonbinding, the rebuke by the CB2 Piers Subcommittee had temporarily brought to a halt the Port Authority and the city's ambitions for the commercial development of Piers 1–6. The subcommittee hearings had also drawn a wide variety of citizens from outside the Brooklyn Heights community into the waterfront debate, broadening support for a park on the piers to include representatives of other Brooklyn neighborhoods; leaders of a diverse group of local, city, and state organizations; and politicians such as Assemblywoman Eileen Dugan and State Senator Martin Connor. And the growing public support of a "pure park" concept, with little, if any, allowance for supplementary commercial development, signaled a significant shift from the diplomatic style of Hand and Pearsall to a less compromising and more confrontational approach to engagement with the public authorities.

For leaders of the Piers Committee, these changes represented both a tremendous opportunity and a brand new set of questions and challenges. How was the Piers Committee to move beyond its role as the representative of Brooklyn Heights and accommodate the priorities and concerns of a vastly broadened constituency? What adjustments would need to be made to the committee's membership and organizational structure? Who should assume the responsibility for leading it? And what were the most effective ways to build the support among the public, the media, and political leaders that would be required to achieve its objective of a public park on Piers 1–6?

THE COALITION

OLLOWING THE REJECTION by Community Board 2 (CB2) of the Port Authority's proposal for the private development of Piers 1–6 and almost unanimous endorsement of the Harbor Park concept proposed by Terry Schnadelbach, the prevailing mood among the members of the Brooklyn Heights Association (BHA) Piers Committee and the community they represented had shifted from compromise to confrontation.

In the minority, Piers Committee chair Scott Hand and vice chair Otis Pearsall struggled in vain to convince their fellow committee members that the public victory over the Port Authority and the Department of City Planning had resulted in "circumstances propitious to try to move toward a compromise deal" with the public authorities.[1] Even in the unlikely event that the Port Authority and its partners in city government could somehow persuade the Board of Estimate to ignore the recent hearings and approve their plans for the piers, the humiliating defeat before the community board would inevitably undermine the confidence of potential real-estate investors and weaken the public authorities' ability to change or bypass local zoning restrictions that limited the commercial viability of the property. Faced with the looming possibility of completely losing control of the dispossession of Piers 1–6, reasoned Hand and Pearsall, the Port Authority would have no alternative but to work with the Piers Committee and other local leaders to agree on a development plan that was both sensitive to the needs of Brooklyn Heights and the surrounding neighborhoods and profitable for the Port Authority and the city.[2]

In spite of their diplomatic assessment of the situation, Hand and Pearsall quickly realized that the community's appetite for negotiation and compromise had passed. After the Port Authority's sudden abandonment of the Piers Committee in favor of CB2 in the final stages of the development review process and its refusal to include the community's concerns in its proposals for Piers 1–6, a growing number of people in the BHA and the greater community no longer considered the agency to be a reliable or trustworthy partner.

Going head to head with the public authorities was a formidable task in New York City, however, and one that would require far more than the local community's growing enthusiasm for a public park along the Brooklyn waterfront and an increasing appetite for confrontation. Since the mid-nineteenth century, the city had gained notoriety for the frequent indifference of its leaders to the concerns of individual citizens and the exclusion of nonelected public representatives from a city-planning process that was often characterized by corruption and scandal. The popular refrain "You can't fight city hall" reportedly originated in New York City during the seventy-year reign of Tammany Hall, the powerful political machine whose power was consolidated by the selection of William M. "Boss" Tweed as the chairman of the New York City Democratic General Committee in 1861, and exerted almost continuous control over city government until 1932.[3]

On the heels of the Tammany Hall political dynasty, the three-decade tenure of Robert Moses as the city's powerful Parks and Public Works Commissioner represented an even further decline in the capacity of individual citizens or groups of citizens to have a meaningful impact on development policy. While Moses's unprecedented transformation of the New York landscape was informed by a genuine commitment to public service and frequently resulted in parks, parkways, and other public projects that were of undeniable benefit to its citizens, the city's powerful planning czar practiced a top–down, nondemocratic approach to urban development, financially rewarding his supporters and punishing his enemies in business and city government, while habitually ignoring the protests and petitions of residents of the neighborhoods that were adversely affected by his massive development schemes.

"Corruption before Moses had been unorganized," explains Moses's biographer Robert Caro, "based on a multitude of selfish, private ends. Moses's genius for organizing it and focusing it at a central source gave it a new force, a force so powerful that it bent the entire city government off the democratic bias. He had used the power of money to undermine the democratic processes of the largest city in the world, to plan and build its parks, bridges, highways and housing projects on the basis of his whims alone."[4]

WHILE THE ABILITY OF THE CITY'S RESIDENTS to influence planning decisions affecting their communities remained a long shot at best in the late 1980s, recent decades had witnessed cracks in the armor of New York City's centralized planning and development process, and disgruntled residents were beginning to find ways to make their voices heard. A major step in the direction of citizen empowerment occurred in the spring of 1956, when Moses encountered unexpected resistance from an unlikely source: a group of Manhattan mothers who staged a public protest over his plans to build a parking lot on the site of a popular playground in Central Park.

The controversy began on the morning of Thursday, April 9, when a young woman named Roselle Davis, who had been sitting on a bench in the southwestern corner of the park just north of the West Sixty-seventh Street entrance while her son played on the lawn in front of her, noticed a group of men with surveying equipment examining the landscape. As she was leaving the park, Davis discovered a blueprint on one of the benches where she and the other mothers usually sat and was shocked to read the heading, "Detail Map of Parking Lot."[5] Davis, the wife of the celebrated abstract painter Stuart Davis, immediately shared what she had seen with the other mothers from the neighborhood, including the wife of Richard C. Wald, a reporter for the *Herald Tribune*, and on the morning of Monday, April 13, the readers of the newspaper were treated to a story describing the planned demolition of the playground and the objections of the Central Park mothers and their children.[6]

In the weeks that followed, the women and children of the neighborhood staged a number of high-profile protests against the proposed demolition, prompting the city to briefly delay its plans for the property. After two weeks of confusion and delay, Moses had had enough, and on April 24, he instructed the park workers under his charge to fence off and bulldoze the area between the hours of midnight and 4:00 A.M. and with a full police guard. The action backfired, however, as the following morning's newspapers featured headlines and editorials disparaging Moses and his harsh tactics, along with heart-wrenching photographs of tearful mothers and their children.[7] By the time the controversy subsided in mid-July, Moses had agreed to rebuild a playground on the site, and the Tavern on the Green was forced to make do with its existing parking lot.[8]

In the years that followed, the Central Park protest would inspire a number of other protests among neighborhood groups throughout the city, including the successful effort in the late 1950s by the BHA and its newly formed Community Conservation and Improvement Council to achieve major concessions in large-scale "slum-clearance projects" that Moses had planned at Cadman Plaza at the intersection of Brooklyn Heights and Cobble Hill and in the tiny Willowtown neighborhood of Brooklyn Heights. By the mid-1960s, the movement generated by these initial protests in Brooklyn Heights had achieved major victories in historic preservation and view protection under the capable leadership of BHA members Otis Pearsall and Scott Hand.[9]

The Central Park episode also reawakened many New Yorkers to the vital importance of public parks and open spaces in the life of the city. For citizens of all social, ethnic, and economic backgrounds, the city's parks, promenades, and playgrounds have traditionally provided a welcome—and, many would argue, indispensable—respite from the daily pressure and stress of life in the metropolis. For residents of Harlem and midtown Manhattan, Central Park exists as a vast, easily accessible oasis of open lawns, reflecting ponds, carousels, and horse-drawn carriages. For Upper West Siders, a leisurely stroll west from Broadway to Riverside Drive opens within minutes onto the flower gardens, shaded paths, and scenic Hudson River views in Riverside Park. And in the Park Slope and Flatbush neighborhoods of Brooklyn, Prospect Park and the Brooklyn Botanic Garden attract thousands of visitors each day with the promise of rose gardens, skating rinks, lush lawns, and tranquil ponds.

For New Yorkers, parks have an emotional and symbolic value that transcends the type of pragmatic, profit-oriented motivations that govern so many other aspects of life in the city. Throughout New York's history, poets and novelists such as Walt Whitman, William Cullen Bryant, Henry James, and J. D. Salinger have reflected on the significance of parks in defining the city's character and revitalizing its residents. In 1967, poet Marianne Moore campaigned successfully for the preservation of a severely injured Camperdown elm near the boat basin in Prospect Park. For Moore, a lifelong New York City park enthusiast who would later work to save the horse stables in Central Park, the Camperdown elm was a living symbol of the park itself, both in its fragility and vulnerability to external destruction and in its vital, irreplaceable importance in the lives of those who enjoyed its shade and admired its beauty. "It is still leafing," Moore observed as the end of the celebrated poem she wrote about the tree,

still there. *Mortal* though. We must save it. It is
our crowning curio.[10]

During the 1980s, with many of the city's public facilities and services
still in decline and disrepair following the recession of the mid-1970s,
neighborhood parks and open spaces served as "crowning curios" for
millions of New Yorkers. For a growing number of Brooklyn residents
and their neighbors, the unprecedented and unrepeatable promise of
a grand public space along the waterfront elicited a similarly profound
emotional response. The mothers of Central Park were facing a choice
between a playground and a parking lot. The residents of Brooklyn
Heights and others in the growing waterfront movement were facing a
choice between a vast public park along the piers and a collection of high-
rise luxury condominiums. The residents in each instance were inspired
to forgo traditional pragmatic concerns and to confront seemingly insurmountable obstacles to achieve their goals.

HAND AND PEARSALL, both of whom had been through lengthy and contentious negotiations with the public authorities in the past, still believed that the pragmatic interests of the Port Authority and the city and
the symbolic aspirations of the community could be harmonized in the
disposition of Piers 1–6, and they continued to advise their colleagues on
the Piers Committee that a large waterfront park and substantial public
housing could be successfully integrated in a hybrid development model
like the "illustrative scheme" "Intensive Mixed-Use Development" included in Buckhurst Fish Hutton Katz's report, *The Future of the Piers:
Planning and Design Criteria for Brooklyn Piers 1–6* (figures 11 and 12).

If the residents of Brooklyn Heights and the surrounding waterfront
neighborhoods wanted a pure park on Piers 1–6, Hand and Pearsall
conceded, then the Piers Committee should redirect its efforts and resources toward that goal. On their departure from the park movement,
the two men reiterated their advice to Anthony Manheim, John Watts,
and the other "pure park" advocates that achieving this goal would require a complete overhaul of the composition, leadership, and structure
of the Piers Committee.

One problem was the identification of the committee with the BHA
and the Brooklyn Heights neighborhood. In the past two years, the Port
Authority had repeatedly emphasized the Brooklyn Heights connection
to discredit the Piers Committee as representing only the needs and priorities of a single community at the expense of the broader public interest. In the CB2 hearings, leaders from other waterfront neighborhoods,

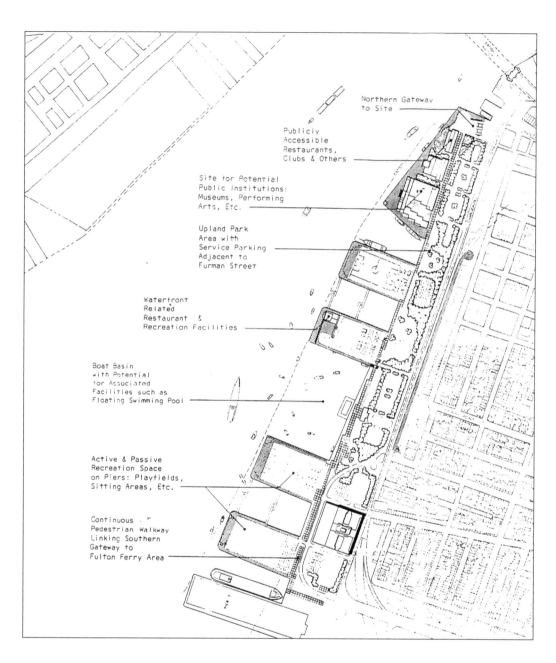

Northern Gateway
to Site

Publicly
Accessible
Restaurants,
Clubs & Others

Site for Potential
Public Institutions:
Museums, Performing
Arts, Etc.

Upland Park
Area with
Service Parking
Adjacent to
Furman Street

Waterfront
Related
Restaurant &
Recreation Facilities

Boat Basin
with Potential
for Associated
Facilities such as
Floating Swimming Pool

Active & Passive
Recreation Space
on Piers: Playfields,
Sitting Areas, Etc.

Continuous
Pedestrian Walkway
Linking Southern
Gateway to
Fulton Ferry Area

FIGURE 11

Commissioned by the Brooklyn Heights Association in 1987, Buckhurst Fish Hutton Katz's *The Future of the Piers* envisioned four different plans for Piers 1–6. Scheme B, "Major Public Park," envisioned forty acres of park, a small marina, playing fields, and restaurants.

COURTESY OF BUCKHURST FISH HUTTON KATZ

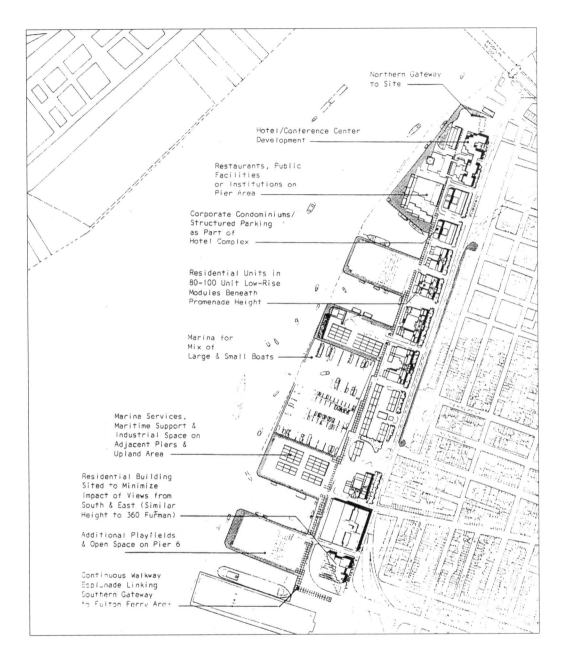

Northern Gateway
to Site

Hotel/Conference Center
Development

Restaurants, Public
Facilities
or Institutions on
Pier Area

Corporate Condominiums/
Structured Parking
as Part of
Hotel Complex

Residential Units in
80-100 Unit Low-Rise
Modules Beneath
Promenade Height

Marina for
Mix of
Large & Small Boats

Marina Services,
Maritime Support &
Industrial Space on
Adjacent Piers &
Upland Area

Residential Building
Sited to Minimize
Impact of Views from
South & East (Similar
Height to 360 Furman)

Additional Playfields
& Open Space on Pier 6

Continuous Walkway
Esplanade Linking
Southern Gateway
to Fulton Ferry Area

FIGURE 12

Scheme D, "Intensive Mixed-Use Development," envisioned twenty acres of park; a hotel and conference center; 50,000 square feet of office space; 40,000 square feet of retail space; and 750 residential units.

COURTESY OF BUCKHURST FISH HUTTON KATZ

such as former Cobble Hill Association president Roy Sloane, had openly questioned the wisdom of the committee's continuing sponsorship by the BHA. If, as its members consistently maintained, the Piers Committee truly represented the interests and aspirations of all the communities that would be affected by the proposed development, then it should sever its formal ties with the BHA and open both its membership and its leadership to a broader base of citizens in and beyond Brooklyn.[11]

Informing Manheim that they would no longer be continuing in their role as leaders in the Piers Committee, Hand and Pearsall recommended that the new committee should have three co-chairs, each one representing a different constituency for the Brooklyn waterfront movement.[12]

As the Port Authority's initial contact regarding its plans for Piers 1–6 and the founder of the Piers Committee (and its earlier incarnation, the Waterfront Committee), Manheim was the obvious choice to represent Brooklyn Heights in the new organization.

To represent the other Brooklyn waterfront neighborhoods outside Brooklyn Heights, Pearsall nominated Cobble Hill resident Maria Favuzzi, with whom he had served on the CB2 Piers Subcommittee. A lifelong Brooklyn resident, Favuzzi had been an active voice in the Cobble Hill community since the late 1970s, as a member of both the Cobble Hill Association and Community Board 6 (which included the neighborhoods of Cobble Hill, Carroll Gardens, Red Hook, Park Slope, and Gowanus), where she served on the Waterfront and Economic Development Committee. In addition to her connections with Brooklyn communities outside Brooklyn Heights and her knowledge of issues relating to economic development and the waterfront, Favuzzi had also proven herself as a determined, imperturbable advocate of the causes she supported—and as someone who was not easily intimidated by public authorities.

"I'm the daughter of Italian immigrants," explains Favuzzi of her lifelong enthusiasm for civic activism and public debate, "and I grew up hearing every so often the phrase, 'You can't fight city hall.' That was the immigrant outlook: 'You can't fight city hall.' Well, somehow that became a challenge to me. And as I became an adult, I began to question more and more, 'Well, why can't you fight city hall?' And I think that may summarize or characterize my view that, 'Yes, people can make a difference.' It may take a very, very long time. And you have to hang in there, and you can't give up, and you've got to be prepared to keep trucking. But you can make things happen."[13]

During the subcommittee hearings, Favuzzi had been frustrated by the commercial-development plan put forward by the Port Authority and increasingly committed to the plans for the Harbor Park proposed by the BHA Piers Committee (figure 13). She eagerly accepted Hand

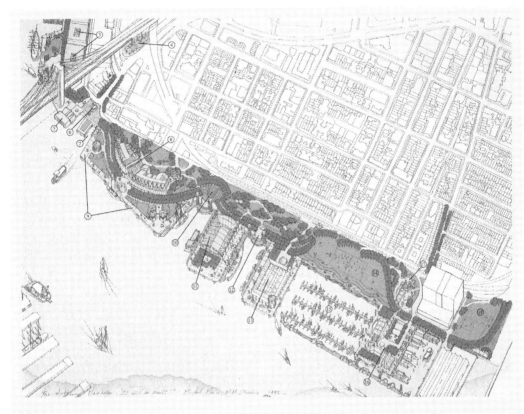

B·R·O·O·K·L·Y·N B·R·I·D·G·E P·A·R·K
A MARITIME AND PUBLIC USE DEVELOPMENT ON THE DOWNTOWN BROOKLYN WATERFRONT

INTERBRIDGE SECTOR

1 • Main Street Pavillion
2 • Floating Swimming Pool
3 • Empire Stores

FULTON FERRY SECTOR

4 • Anchorage
5 • River Cafe
6 • Fireboat House
7 • BargeMusic

PIERS SECTOR

8 • Resort Hotel/Conference Center
9 • Public Terrace
10 • Amphitheater
11 • Crystal Palace/Active Recreation
12 • Landing Stage
13 • Cultural & Educational Pier
14 • Great Meadow
15 • Marina
16 • Marine Center/Catering Hall/Restaurants
17 • Adventure Playground
18 • Ballfields

FIGURE 13

Praedium's *Economic Viability Study* (1997) of Terry Schnadelbach's "Harbor Park" (1988) called for 1 million square feet of commercial development (32 percent of the Piers Sector), plus a 300-boat marina and 1,500 parking spaces to provide $4 million in revenue to support the forty-eight-acre park's projected $3.4 million maintenance budget.

COURTESY OF R. TERRY SCHNADELBACH, FAAR

and Pearsall's invitation to serve as a co-chair of the new waterfront organization.

"It was inspiring to think of that as being open to the public," she recalls of her early attraction to the Harbor Park concept. "We New Yorkers lived at a time when you didn't have access to the waterfront, when the waterfront was virtually walled off from us. This was an incredible opportunity, and people could see that the proposal that the piers be used as a housing property was just so insipid. We saw the potential for something grand, whereas we were being offered something small and uninspiring."[14]

The final co-chair in the new organization was Manhattan resident Tom Fox, the executive director of the Neighborhood Open Space Coalition and the driving force behind the public's successful resistance to the Westway development project along the banks of the Hudson River in Manhattan. During the CB2 Piers Subcommittee hearings, Fox had served on the Advisory Committee to the BHA Piers Committee and had testified before the subcommittee regarding the public benefits of having a park on the west Brooklyn waterfront. As leader of the Neighborhood Open Space Coalition, Fox worked with 123 organizations representing a broad and diverse constituency, from the blue-blooded Municipal Art Society of New York to the insurgent Green Guerillas, for which he had served as vice president. He also had the advantage of being a non-Brooklynite, providing the new organization with an invaluable link to the rest of New York City. "I saw my role in this whole thing as the broker, who didn't represent Cobble Hill or Brooklyn Heights," Fox remembers. "I represented that overall idea of the expanding park system, of capturing the waterfront as a place that would be useful to all of these other people because there would be recreational facilities and marinas and open places to relax and skip and hop and jump and look at the stars and the birds."[15]

A Vietnam War veteran and former National Park ranger who had spent his childhood in Brooklyn, Fox was a seasoned and savvy environmental activist who understood the necessity of combining confrontation and compromise in influencing public policy and urban planning: "There are times when you have to be willing to say: 'This just isn't going to work,'" he explains. "'We're going to make you look like fools, and we're going to be proud of it.' But then you also have to learn to speak in the language of the elected officials, the unions and the real-estate developers. Finding a way to show your adversaries the value in the work is a critical part of any kind of successful advocacy movement. You can't just say, 'You can't do it because I want something else.' You have to say, 'You know that other thing that I want to do is really in your interest.'"[16]

In addition to his skills as a negotiator with public officials, Fox had a passion for promoting and facilitating community involvement in park development and environmental activism, particularly among groups with diverging opinions about what should and should not be done. "The public participation process takes patience," he explains, "and people don't have patience to listen to everybody. But you have to. If you don't listen to them, then you've left them out. Even if you don't agree with them, spend time with them. We would have meetings that would last until two o'clock in the morning and just let people talk. Give them respect."[17]

Once the new co-chairs had been selected, the next task was coming up with a suitable name for the new organization—one that would capture the imagination of the general public and dispel any lingering suspicions that the park was the pet project of the Brooklyn Heights community. All the new co-chairs supported the conviction of Frederick Law Olmsted, the father of the New York City park tradition, that the names of public parks and public spaces should directly reflect the location or physical form of the park itself. "It's the fine Olmsted tradition of simple names that describe the place or the function of the property," says Fox. "We had Ocean Parkway, which went out to the ocean. Eastern Parkway, which went out to Long Island. And the Long Meadow was a long meadow. And the Sheep's Meadow where you grazed sheep."[18]

With Olmsted in mind, the original choice was to continue to refer to the proposed space as Harbor Park, following the example of Terry Schnadelbach's report (figure 14), and to name the organization Coalition for a Harbor Park on Brooklyn Piers 1–6. Stretching along the mouth of the East River, Piers 1–6 occupied a substantial part of the eastern shore of the entrance to the great New York Harbor, after all, and would inevitably provide visitors with spectacular views of the maritime activities that took place in the harbor each day.

While the new co-chairs continued to champion Olmsted's principle of naming a park after the physical characteristics of the site it occupies, the name Harbor Park soon gave way to Brooklyn Bridge Park, reflecting the decision to expand the property that would be included in the park plan. The new name and the proposed additions to the park property were greeted with great enthusiasm by everyone involved. "Branding is important, and the Brooklyn Bridge Park Coalition was a little catchier than the Coalition for a Harbor Park on Brooklyn Piers 1–6," says Fox of the public-relations advantage of the Brooklyn Bridge association. "It seemed more press worthy and easier to sell, saving the setting around the Brooklyn Bridge and nestling it in a park, like the Golden Gate, which gave its name to the National Recreation Area in San Francisco."[19]

HARBOR PARK
A MARITIME AND PUBLIC USE DEVELOPMENT ON THE BROOKLYN PIERS

FIGURE 14
Schnadelbach's "Harbor Park" featured forty-eight acres of park, including open spaces, playing fields, seating areas, interactive waterfalls, a skating rink, a conference center and hotel, an expansive marina, and a continuous walkway.
COURTESY OF R. TERRY SCHNADELBACH, FAAR

The new name and expanded park concept quickly gained momentum both within the new organization and throughout the broader community, providing park advocates with an immediately recognizable name that matched the public's growing enthusiasm for the park concept. "We finally had something that we could use to get the community excited about what we were doing," recalls Favuzzi.[20]

WITH A NEW NAME AND NEW LEADERSHIP for the organization, the next challenge facing the co-chairs was to create a legal entity for the organization that was fully independent of its old associations with the BHA and the Brooklyn Heights community. The incorporation of the Brooklyn Bridge Park Coalition was notable for the involvement of Brooklyn Heights resident Mark Baker, a young attorney who had recently assisted Tom Fox in the Westway negotiations in Manhattan. As his first task for the Coalition, Baker filed a Certificate of Amendment to New York State, through which the newly formed organization was granted the not-for-profit status previously awarded to the Friends of Fulton Ferry Landing, a dormant group formed by Scott Hand a few years earlier. Baker would continue to provide legal guidance and various other types of assistance for the Coalition during the next twenty-five years.

"I was a young lawyer, and I was looking for pro bono work," Baker recalls of his initial foray into the controversy over Piers 1–6. "Tom was a Green Guerilla and had become the leader of the community-garden organizations in the city. I worked as his lawyer in the community-garden movement, and then he became very interested in parks and open spaces, and we worked extensively in Hudson River Park, where I got my firm to write opinions that underpinned turning that into a park in the aftermath of the whole Westway debacle.

"After Tom ended up being one of the three co-chairs here," Baker continues, "he called me up and said, 'They need a good lawyer over here, and it's right in your backyard. Why don't you meet Tony Manheim?' So I met him and seemed to hit it off with him, and he said, 'Okay, why won't you be our lawyer?' And then Tony said, 'Call Scott Hand.' And I called Scott, and he had this organization that had Fulton Ferry Landing in the title, and he said, 'Why don't you use that organization?' So we changed the name of that organization to the Brooklyn Bridge [Park] Coalition, and that's the legal entity that is today the Brooklyn Bridge Park Conservancy."[21]

DURING THE FIRST MONTHS of its operation, the Brooklyn Bridge Park Coalition operated largely outside the scrutiny of the media and the general public, with Manheim, Favuzzi, and Fox working behind the scenes to enlist the support of leaders of local, city, and state organizations (with more than sixty recruited by the end of the year) and cultivate relationships with political and community leaders, including State Senator Martin Connor, Assemblywoman Eileen Dugan, Congressman Stephen Solarz, Brooklyn Borough President Howard Golden, and Jerry Renzini and Stephanie Twin, the chairs of Community Boards 2 and 6, respectively.[22]

Another important task facing the newly formed Coalition was the formulation of a set of shared guiding principles for the development of the west Brooklyn piers, which would collectively reflect the priorities and expectations of the organization's increasingly diverse constituency. Although not everyone who supported the general aims of the Coalition could agree on a single vision for the park, Manheim, Favuzzi, and Fox recognized that a consensus had begun to emerge throughout the park movement regarding a variety of factors relating to the appropriate disposition of the piers property (public benefit, substantial allocation of public space, the need for comprehensive planning, limitations on private development, view preservation, maximum public access and use, self-sustainability, and so on).

By clarifying, assembling, and disseminating these shared principles, the Coalition could simultaneously unify its diverse membership (who might disagree regarding specific aspects of a detailed park design), recruit new supporters for the emerging park movement, and resist forthcoming plans for private development that failed to address shared public concerns for the piers property. The difficult and time-consuming process of developing and building public consensus around the guiding principles for the park would be a central occupation of the Coalition over the next several years and would become one of its signature contributions to the park movement.

THE COALITION ENCOUNTERED its first major challenge toward the end of 1989, when the Port Authority announced tentative plans to lease Piers 1–5 to real-estate developers Larry A. Silverstein and Arthur G. Cohen, the owners of a three-acre slice of upland property between Piers 3 and 5, with an option to purchase the property outright after four years. At the time, the decision had not yet been approved by the Port Authority board, which was scheduled to meet the following January. If approved by the board, the decision would also require the approval of Governor Mario Cuomo.

In a *New York Times* report announcing the proposed development, the Coalition urged Governor Cuomo and Mayor David Dinkins to delay a decision until the Brooklyn community was allowed to present an alternative plan providing greater opportunities for public use of the waterfront property. "This is a very critical site to the city as a whole," Manheim explained to David Dunlap of the *Times*. "It cries out for planning, and that is what has not been done. Our program goal is maximum feasible public benefit. You just don't turn over a site, with no controls, to a development team. These are public assets."[23]

In a letter to Manheim, Hugh B. O'Neill, the Port Authority executive in charge of the Brooklyn piers project, tried unsuccessfully to reassure the Coalition that, in contrast to the plans supported by the Port Authority in the past, the proposed development by Silverstein and Cohen was sensitive to the community's concerns and that the two real-estate titans had actually "come up with an attractive concept for developing the site that will balance the various public interests involved (the need for housing, the need for open space, continuation of maritime-related activity) in a financially feasible way."[24] "The result could be a mixed-use development of a size and density that's consistent with good planning and the needs of the community," explained Silverstein in the *Times* report. "We could not in any way violate the view planes."[25]

Not surprisingly given its past experience, the Coalition's leaders were unimpressed with the assurances by the Port Authority and the potential developers. "I don't think the city should lose the opportunity to create a major public facility," Tom Fox said at the time. "I can't believe a resource like this would be piddled away on a housing development that could be built anywhere."[26]

By the time of the public announcement of the Port Authority's new plans for Piers 1–5, the Coalition was prepared to do far more than argue its case through the media. On hearing of the proposed Silverstein–Cohen development project, the Coalition leaders immediately alerted the public officials with whom they had been cultivating relationships during the preceding months, including Howard Golden. While Golden had reservations about the Coalition's proposal for a park on the west Brooklyn piers, he shared the organization's revulsion to the prospect of turning the area beneath the Brooklyn Heights Promenade into a vast residential development, and he was quickly enlisted into the current conflict with the Port Authority.

On December 4, 1989, the same day that the *Times* article announced the Port Authority's consideration of the Silverstein–Cohen development scheme, Golden wrote to Mario Cuomo, explaining his objection to the proposed project and urging the governor to veto any plans for Piers 1–5 that were based solely on financial considerations, without attention to the impact of the proposed action on the adjacent communities and the city as a whole. "This great Brooklyn resource must not be the subject of a dollar and cents negotiation in the absence of a shared set of development guidelines, acceptable to all," Golden reasoned. "I firmly believe that development guidelines directed toward implementation of a comprehensive plan must precede any financial disposition of the property."[27]

As an attachment to his letter, Golden included a set of sixteen guidelines for the development of the piers that he had drawn up with the assistance of his staff and the informal guidance of the Coalition, which had briefed him on the guiding principles that they were currently developing with their constituents.[28] Motivated by both the letter from Golden and the request from the Coalition, the governor subsequently instructed the Port Authority to abandon the terms of the proposed arrangement with Silverstein and Cohen, while also demanding that all future negotiations between the Port Authority and private developers reflect a greater sensitivity to the needs and interests of the Brooklyn community.[29]

FOUR

THE "13 GUIDING PRINCIPLES"

> We were all arguing over things that might never happen and fo-
> cusing on where we disagreed. I, in my naiveté or wishful thinking,
> basically invited in a lot of the community players to my office in
> Borough Hall and said, "Why don't we focus on what we agree on,
> instead of all the things we keep fighting about?"
>
> **MARILYN GELBER**

GOVERNOR MARIO CUOMO'S REJECTION of the Port Authority's tentative arrangement with real-estate developers Larry A. Silverstein and Arthur
G. Cohen brought the agency's plans for the private development of the
west Brooklyn piers to a grinding halt at the end of 1989. Faced with the
governor's call for a revised development plan that reflected a greater
sensitivity to the needs and interests of the Brooklyn community, the
Port Authority and its partners in city government, having spent the previous five years ignoring the community's recommendations and concerns, were forced to go back to the drawing board in their plans for the
Brooklyn piers. Nearly a year would pass before the public entities would
be prepared to offer a new proposal for the disposition of the waterfront
property.

The temporary hiatus in the public confrontations with the Port Authority and the city provided Brooklyn Bridge Park Coalition co-chairs
Anthony Manheim, Tom Fox, and Maria Favuzzi with invaluable time
to focus their attention on the important task of building their new organization, generating support for the park concept in and beyond the
neighborhoods adjacent to the west Brooklyn waterfront, and devising

an effective strategy for promoting the development of a public park along the piers.

THROUGHOUT THIS PERIOD, the members of the Brooklyn Bridge Park Coalition continued to discuss and debate the core principles that would ultimately guide the development of the park. The task at hand was to formulate a set of guidelines that would simultaneously address the concerns of the Brooklyn communities immediately adjacent to the piers; satisfy the public entities' demand for a fiscally responsible, self-sustainable use of the site; preserve the physical and environmental integrity of the entire waterfront property; and continue to generate enthusiasm for the park concept among residents citywide.

If balancing the competing interests and priorities of these various constituencies wasn't difficult enough, the Coalition members often had difficulty agreeing among themselves about the guidelines for developing the park. Disagreements about residential housing on the waterfront had already been responsible for a change in the leadership of the west Brooklyn piers movement in January 1989, when Brooklyn Heights Association (BHA) Piers Committee chair Scott Hand and vice chair Otis Pearsall, both of whom supported the construction of limited housing on the piers, resigned their positions in deference to the anti-housing majority on the Piers Committee.[1]

The resignations of Hand and Pearsall had not been the end of the housing debate. Following the formation of the Brooklyn Bridge Park Coalition, a growing number of west Brooklyn residents and some Coalition members had begun to believe that limited housing was not only acceptable as part of the waterfront development plan but also necessary to the safety and security of a park along the piers. In reaction to the growing support for a park on Piers 1–6 following the Community Board 2 (CB2) Piers Subcommittee hearings, Brooklyn Borough President Howard Golden had repeatedly warned that without the inclusion of at least some amount of housing, the waterfront property would soon become a haven for drug dealers at night. Even some of the members of the Coalition had begun to warm to the prospect of private residences providing twenty-four-hour "eyes on the park," increasing the safety and accessibility of the piers property for everyone. In contrast, other Coalition members and longtime park supporters continued to view residential housing on the piers as unacceptable on any scale, insisting that private residencies on the waterfront would inevitably privatize the park, with park residents viewing the open space as an extension of their own property, while the lights from the high-rise dwellings would also obscure the nighttime views of the Manhattan skyline and the East River from the Brooklyn Heights Promenade.

Coalition members also disagreed about the most appropriate method for visitors to gain access to the park. Most Brooklyn Heights residents in the Coalition were committed to preserving the cul-de-sac design of the neighborhood and consequently opposed the construction of any type of public corridor linking the elevated Promenade with the waterfront property. In contrast to this position, co-chair Tom Fox was far more concerned about maximizing access to the park for people from outside Brooklyn Heights, promoting increased public transit and a broad pedestrian thoroughfare for visitors to the park, even if it meant disturbing the tranquility of the neighborhood's streets and sidewalks. "One of the things I lost on was a pedestrian connection for Montague Street," Fox remembers of the compromises that were ultimately required to create a common set of guiding principles around which the Coalition could unite. "Where are all the trains? Where's all the mass transit? Right here. It's a beautiful street whose store owners could all benefit from pedestrian traffic."[2]

Resolving these and many other issues relating to the design, use, and funding of the piers property was a difficult and time-consuming process. Working Group meetings and informal discussions often lasted late into the night, with little or no apparent progress toward a consensus. "I was coming there as a Wall Street lawyer, and my deals were going a hundred miles an hour," recalls Mark Baker of the lengthy, exhausting, frequently unresolved discussions that occupied the Coalition members during the early years of its existence. "And then I would come into that room, and we would debate and it felt like I was moving in molasses. But then I began to learn, 'No, this is how it gets done. This is how you build it.' Late at night. In the back of Wolf Spille's offices. And we talked about everything under the sun."[3]

ON MARCH 11, 1990, Maria Favuzzi, who had served as the Community Board 6 representative during the CB2 Piers Subcommittee hearings, announced her resignation as Coalition co-chair "with confidence in knowing that the Coalition is strong, that its membership is dedicated, and that there is inherent logic, foresight, and persuasiveness in the proposal that the splendid piece of waterfront from Atlantic Avenue to the Manhattan Bridge be used for maximum public benefit in a fiscally responsible way."[4] Manheim and Fox continued serving as Coalition co-chairs, and no attempt was made to find a replacement for Favuzzi. Following her resignation, Favuzzi fulfilled her commitment "to doing what I can do, within the constraints of time on me, to promote the goal of the Coalition," continuing to meet regularly with the Coalition and serve as a conduit with residents of Cobble Hill and other neighborhoods outside Brooklyn Heights.

IN OCTOBER 1990, the public entities reentered the planning discussions for the west Brooklyn piers, when the New York State Urban Development Corporation (UDC) and the New York City Public Development Corporation (PDC) released the results of a jointly commissioned study prepared by consultant Gary Hack of the Boston urban-design firm Carr, Lynch, Hack and Sandell.

Representatives from Carr, Lynch, Hack and Sandell provided Coalition members and other Brooklyn Heights residents with summaries of the findings from the report at community workshops on October 27 and November 28, 1990. After the repeated neglect that the Coalition and other neighborhood representatives had received from the public entities in the past, the Coalition members were encouraged by the announcement of the forthcoming report and the efforts that the UDC and PDC were making to include the local community in the discussion and evaluation of the proposed alternatives for the piers. Following the initial meeting with representatives of the Boston firm, Manheim reported to the members of the Brooklyn Bridge Park Coalition Working Group that all the public bodies with which the consultants had met were awaiting the full results of the forthcoming report "with positive expectations."[5]

One factor that did not go unnoticed during the community workshops was the absence of any representatives from the Port Authority. In a meeting with Manheim following the announcement of the preliminary findings from Hack's report, Port Authority executive director Stan Brezenoff reported that the agency was not directly involved in the project, assuring the Coalition that it would not initiate any additional plans for the disposition of the west Brooklyn piers "in the near future."[6]

On January 10, 1991, Gary Hack introduced five alternative plans for Piers 1–5 to an audience of more than 100 neighborhood leaders, elected officials, and other Brooklyn residents at a special communitywide meeting at St. Francis College in Brooklyn Heights. Hack's plans for the piers included

⊙ A modified "Brooklyn Bridge Park" plan, featuring 37 acres of landscaped open space with 30,000 square feet of light-industrial space, a 200-boat marina, 160,000 square feet of structured parking, and a large skating rink

⊙ An "Urban Waterfront" plan, featuring a conference center, offices, hotels, and a marina, as well as 22 acres of open space

⊙ A "Hillclimb" plan, featuring a combination of commercial developments (a conference center, a boatel, retail showrooms, and office space), light-industrial use of existing spaces, a 150- to 200-boat marina, and 22 acres of open space

⊙ A "Break Even" plan, consisting of 1.9 million square feet of housing, office space, retail shops, and other commercial constructions

⊙ A "Warehouse Re-use" plan, through which existing structures would be repurposed for storage and light-industrial uses, along with a 150- to 200-boat marina and 8 acres of open space[7]

A thirty-minute slide presentation depicting the layout and specific features of the five alternatives was accompanied by a detailed financial analysis of each plan. In spite of the community's positive expectations for Hack's report, Manheim and many of the others in attendance were distressed to learn that the study favored housing over other commercial-development options for revenue production and to hear the consultant question the financial viability of the modified "Brooklyn Bridge Park" plan favored by the Coalition, for which he projected an $88.9 million gap between total costs and revenues (compared with the $8 million gap projected by the Coalition).[8] "I regret that analysis of our proposal was not more informed by an interactive dialogue," Manheim complained to reporter Michael Clark following the meeting.[9]

In spite of his frustration with Hack's recommendations and financial analysis, Manheim was unperturbed, joining with fellow Coalition Working Group members John Watts, Terry Schnadelbach, Robert Rubin, and Ted Liebman on February 12 to meet with Hack and financial consultant Lynne Sagalyn to discuss the two groups' conflicting projections of the costs for the alternative plans for the piers. "I believe this meeting presents a rare opportunity to attempt a truly collaborative endeavor in seeking consensus on a redevelopment approach for the downtown Brooklyn waterfront," Manheim explained to his colleagues in the Working Group a few days before the meeting.[10]

ON APRIL 6, 1991, Borough President Howard Golden convened a special meeting at St. Francis College with elected officials, community board officials, and other residents from the neighborhoods adjacent to the west Brooklyn piers. Golden's purpose in calling the meeting was twofold:

1   To generate support for the creation of an independent public authority to acquire, operate, and supervise the planning and development of the public use of the Piers 1–5 site
2   To announce his endorsement of and request the community's support for the $67.4 million "Warehouse Re-use" plan

As described in Gary Hack's report, the "Warehouse Re-use" plan would convert the piers' existing warehouses for trade shows, exhibition halls, restaurants, retail markets, and office space, while also creating a 150- to 200-boat marina, light-industrial lofts, and eight acres of open space along the East River (figure 15).[11]

Golden's proposal for the creation of an independent public authority to oversee the piers was well received by both the Brooklyn elected officials and the community leaders attending the meeting, as well as by representatives of the public entities who were later informed of the idea. "We could live with a less-than-ideal [project] if we got public site control upfront," Manheim commented at the time. "It's awfully hard to get a private developer to the do the public's business."[12]

State and city officials, many of whom had grown weary of the routine setbacks and constant conflicts with the local community, publicly welcomed the idea of relinquishing control of—and responsibility for—the disposition of the west Brooklyn waterfront. "We'd like to have the site ready for development when somebody's ready to develop it," said a PDC spokesperson after having been informed of Golden's proposal.[13]

For Golden, who opposed the predominantly private development of the west Brooklyn waterfront but remained unconvinced about the safety and financial feasibility of the "Brooklyn Bridge Park" plan, the "Warehouse Re-use" plan represented the ideal alternative, ensuring that the scenic views and tranquil streets of his constituents in Brooklyn Heights would be preserved until a compromise agreeable to both the local community and the public authorities could be achieved. While other elected officials and community leaders welcomed a temporary solution that would forestall additional actions by the Port Authority until a suitable plan could be realized, they also worried that Golden's temporary solution, without the benefit of long-term comprehensive planning, might end up becoming a permanent plan for the piers.

On first hearing, Manheim, Fox, and the other Coalition members, who had already had private discussions with Golden about the potential viability of an interim proposal for the disposition of the piers, were

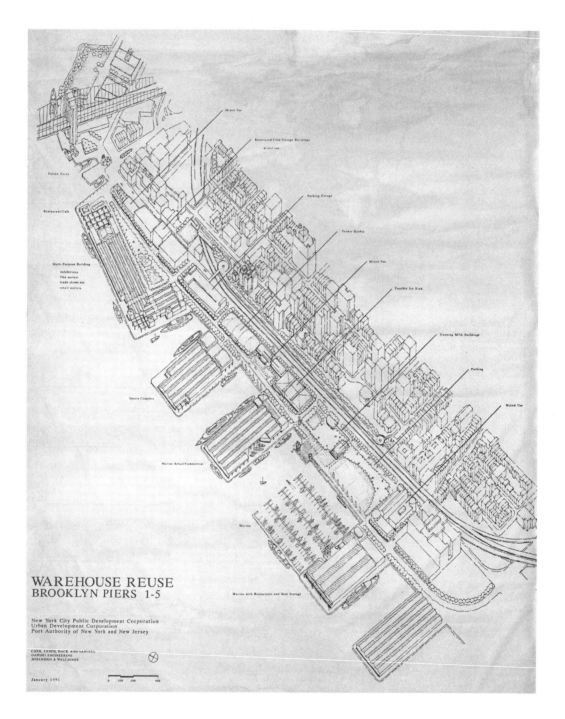

Mixed Use

Renovated Cold Storage Buildings
mixed use

Parking Garage

Tennis Bubble

Mixed Use

Possible Ice Rink

Existing MTA Buildings

Parking

Mixed Use

Fulton Ferry

Restaurant/Cafe

Multi-Purpose Building
exhibitions
flea market
trade shows etc.
retail outlets

Sports Complex

Marine Retail/Commercial

Marina

Marina with Restaurants and Boat Storage

WAREHOUSE REUSE
BROOKLYN PIERS 1-5

New York City Public Development Corporation
Urban Development Corporation
Port Authority of New York and New Jersey

CARR, LYNCH, HACK AND SANDELL
GANDRI ENGINEERING
JOHANSSON & WALCAVAGE

January 1991

0   100   200   400

FIGURE 15

In 1991, the Port Authority introduced four new plans for the Brooklyn piers. The "Warehouse Re-use" design was supported by Brooklyn Borough President Howard Golden as an interim solution to the disposition of the piers.

COURTESY OF CARR, LYNCH, HACK AND SANDELL, INC.

guardedly supportive of the "Warehouse Re-use" plan. "I think it is a very constructive idea to use this window of opportunity to have somebody own the land until public funding is readily available," Manheim confided to a reporter before the meeting with Golden.[14] Manheim was careful to add in subsequent statements, however, that the interim plan was not an end in itself and should not represent a halt in community activism in support of a park on the piers: "An interim use would make sense, if we see it as a stepping-stone on the way to building the park."[15]

Elected officials from Brooklyn Heights and the neighboring communities agreed with Manheim's assessment of the "Warehouse Re-use" plan. "It's an exciting possibility if it's truly an interim use," said Stephen DeBrienza, who represented Red Hook and Carroll Gardens on the City Council and chaired the council's Subcommittee on Waterfront Development. "The danger is that it might become the only plan."[16]

THE DISCUSSIONS BETWEEN Borough President Golden and the Coalition intensified after the meeting at St. Frances College on April 6. On April 16, under pressure from Vincent Tese, executive director of the Urban Development Corporation, to reach a communitywide consensus on the appropriate plan for the piers within sixty days, Golden sent a letter to the Coalition soliciting a formal response by the end of the month to his proposal for the creation of a public authority for the piers, his call for support of the "Warehouse Re-use" plan, and his request for input into the formulation of the "planning principles" that would guide the development of the piers under the new public entity.[17]

The Coalition took Golden's request for a timely response seriously, with Manheim and Fox convening a special Coalition meeting at the Brooklyn Club at 75 Montague Street in Brooklyn Heights on April 22 to consider Golden's proposals. The first order of business was Golden's recommendation for the communitywide adoption of Gary Hack's interim "Warehouse Re-use" plan for Piers 1–5. The Coalition members had continued to discuss the strengths and weaknesses of the plan, with a consensus gradually emerging that the interim plan, which dedicated only eight acres of the piers property to open space (the lowest percentage of any of the five alternative plans), would do more to hinder than to help the Coalition's ultimate objective of a park on the waterfront. In the end, the thirty members in attendance voted unanimously to reject Golden's proposal for an interim plan for the piers. Manheim clarified to a reporter after the meeting that he and his fellow Coalition members remained open to an interim use of the piers property "so long as it does not interfere with the achievement and accomplishment of the long term goals" for the site.[18]

In spite of the unanimous rebuke of Golden's proposal to adopt an interim-use plan for Piers 1–5, the Coalition members fully endorsed Golden's call for an independent public entity to oversee the future development and maintenance of the piers, with the additional recommendation that the Coalition's "Sixteen Guiding Principles" (as they existed at the time) should serve as the charter of the new public agency. "They are broad enough to encompass almost every public figure's stated objectives," Manheim and Fox explained in a letter to Golden a few weeks after the meeting, "and precise enough to avoid papering over fundamental differences that might arise."[19]

In the event that a new public entity was created, the Coalition insisted that its authority should include the right to ownership, development, and oversight of "the entire downtown Brooklyn waterfront." The emerging consensus among Coalition members was that, in addition to Piers 1–5 and the adjacent upland areas, the site should include "the Brooklyn Bridge Anchorage, Fulton Ferry Landing and the old fireboat station, and Empire–Fulton Ferry State Park."[20]

THE COALITION'S UNANIMOUS REJECTION of Golden's proposal for an interim-use plan for the piers was an early volley in a cycle of public disputes and private negotiations between the Coalition and the Brooklyn borough president that would continue for the next several years. "Howard was very nervous about this becoming what would be known as a jeweled necklace for the Brooklyn Heights community and no one else," recalls Golden's chief of staff, Marilyn Gelber, of the borough president's frequent clashes with the Coalition over the best plan for the piers. "He wasn't ready to simply accept their vision for the park."[21]

In addition to his general mistrust of Brooklyn Heights, Golden's unwillingness to relinquish control of the park project to the local community was also rooted in his sense of what would actually be required to bring a public park to the west Brooklyn waterfront. "We thought it's great that the community feels that sense of ownership and that they're out there fiercely defending their point of view," explains Gelber, "but being in government—and you know government can be arrogant at times—we felt that we owned it and it was our job to make something happen. We realized that ultimately it was only by getting city government and state government to work together that we would have some leverage over the Port Authority."[22]

Shortly after learning of the Coalition's negative vote on the "Warehouse Re-use" plan, Golden fired back, publicly reiterating his lack of confidence in the "parochial plan" for a park along the piers supported by the Coalition. "I wasn't committing to any plan until I had the opportunity to have all the factors looked into," Golden explained to Brooklyn reporter Michael Clark. "I wanted some kind of consensus because we want to bring in the larger interest of Brooklyn. You can't just have one group proposing a plan and then go accept it. We need further discussion on this thing."[23]

"There has historically been this tension about whether the park was for everybody or whether the park was for Brownstone Brooklyn," explains former City Council member Ken Fisher regarding the mistrust of Golden and other Brooklyn residents for the Coalition's plan for the park. "The Coalition has virtually always been an organization of elites. And the thing about elites is that they make up their minds about what's right for everybody else and then they execute on it."[24] At this stage in the planning process, the majority of Brooklynites were either, like Golden, resistant to the prospect of having the public park designed on their behalf by representatives of the affluent neighborhoods adjacent to the waterfront or completely indifferent to or unaware of the proposed project. While the *New York Times* and the local newspapers in Brooklyn Heights and Cobble Hill provided their readers with regular coverage of important developments related to the piers, the *New York Post*, which represented a blue-collar readership more typical of the rest of Brooklyn, and other local Brooklyn newspapers ignored the proposed development altogether.

Golden's resistance to the Coalition's plan for a park on Piers 1–5 was echoed by the Port Authority, with which the borough president had recently begun negotiations on the transfer of the ownership and oversight of the property to an independent public entity. "The Coalition is not the only voice being heard," said PDC spokesperson Lee Silberstein, "and I don't think the Coalition is as broad based as they would like to believe."[25]

Informed of the comments by Golden and Silberstein, Manheim maintained that the "Brooklyn Bridge Park" plan—not Golden's preferred "Warehouse Re-use" alternative—represented the true consensus among Brooklyn residents. The borough president, Manheim insisted, was the "lone dissenter" in the public discussions regarding the future of the piers. "We have to do a major education job on Golden," said Manheim.[26]

In spite of the public disagreement about the appropriate plan for the Piers 1–5, Golden, Manheim, and Silberstein expressed optimism that the issue would soon be settled and a suitable plan for the piers would be adopted.[27] To this end, a Coalition Working Group (composed of Manheim, Fox, John Watts, Ted Liebman, Roy Sloane, and Robert Rubin) began meeting regularly throughout the summer to discuss the integration of the two groups' respective guiding principles for the park.[28] During the same period, Golden and his staff were similarly occupied, adapting the guidelines for the development of the piers that the borough president had sent to Governor Mario Cuomo a year and a half earlier to incorporate the concerns expressed in the guiding principles supported by the Coalition.

At the suggestion of Golden's chief of staff, Marilyn Gelber, the two groups soon began to meet together regularly with the objective of developing a set of principles for the park that would be acceptable to everyone. "The idea was to try to make peace between Howard and Tony by focusing on the things we agreed on," explains Gelber, "and to show Vincent Tese at the UDC that we had a sense of unity between the local community and Borough Hall. We were all arguing over things that might never happen and focusing on where we disagreed. I, in my naiveté or wishful thinking, basically invited in a lot of the community players to my office in Borough Hall and said, 'Why don't we focus on what we agree on, instead of all the things we keep fighting about?'"[29]

IN AN ADDRESS to business and civic leaders in New York City on September 24, 1991, Mario Cuomo reaffirmed his support for a public solution to the controversy over Piers 1–5 and called for all the parties involved in the disagreement over the disposition of the piers to reach a consensus and follow through on the proposed development.[30] By this time, both the Coalition and Borough President Golden were satisfied that significant progress had been made toward the formulation of a set of common principles to be used to guide the charter for the proposed independent public entity in charge of the piers.

Although no final consensus had been achieved, the list of common principles on which the Coalition Working Group and Golden's office had agreed was impressive and featured many of the key concerns that had been raised by the various competing parties in the piers controversy during the previous seven years, including protecting the scenic-view plane, encouraging public participation and review at each stage of planning through public hearings, maximizing public recreation space, promoting water-related development, providing meaningful jobs for the local community, minimizing noise and pollution, and exploring possibilities for commercial development (including limited housing) that would ensure the sustainable fiscal viability of the plan.[31]

However, the two groups had yet to reach an agreement on which of the revised versions of the guiding principles most adequately reflected the priorities and interests of all the parties involved. "Our goal is to crystallize the thinking on the piers so there can be a unified Brooklyn position," Gelber explained to a local reporter following Cuomo's speech. "I think you see the Coalition guidelines already in this [Golden's] working document."[32] In spite of the governor's public call for an immediate solution to the piers debate, the process of revisions and negotiations continued well into the following year.

ON APRIL 3, 1992, the Port Authority announced a new set of plans to sell Piers 1–5 for private development. According to Port Authority executive director Stanley Brezenoff, the agency's decision to bypass the negotiations currently being conducted within the Brooklyn community was motivated by the fragility and vulnerability of the piers themselves. According to Brezenoff, one of the piers was in immediate danger of collapsing on top of an underwater subway tunnel, and all the piers were in urgent need of major repairs. From the perspective of the Port Authority, which still retained final responsibility for the oversight of Piers 1–5, the stalled negotiations among local elected officials and other leaders in the adjacent waterfront communities threatened to endanger the future viability of the property, whatever the intended use. "It isn't a question of negotiation," Brezenoff insisted. "After all this effort it seems doubtful than an approach that is acceptable to all parties will ever emerge."[33]

Whatever internal disagreements had kept the Coalition and the borough president from reaching a consensus on the appropriate planning and principles for the Brooklyn waterfront, the two groups were immediately united in their resistance to the reemergence of the Port Authority as a player in the disposition of Piers 1–5. "We've made great strides," Golden insisted to a reporter at the time, countering Brezenoff's claim that stalled local negotiations were endangering the waterfront property. "We've listened to every community. And we have gotten to the point where we are almost unanimous in the usage of the piers. The greatest mistake that could be perpetrated now is to give those piers away. Rome wasn't built in a day and our piers won't come back in a day."[34]

"We are going to go to the governor again and to Vincent Tese in hopes of getting them to stop the Port Authority from selling the land," announced Assemblywoman Eileen Dugan regarding the shared commitment of the community's elected officials to do whatever was necessary to resist the agency's plans. "We think it is a natural resource for Brooklyn and we are not going to stand still while they give it away."[35]

Following public outrage from community leaders and local elected officials—and a formal request for additional time for the completion of a public development plan from UDC executive director Vincent Tese, who was also serving as Governor Cuomo's chief economic adviser—the Port Authority quickly backed off its plans to sell the property for private development. "Frankly, it's something that I'm more than happy to do," explained Brezenoff. "The priorities for us involved here are that the property be put to good use, that it not be a drain on our budget and that our capital expenditures be reimbursed."[36]

THE REEMERGENCE of the Port Authority as a potential adversary in the disposition of the west Brooklyn waterfront property turned out to be the final nudge that the Coalition and Borough President Howard Golden needed to reach consensus on the common principles to guide a new public entity in charge of the piers. On June 29, 1992, the "13 Guiding Principles to Govern Redevelopment on the Downtown Brooklyn Waterfront" were approved by Coalition members, local elected officials, and other community leaders at a special meeting held at Borough Hall on 209 Joralemon Street in Brooklyn Heights.[37]

The "13 Guiding Principles" represented a comprehensive synthesis of the full range of issues and concerns of all the relevant parties in the proposed disposition of the Brooklyn piers, from the Brooklyn Heights community's original concerns about protecting the scenic view and the cul-de-sac design of the neighborhood to the public entities' insistence on the financial prudence and self-sustainability of the development plan to the maximization of access and opportunities (including job creation) for residents living outside the neighborhoods immediately adjacent to the piers property.

13 GUIDING PRINCIPLES TO GOVERN REDEVELOPMENT ON THE DOWNTOWN BROOKLYN WATERFRONT

1. **COMPREHENSIVE PLANNING;**

a) The Plan shall celebrate the unparalleled vistas and historic nature of the site with a world-class design affording spectacular entry into Brooklyn;

b) The Plan shall be conducted by a public entity which holds title to the site which includes Port Authority and other public and private parcels;

c) The Plan shall encompass the waterfront area between Manhattan Bridge and Atlantic Avenue including Empire–Fulton Ferry State Park, the Brooklyn Bridge area and the upland of Pier 6;

d) The Overall Plan shall be agreed to before permanent use or construction is authorized;

2. **FULL PUBLIC PARTICIPATION AND FULL PUBLIC REVIEW THROUGHOUT THE PLANNING, DEVELOPMENT AND MANAGEMENT PROCESS;**

a) Including representatives of the Brooklyn Bridge Park Coalition, Citywide and Brooklyn groups who have devoted years to public involvement and professional planning for the site;

b) Including Citywide and Brooklyn-area business, labor, civic and educational leaders;

3. **RETAIN AND ENHANCE SCENIC VIEWS;**

a) Preserve existing street-end view corridors including Atlantic Avenue and Old Fulton Street;

b) Protect and enhance the view of the Brooklyn Bridge and its towers, the Statue of Liberty and New York Harbor from the adjacent communities and the Promenade;

4. **PUBLIC OWNERSHIP TO PLAN, DEVELOP AND MANAGE THE SITE;**

a) In accordance with the overall Plan, issue carefully phrased sequential requests for proposals to construction and operation through ground lease for commercial developments;

5. **MAXIMIZE DEDICATED PARK LAND AND OPEN SPACE FOR YEAR-ROUND PUBLIC RECREATION, BOTH ACTIVE AND PASSIVE;**

a) The goal for the redevelopment is public access and use in a mixed-used development consisting predominantly of, and including the maximum level of, dedicated park land and open space, for both active and passive recreation;

6. **FOSTER PUBLIC ACCESS AND USES FROM BROOKLYN AND THROUGHOUT THE REGION WHILE RESPECTING AND PROTECTING THE CHARACTER OF, AND IMPACTS ON, ADJACENT COMMUNITIES;**

7. **DEVELOP AND PROVIDE FOR ENFORCEMENT OF DESIGN AND CONSTRUCTION GUIDELINES EMPHASIZING DESIGN QUALITY AND PROVIDING ENFORCEABLE LIMITS ON THE HEIGHTS, BULK, MASSING AND FOOTPRINT;**

8. **DEVELOP A FISCALLY PRUDENT PLAN;**

a) Specialized commercial uses (e.g., executive conference center/destination resort, restaurants, maritime center) shall be encouraged and residential and office uses shall be discouraged;

b) The site shall have only so much commercial development in a park-like setting as is necessary to enliven the area, to provide security and to finance ongoing operation;

c) The revenues from such commercial uses shall be committed to the operation and maintenance of dedicated park and open space areas and contribute to capital development costs;

d) The development of commercial uses, open space and park areas specified in the overall Plan shall be implemented in an incremental and coordinated manner;

9. **FOSTER JOB DEVELOPMENT;**

a) Favor development that generates permanent skilled jobs especially based on marine repair, hotel-conference and restaurant services and maritime activities;

10. **FOSTER WATER-RELATED DEVELOPMENT;**

a) Encourage uses that are enhanced by a waterfront location and/or that will enhance the waterfront;

11. **REQUIRE A SCALE AND BUILT FORM THAT RELATES CLOSELY TO THE SURROUNDING NEIGHBORHOODS;**

12. **FOSTER THE RELATIONSHIP BETWEEN THE SITE AND DOWNTOWN BROOKLYN, INCLUDING INCREASED TRANSPORTATION OPPORTUNITIES;**

a) Trolleys, buses and other public transportation to connect the site to rail and subway services;

b) Encourage the provision of pedestrian and bicycle access to, and usage within, the site;

13. **MINIMIZE NOISE AND AIR POLLUTION;**

a) Minimize vehicular traffic congestion and pollution impact on neighborhoods to the north, east and south.

Source: Brooklyn Bridge Park Coalition, "13 Guiding Principles to Govern Redevelopment on the Downtown Brooklyn Waterfront," June 29, 1992.

Even after the final document had been adopted and distributed, the "13 Guiding Principles" continued to have its detractors, both inside and outside the Coalition. A few months after the principles were adopted, Manheim confided to State Senator Martin Connor and Assemblywoman Eileen Dugan that several members of the BHA, Cobble Hill Association, and Fulton Ferry Landing Association on the Coalition had expressed frustration "at the whittling down of the Parks commitment in our own 16 Guiding Principles (already too weak, some thought) to get to the 13 Common Principles."[38] One of the key concerns was the issue of housing, with residents from the neighborhoods adjacent to the piers complaining that the document failed to ensure the complete absence of luxury condominiums and other private residences on the site, since Guiding Principle 8.a mandated that "specialized commercial uses (e.g., executive conference center/destination resort, restaurants, maritime center) shall be encouraged and residential and office uses shall be discouraged"—but not prohibited.

ON JULY 15, 1992, the newly adopted "13 Guiding Principles" were submitted to the UDC by the Coalition and the elected officials from Brooklyn. With the guiding principles for the new public entity approved and the Brooklyn community finally united around a common vision for the piers, it was the public entities' turn to delay the disposition process. In February 1993, more than six months after the joint submission of the "13 Guiding Principles" to the UDC, Manheim expressed frustration that he had still not received formal acknowledgment that the document had been received, much less a response to its contents.[39]

Manheim's frustration was further exacerbated by the recent release of the "Comprehensive Waterfront Plan" by the New York City Department of City Planning, which proposed splitting the Brooklyn Bridge Park site into two separate sites, Piers 1–5 and the Empire Stores/Fulton Ferry, only the latter of which was formally designated as a "Public Waterfront." The private nature of the study and its recommendations were in violation of Guiding Principle 2, which called for "full public participation and full public review throughout the planning, development and management process" and increased suspicions within the Brooklyn community that the public entities, which had repeatedly complained about delays in the adoption of the guiding principles for the piers, had no intention of following the newly adopted principles.

"Moving into our 5th year as a 52-organization-strong Borough- and City-wide Coalition, it is appropriate to be encouraged at the progress we have made—but disappointed at the pace!" Manheim wrote in his "Summary Progress Report" for 1993. "City and federal governments need to be much more actively involved and adopt a long-range public benefit perspective appropriate for a capital project that pays its own way, once built. The State needs to redeem, in a timely fashion, the promise implicit in Governor Cuomo's various statements of support. We are impatient to see interim public uses on the site, and detailed master planning get under way, in accord with our Bible—the PRINCIPLES."[40]

FIVE

BANGING THEIR CUPS
ON THE HIGH CHAIR

I remember that Tony's favorite phrase was "We've got to bang our cups on the high chair. We've got to bang our cups on the high chair." And that's what we did. We banged a few cups, and we got people's attention.

MARK BAKER

N JULY 1993, a year after the Brooklyn Bridge Park Coalition and the elected officials in Brooklyn had approved and submitted the "13 Guiding Principles" to the New York State Urban Development Corporation (UDC), the agency still had not endorsed the document, nor had it formally acknowledged receipt of a follow-up letter from Anthony Manheim, dated January 15, urging the adoption of the "13 Guiding Principles" and requesting the opportunity to discuss the appropriate composition of the board of directors for the proposed independent public entity for the disposition and oversight of the piers.[1]

After almost ten years of involvement in the piers controversy, Manheim had become increasingly frustrated with the frequent delays in the negotiation process, from both the public entities and the Coalition's partners in the Brooklyn community, and his private and public statements had begun to reflect the strain and impatience that he felt.

"It's extremely irresponsible," Manheim had complained to local reporter Anne-Marie Otey the previous July, shortly after he learned of the Port Authority's short-lived decision to sell the piers to private developers in the midst of the ongoing negotiations between the Coalition and elected officials in Brooklyn and the UDC. Later in the same interview, Manheim implicated both Brooklyn Borough President Howard

FIGURE 16
Anthony Manheim and
Brooklyn Borough President
Howard Golden, 1996.
COURTESY OF ANTHONY MANHEIM

Golden and UDC executive director Vincent Tese, two critical allies in the community's push for an independent public entity to take charge of the piers, for the failure of the park alternative to gain traction with the public authorities, in spite of the good faith and ongoing diligence of the Coalition and its supporters (figure 16). "We [the Coalition] have not had any contact with the PA [Port Authority], UDC, or EDC [Economic Development Corporation]," complained Manheim. "All discussions have gone on between the borough president's staff and the agencies. Everyone has said, we're giving Golden an opportunity to see if he can work it out. Now there's the perception that Golden's effort has failed," said Manheim, before directing his ire at Tese. "We heard the UDC thought it was too park-y. Tese has an absolute fear and hatred of parks."[2]

Now that the Coalition had finally gained some leverage with local elected officials and in the governor's office, Manheim was acutely aware that stalled negotiations and other delays could also work to the disadvantage of the community and the park movement and to the advantage of those favoring the private development of the piers. On the political level, the public support of even the most trusted allies in borough, city, and state government were only as reliable as the results of the latest election, while the hard-earned assurances of the Port Authority, the UDC, and other public agencies were always vulnerable to the changing priorities of private developers, who were continually warming to or shying away from the city's waterfront properties, depending on fluctuations in real-estate markets, political loyalties, and regulatory environments. As the UDC continued to delay the process by withholding its endorsement of the "13 Guiding Principles," Manheim grew to view the situation in "now or never" terms. If the hard-earned victories achieved by the Coalition and its antecedents in the west Brooklyn piers movement over the previous ten years were to slip away, with the promise of an independent public entity to control the piers in plain sight, the opportunity would almost certainly not be repeated.

The pressures on Manheim as the spokesman for the Coalition increased significantly in May 1992, when Coalition co-chair Tom Fox left the organization to become director of the newly formed Hudson River Park Conservancy, a subsidiary of the UDC, which was to oversee the planning and construction of the West Side waterfront between Battery Park City and Fifty-ninth Street. Now that Manheim was alone at the helm of the Coalition, he doubled his efforts to ensure the realization of the park that he had first envisioned almost a decade earlier.

"You have to understand how inspiring it was to think of [the waterfront] as being open to the public," recalls Manheim of the passion and urgency that drove him at the time. "We New Yorkers lived at a time when you didn't have access to the waterfront, when the waterfront was virtually walled off from us. And we realized that this was the one chance we would have, this one tremendous opportunity to create an enormous public resource in the center of the city and to take advantage of an opportunity that would never present itself again."[3]

If the Coalition were to fail in its efforts to create a public park on the west Brooklyn piers, Manheim reasoned, it would not be because its members had failed to make their voices heard. In each subsequent public pronouncement and private correspondence, Manheim's vision for the piers—and his assessments of the reasons that the Coalition's goals had not yet been achieved—became clearer, more emphatic, and more confrontational, and he urged his fellow Coalition members to act accordingly.

"I remember that Tony's favorite phrase was 'We've got to bang our cups on the high chair. We've got to bang our cups on the high chair,'" Mark Baker remembers of Manheim's increasing flair for drama and public confrontation. "And that's what we did. We banged a few cups, and we got people's attention."[4]

"Every time we had a fight it seemed to increase the attention," agrees John Watts. "We didn't stage any of this, but that's the effect it had. People in Albany said, 'Those people in Brooklyn, they never are satisfied.'

And the answer was, 'Yes. We're not until we get what we think ought to be done.'"[5]

According to other Coalition members from the period, Manheim was not the only one willing to challenge the authorities. Watts describes one particular meeting in the mid-1990s with the Port Authority and the UDC (at UDC headquarters on Third Avenue in midtown Manhattan) in which Coalition Working Group member Robert Rubin, a partner with Lehman Brothers who had overseen the financing of numerous Manhattan construction projects, stood up to UDC executive director Vincent Tese. "Tese was constantly giving us deadlines," Watts remembers. "He would say, 'I'll give you till the end of year and if you don't have it all figured out, I'm going to fast track the property back on the market.' It was clear he didn't think any of us had any idea what we were doing. And in one of the meetings, he looked at us and said, 'How many of you people here have ever built a building?' And Robert said, 'I have.' And Tese responded, 'Oh, yeah? What have you built?' And Robert replied, 'This building we're in right now.' And that was the end of the conversation."[6]

THE CONFRONTATIONAL APPROACH displayed by Manheim and other Coalition members gained the attention of elected officials at both the local and state levels. One of the first to respond in a positive way was Assemblywoman Eileen Dugan (figure 17). In 1993, Dugan, who had been supportive of the park plan since the Community Board 2 (CB2) Piers Subcommittee hearings in 1998, secured the first major financial assistance for the Brooklyn Bridge Park Coalition, a $250,000 contract awarded by the New York State Department of Economic Development.[7] For the Coalition, which had been dependent primarily on direct-mail campaigns and other local fund-raising efforts to fund its studies and cover its expenses, the state contract was both a vital source of funding and an enormous encouragement that the Brooklyn community's seemingly quixotic ambitions for a park on the piers might actually be achievable.

ON JANUARY 5, 1994, Governor Mario Cuomo finally announced during his annual State of the State message that an agreement had been reached among all the parties in the west Brooklyn piers negotiations: "The UDC will take the lead in implementing a plan developed by the city and Borough President Golden's office and long supported by Assemblywoman Eileen Dugan to create a mixed-use development on the Brooklyn waterfront, at Piers 1 through 5."[8]

While Manheim noted—and representatives of the Cuomo adminis-tration acknowledged—that the agreement was limited to the guidelines and did not include a specific development plan, he was gratified that the community's demands for the creation of an independent public au-thority for the piers had begun to progress—even though the public au-thorities cautioned that the actual development of the piers would still be years away. "The engine has been running, but the brakes have been on," Manheim said of the long-delayed but now completed negotiations. "Now, the brakes are being released and the project is being allowed to move forward. We just hope that the focus will be more on parkland."[9]

THE COALITION WASTED LITTLE TIME celebrating the governor's statement of support for "a mixed-use development" of the west Brooklyn water-front, with Manheim writing to Cuomo a few weeks after the State of the State message to remind him of the community's ultimate objective for the piers. "The goal of the universally endorsed program is public use and access," Manheim reminded the governor. "Mixed use is the means to that end: a technique for creating a major regional public amenity in a financially responsible way. . . . Controlled, limited and relevant 'concessions,' subordinate to the park's central purpose, are welcome—but only so much as needed to support and sustain a soft and green park, and subject to a comprehensive plan, developed with meaningful community input and controlled by the '13 Guiding Principles.'

"Appreciative as we are of your past actions in vetoing Port Authority disposition of these public assets and arresting inappropriate development schemes," Manheim explained, tempering his gratitude with a note of frustration, "we trust you will understand our impatience to move ahead now to begin recycling this underused land for new, higher and better public purposes—and at minimum public cost."[10] As important as the governor's past interventions with the Port Authority had been, a stronger and more focused commitment of state government would be necessary before the Brooklyn community's goal of "public use and access" of the piers could be achieved.

In addition to more aggressive support from state government, the success of the Brooklyn waterfront movement would require increased support from local residents and elected officials. In March 1994, the Coalition hosted an outdoor rally in blizzard conditions beneath the Manhattan Bridge on Fulton Ferry Landing to raise public support for the formation of an independent public entity to take control of the west Brooklyn waterfront. In spite of the heavy snowfall, a representative for Borough President Golden was in attendance, along with Karen Johnson, an aide to Congressman Edolphus Towns, who recently had secured a $500,000 federal grant for a study conducted by the U.S. Army Corps of Engineers that would contribute to the development of an erosion-control plan to stabilize and repair Piers 1–5.[11]

In spite of the generally positive tone of the ceremony and the gratitude expressed to Towns and other elected officials for their past support of the waterfront project, Manheim cautioned that past contributions would not be sufficient to achieve the community's goals for the piers property. "We will not allow this election year to pass with just words," he informed the crowd, clearly signaling that the Coalition would not hesitate to withdraw its support from elected officials who failed to follow through on their commitment to community ownership and development of the piers. "We will not let this opportunity go by without significant irreversible progress."[12]

WITH THE INTERCESSIONS AND VOCAL SUPPORT of Governor Cuomo, the formal endorsement of the "13 Guiding Principles" by the UDC, an expanding Coalition membership (that now included almost sixty borough, city, and state organizations), and the increased financial resources resulting from the grant secured from the Department of Economic Development by Assemblywoman Dugan, the Coalition's vision of a park along the west Brooklyn waterfront actually seemed within reach. The crucial remaining step was the formation of an independent public entity to manage the disposition of the piers and the construction and maintenance of a public park on the property. After more than a decade of leadership in the park movement, Manheim and the other Coalition members understandably believed that the organization would ultimately play a crucial role in the creation and leadership of the new public entity, along with the design, construction, and maintenance of the park over time.

Beginning in 1994, a series of personal, political, and economic events seriously threatened not only the Coalition's power and credibility in the Brooklyn piers movement but also the continued existence of the organization itself. The first major blow to the Coalition was the defeat of Mario Cuomo, the Democratic incumbent, to Republican challenger George Pataki in the gubernatorial election held on November 8, 1994. Not only had Cuomo championed the Brooklyn Bridge Park concept in his State of the State message at the beginning of the year, but he had included support of the Brooklyn waterfront park and other public spaces as a feature in his campaign, and the election of Pataki signaled a potential defeat for the park movement in Brooklyn.

According to Coalition board member John Watts, "Cuomo was always reassuring Tony. He'd say, 'Don't worry, Tony. You'll get your park.' And then when Cuomo wasn't reelected—and he didn't do anything to get it done in the interim between the election and the end of his administration—I think Tony took that really hard."[13]

Fortunately, Pataki, a longtime admirer of President Theodore Roosevelt's efforts to protect the natural environment and open public space, would soon warm to the concept of a public park along the west Brooklyn waterfront, listing Piers 1–5 among a roster of ninety tracts of "open space" that the state government intended to purchase or protect from development, with the state to provide a $250,000 grant for a preparatory study for the optimal development of the site.[14]

THE SECOND MAJOR BLOW to the Coalition and the Brooklyn Bridge Park movement—and to the Brooklyn community as a whole—was the death of Eileen Dugan on November 8, 1996, after a long battle with cancer. As a local member of the New York State Assembly and the chairwoman of the Committee on Economic Development, Job Creation and Industry,

Dugan had been among the earliest and most committed supporters of the concept of a park on the piers, lending her name and support to the CB2 Piers Subcommittee's endorsement of the Harbor Park plan, publicly criticizing each of the Port Authority's repeated attempts to lease the property for private development, urging UDC director Vincent Tese to endorse the "13 Guiding Principles," and securing a $250,000 contract for the Coalition from the New York State Department of Economic Development in 1993.

A few months earlier, on July 23, 1996, Dugan had announced that she and State Senator Martin Connor had secured a $500,000 grant through the state legislature to support the Coalition's planning, education, and advocacy on behalf of the park. "The grant will cover a portion of the Coalition's expenses in seeking public access redevelopment of the Downtown Brooklyn Waterfront from Manhattan Bridge to Atlantic Avenue for both active and passive recreation," wrote Dugan in a press release to announce the grant. "Fighting for this park has been a long and sometimes exhausting struggle. However, Senator Connor and I remain firmly committed to this project, and we along with the Coalition believe that one day the downtown Brooklyn waterfront will be enjoyed by everyone for recreational use."[15]

IN JUNE 1997, the Coalition's ambitions for the area of the park north of the Brooklyn Bridge received yet another major blow when David Walentas of Two Trees Management Company announced that he was seeking city and state approval to resume his decade-old plans to construct an investor's paradise of restaurants, retail stores, and movie theaters on the nine-acre Empire–Fulton Ferry State Park and its seven dilapidated Civil War–era warehouses (the Empire Stores) between the Brooklyn and Manhattan Bridges (figure 18). Walentas was reportedly the only developer to respond to a request, in February, from the New York State Office of Parks, Recreation and Historic Preservation for proposals to refurbish the parkland and warehouses. Walentas had originally been chosen to develop the waterfront property in 1982, with plans for more than 2 million square feet of office space, a 100-boat marina, and a 330-foot observation tower, but his plans were derailed in 1984, when Kenneth Lipper, the Deputy Mayor for Finance and Economic Development, ruled that he did not have sufficient financial backing to ensure the completion of the project. In the face of public resistance for his private development plans and growing support for a public park along the west Brooklyn waterfront, Walentas had shelved his proposals for a number of years, waiting for a resurgence of the local real-estate market. In 1996,

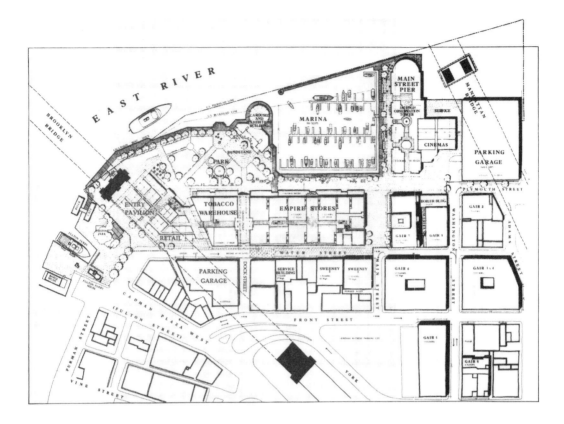

Mayor Rudolph Giuliani designated Walentas as prime developer of the property between the two great bridges, and the real-estate developer decided that the time was right to resurrect his plans for the site.

In a further setback, Borough President Howard Golden publicly endorsed Walentas's project, contributing an op-ed piece to the *New York Times* contesting the assertion of *Times* reporter David Rohde that Walentas's plan "could delay or alter a decade-old effort by the Brooklyn Bridge Park Coalition to convert the abandoned piers into a public park."[16] "In fact," insisted Golden, "the uses proposed by Mr. Walentas for the inter-bridge area—retail outlets, a restaurant and multiplex movie theater—are not in competition with the uses envisioned on Piers 1–5. The Brooklyn Bridge Park plan calls for the development of a conference center and hotel, a maritime support center and marina, and catering and restaurant facilities, all within a park setting."[17]

IN DECEMBER 1996, the Coalition encountered yet another obstacle when the Strober Organization, a large building-supply company, opened a massive wholesale showroom, lumberyard, and offices for its corporate headquarters on Pier 3. The Strober Organization had recently shut down its main headquarters on Hamilton Avenue in Brooklyn, having been granted a ten-year lease by the Port Authority in June 1996 to re-open its facilities on the pier.

For the Coalition, the installation of a massive lumberyard on Pier 3, near the center of the Brooklyn Bridge Park site, would violate the integrity of the proposed site and inevitably discourage private developers from investing in the creation of the park and the supplemental commercial ventures required to support its construction and ongoing operation. "Ten years is a long time," Manheim explained to a reporter about the inevitable impact of positioning a building-supply storage facility at the center of a public park. "'It's a new and unnecessary hurdle for any kind of constructive development. Who wants a site with a lumberyard in the middle of it?"[18]

In January 1997, the Brooklyn Bridge Park Coalition filed a suit in the United States District Court in Brooklyn against the Port Authority of New York and New Jersey and the Strober Organization of Brooklyn, challenging the Port Authority's decision to lease Pier 3 to the supply company. In addition to the papers submitted by the Coalition's pro bono attorneys, the prominent New York law firm Cravath, Swaine & Moore, State Senator Martin Connor; Assemblywoman Eileen Dugan; Representatives Edolphus Towns, Jerrold Nadler, and Nydia Velázquez; and City Council members Kenneth Fisher, Stephen DiBrienza, and Joan Griffin McCabe had filed a brief by *amici curiae* in opposition to dismissal of the case.

Although various procedural challenges were included in the suit, the foundation of the Coalition's case was that in allowing the Strober Organization to use Pier 3 as an office and a warehouse—and not as a "marine terminal facility" for the offloading of goods delivered by ship to the site—the Port Authority "would be acting *ultra vires* [beyond] the powers conferred upon the agency by its compact in leasing the property to this codefendant."[19]

On January 21, 1997, Judge Reena Raggi rejected the Coalition's argument that the Port Authority's charter of 1921 restricted the site to "marine-related uses" and would hence not radically alter the character of the property, which had originally been "designed" for the unloading of freight at the waterfront.[20]

Although the Coalition's claim was denied, the lawsuit resulted in an unexpectedly positive outcome for the organization and the park movement. On August 1, 1997, Lillian C. Borrone, director of the Port Commerce Department, authorized the Port Authority to enter into a five-year, rent-free lease with the Coalition for a vacant building at 334 Furman Street in exchange for the discontinuation of a planned appeal of the Strober decision.[21] The building, which today serves as the headquarters for both the Brooklyn Bridge Park Conservancy and the public entity in charge of the construction of Brooklyn Bridge Park, was the park movement's first footprint on the piers property.

IN DECEMBER 1997, Manheim and the Coalition received a final—and seemingly insurmountable—blow when Borough President Howard Golden, with the support of other local elected officials, finally proposed the formation of the Brooklyn Waterfront Local Development Corporation (LDC) to prepare studies to facilitate the development of Piers 1–5. During the 1997 session of the New York State Legislature, State Senator Martin Connor and Assemblywoman Joan Millman, who had replaced Eileen Dugan, secured a $1 million grant to support the formation and operation of the new entity.

According to Golden's chief of staff, Greg Brooks, the timing and design of the LDC were motivated by the frustration of Golden and other political leaders over a conflict with the Coalition earlier in the year. "The catalyst for the LDC was at the opening of the Coffey Street Pier in Red Hook [on February 5, 1997]," recalls Greg Brooks. "There was a discussion among the elected officials in attendance—Howard Golden, Martin Connor, and Ed Towns were there; I can't remember who else—and they were all wringing their hands over some controversy [involving the Coalition] that had recently happened. I said, 'What we really need is something to give this thing a push,' and I recommended that we form a local development corporation that would involve every community and whose first goal would be to create a master plan for the park."[22]

The decision by Golden and the other officials to form the LDC at the time was also motivated by pressure from community groups frustrated with the Coalition's inability to move the park forward. "On behalf of the Cobble Hill Association," recalls Franklin Stone, former president of the Cobble Hill Association, "I wrote a letter to Howie Golden, and I withdrew the Cobble Hill Association from the Coalition. Both in writing and person, we [at the Cobble Hill Association] and others went to Howie Golden and asked him to set up a new organization to move the park forward. At that time, there was no sign that the Coalition was making any progress on the park or that it would be making any progress in the future. We also did not feel that it was representative of all the communities that would be using the park and affected by the park as a new more-representative organization would be. I'll say as a shorthand, it was too Brooklyn Heights–centric. And Golden did set up the LDC so that there was broader representation."[23]

The LDC would be governed by a board of directors and the leaders of Community Boards 2 and 6, the Brooklyn Heights Association, the Brooklyn Chamber of Commerce, and a number of other groups from the community. With the Coalition having worked tirelessly for the creation of a public entity in charge of the piers, the formation of the LDC should by all rights have been regarded as a major victory for Manheim and the other Coalition board members—if not for the fact that the Coalition was not included among the groups that would be involved in the governance of—or in the selection of directors for—the LDC. "It didn't make sense to us to include the Coalition," recalls Brooks, "which was composed of members of other communities that would already be included. Our hope was that people would understand that the 'electeds' were very serious about having something happen at Brooklyn Bridge Park, and that they would come into the fold because they didn't want to be excluded from it. The communities that the Coalition represented would naturally be a part of that."[24]

The Coalition's objections to the LDC were compounded by a disagreement over the $1 million grant that Connor and Millman had recently secured to fund the new organization. Coalition president Anthony Manheim and other Coalition members maintained that the newly appropriated funds were actually a continuation of the remaining funds that Connor and Dugan had received the previous year. According to Manheim, Dugan had privately assured him at the time of the $500,000 award that the entire $1.5 million was "intended wholly" for use by the Coalition.[25] The previous March, Manheim had submitted a $1.5 million budget grant proposal to Frank McNally, counsel of the UDC, to support the Coalition's planning, education, and advocacy activities on behalf of the piers.[26] The proposal was not granted, however, and the LDC was formed a few months later, its funding provided by what Manheim believed to be money intended for the Coalition.

According to Connor, however, Dugan had originally intended the funds that she secured from the state budget to be used by a special Waterfront Task Force created by Borough President Howard Golden—and not by the Coalition. "In 1996," recalls Connor, "the Assembly had extracted from the governor a lot of capital money through UDC [Urban Development Corporation], which is now called ESDC [Empire State Development Corporation]. And Eileen called me up as we were doing the budget and said, 'I got a commitment for a million bucks, and I'm going to give it to the Brooklyn Waterfront Task Force,' which was something that Howie Golden had set up a couple of years before. It hadn't really done anything, but it was there.

"Eileen called me up that summer," says Connor of a conversation he had with Dugan after she was diagnosed with cancer, "and she said, 'You have to promise me one thing if anything happens to me, if I don't make it.' And I said, 'What?' And she said, 'Don't you let Tony Manheim and the Coalition get my million dollars.' And I've never told anyone this before, because she passed away and I didn't want to say anything. And I've endured years of Tony saying that I stole his million dollars.

"She never intended for them to get the money," concludes Connor. "If she had intended for them to have it, she would have put 'Brooklyn Bridge Park Coalition' into the budget."[27]

WITH THE MAJORITY OF LOCAL RESIDENTS either unaware of or unconvinced by the reasoning behind the LDC's governance structure, news of the exclusion of the Coalition from any and all involvement in the public entity that it had labored so diligently to achieve ignited a fury of protests throughout the Brooklyn Heights community, as well as among the representatives of the sixty-one local, city, and state organizations contributing to its membership. In addition to the exclusion of the Coalition from its leadership, many park supporters were also disturbed to learn that the LDC's mandate also denied the use of its funding to plan for waterfront development on the property between the Brooklyn and Manhattan Bridges owned by Manhattan real-estate developer David Walentas.

Gary VanderPutten, a local activist from the Fulton Ferry neighborhood and a Coalition board member since 1995, remembers how he first learned about the creation of the LDC and its goals for the Brooklyn piers. "I get a call from Joan Millman, my assemblywoman, who knows me very well," says VanderPutten, "and she says, 'Here's what we're going to do. We've got $1.5 million and we're going to form a local development corporation under the ESDC. And we're going to start the park process. But we're only doing Piers 1 to 5, because 6 was still considered a parcel for commercial use by the International Longshoremen's Association. And we're not doing the inter-bridge sector; Walentas is going to do that. We're going to have a new board, and it's going to have representation from public officials and the local community. We want you to be on it. And we also feel there's no need for the Coalition to exist anymore. That's what we're doing, and we'd like your support on it.' And, of course, I didn't support it. But we did end up losing some really valuable people, including the entire Cobble Hill contingent on the Coalition board."[28]

At an emergency meeting held on January 13, 1998, at the First Presbyterian Church on Henry Street in Brooklyn Heights, Borough President Howard Golden and Brooklyn Heights City Council member Ken Fisher did their best to maintain order among a crowd of angry Brooklyn Heights residents, many of whom were troubled by the exclusion of the Coalition from the LDC and threatened to withhold their support from the newly formed organization. Order was finally restored and public endorsement of the LDC achieved when Fisher, after trying to persuade those in attendance that the Coalition had been properly excluded from the leadership of the LDC because of its lack of "accountability to anyone" in dispersing public funds or making decisions about the planning and construction of the park, offered his own seat on the LDC board to John Watts of the Coalition. Only after the announcement of the inclusion of Watts (and hence the Coalition) on the LDC board did the Brooklyn Heights Association and the Fulton Ferry Landing Association agree to participate as well.[29]

"Howie Golden put me in a very difficult position early in my first term," recalls Fisher of the Brooklyn Heights community's initial response to the announcement of the creation, membership, and funding of the LDC. "There was an important meeting held at the Presbyterian Church to discuss what Brooklyn Heights was going to do. It was certainly an important meeting for me, because I could see my political future passing before my eyes.

"I remember the meeting pretty clearly," he continues. "It was a packed house. I went in and deliberately sat down in the middle without making a fuss about being there. People were alternating between being outraged and wanting to know what I was going to do about it. I think that most people didn't even realize that I was there. I was the new kid on the block, and expectations were higher for me than they were for the other elected officials.

"I found myself in a position where I actually got to decide what *I* thought was important, because I was caught between these two important constituencies: the borough president, who was my most important political supporter, on one side and the neighborhood of Brooklyn Heights, which was one of my most important constituents, on the other side. I didn't know what I was going to say until I stood up and said it. What I said was, 'I didn't think it was appropriate for the Coalition or any private organizations to control the money, because these were public funds and, at the end of the day, we [the elected officials] were all accountable and they [the Coalition] weren't.' On the other hand, since I had an appointment to the LDC, I was prepared to nominate John Watts, who was a co-chair of the Coalition, as my representative."[30]

Even after Fisher's generous concession, the lack of regard shown to the Coalition by Golden and the other elected officials was devastating for Manheim and the other Coalition members—though not completely unexpected. "The Local Development Corporation that the government created included no role for us—zero role," explains Mark Baker. "But the history of the Coalition has always been that government is constantly coming up to us and saying, 'You guys have done great work. Now we'll take it from here.' I can't tell you how many 'We'll take it from here' conversations we've had. And here they were saying it again, 'We'll take it from here.' "[31]

The attempt to exclude the Coalition from participation in the LDC was also intended as a rebuttal of Manheim and his leadership of the emerging movement for a park on the west Brooklyn piers. For the past several years, Manheim's public indictments of the public entities in control of the piers and private challenges of elected officials to live up to their commitments had enabled the Coalition to overcome the forceful opposition of the Port Authority, the Department of City Planning, and the Public Development Corporation to the park concept, as well as potentially crippling delays from the UDC in the adoption of the principles to guide the formation of the park. In spite of his undeniable achievements, however, Manheim's outspokenness and increasingly strident tone had also angered many of those whom he had criticized or held accountable.

"It was around this same time that I got a call from the borough president, whom I'd only met through the ribbon-cutting ceremonies I'd attended," remembers VanderPutten. "All of a sudden, I get word that he wants to meet with me. And so I go down to Borough Hall in the borough president's office to meet him, and I think to myself, 'This must be very important.' And he starts to talk, and it's like the scene out of *Network* when Ned Beatty comes in and says, 'You are meddling with the primal forces of the universe!' And Golden says, 'There's a single reason why this is not going to go anywhere with your organization, and it's because of Tony Manheim.' "[32]

According to others on the Coalition, the elected officials' decision regarding the governance of the LDC was more than just a rejection of Manheim. "There was hostility and a lot of it was directed at Tony, but it was really about us," insists Baker. "Who were we to say what ought to happen on the site? Our authority was definitely being questioned.

"When we were small and the idea was new," continues Baker, "it wasn't threatening to anybody. But when the idea began to gain currency and people began to say, 'Yeah, there should be a park down there,' then all of a sudden people were saying, 'Why are they in charge?' "[33]

THROUGHOUT THIS CHALLENGING PERIOD, Manheim continued to work faithfully toward the realization of Brooklyn Bridge Park, appearing at the Coalition's office at 75 Montague Street every day with his assistant, Barbara Brookhart, to request funding from members of the local community, write letters to elected officials and public authorities, and review plans and recommendations for the park.

On February 26, 1997, the Coalition released the *Economic Viability Study: Piers Sector, Brooklyn Bridge Park*, which included a real-estate and market-conditions overview, a construction-cost estimate, a financial-feasibility analysis, and an economic-benefits analysis for the proposed park. The six-month study, which was funded by the $250,000 grant provided to the Coalition by Governor Pataki in 1995, had been undertaken by the real-estate consulting firm Praedium Group, the accounting firm Ernst & Young, and Federman Design + Construction Consultants. The study was based on interviews conducted with seventy-five individuals, including government representatives; hotel and conference operators and developers; directors, promoters, and developers of amateur-sports operations and facilities; real-estate and professional developers; marina operators and developers; and restaurant and catering operators and developers.[34]

The findings from the study, which were shared with elected officials and other attendees at the Brooklyn Bridge Park "Coming of Age" benefit on March 29, reported extensive market support for the specific features of the park plan (including strong interest from national and local companies in operating the hotel, marina, restaurants, skating rink, and other recreational facilities proposed in the park plan), the potential for adequate cash flow to cover the ongoing maintenance of the park (with projected annual revenues of $4 million, compared with an estimated $3.4 million annual maintenance cost), and a variety of public economic benefits that would result from the proposed use of the property (including $100 million of increased economic activity for the borough, the creation of 1,200 permanent jobs, and $25 million in annual tax revenues).[35]

IN SPITE OF THE POSITIVE FINDINGS from Praedium's study, Manheim was reportedly demoralized by the legal impasse with the Strober Organization and the rejection of the Coalition by the elected officials in charge of the formation of the LDC. In response to past snubs or disappointments, he had always become more determined and outspoken in his support for the park. Now, after almost fifteen years as the central figure in the waterfront park movement, he began to withdraw from the day-to-day challenges of the Brooklyn piers movement.

As Mark Baker recalls, the first real sign of the shift in Manheim's attitude toward the Coalition involved an argument over a boiler. "We got this building [the headquarters of the park and the Brooklyn Bridge Park Conservancy on 334 Furman Street] when I settled the lawsuit with the Port Authority over Strober," Baker explains. "It was our first footprint on the site, and I thought it was critical for us to be there. How could we pass up on this opportunity to sit on the site in a building we're being given? How could we pass that up?

"It was a real test of our organization as to our ability to take this building over," Baker continues, "and Tony fought it. He didn't want to do it. He was at the end, and here I'm saying, 'Look, the Port Authority is offering us this abandoned building. And why don't we take it? We'll put our offices in there, and we'll be on the site finally.' And he's like, 'How much work is that?' He was just ready to go, and here was this new project, which meant that the organization would continue."[36]

WITH THE COALITION MARGINALIZED from the public entity on behalf of which it had spent the previous several years lobbying and with the LDC assuming responsibility for the design and funding structure of the park, while also serving as the official conduit between the planners of the park and the residents of the adjacent communities, the members of the Coalition were left with the inevitable question: What, if anything, was left for them to do?

"Looking back," Baker confides, "the creation of the LDC was definitely an important moment for the park, moving the park forward. But for the Coalition, it was the opposite. It was like we were being made redundant."[37]

Shortly after the formation of the LDC, the Coalition's remaining board members assembled to decide if there was a legitimate reason for the organization to continue. "There's only like seven or eight of us at the time," recalls Gary VanderPutten, "because everybody else had left or were part of the LDC. And we're like, 'Is this the last meeting we're going to have? What are we going to do?' There was no need for an advocacy organization at this point. The LDC had that under control."[38]

After learning of the LDC's decision to leave the area between the Brooklyn and Manhattan Bridges out of the park design, VanderPutten had recently joined forces with residents in Fulton Ferry and Brooklyn Heights to resist Two Trees Management's plan for the waterfront property. "I had innocently taken a picture of the Manhattan Bridge, and I put a building in front of it, saying, 'This is what's going to happen.' And Allen Swerdloe, the architect, says, 'No. That's terrific, but it's wrong. What you really need to do is go put together a graphic study of what's going to change if they do this. And it has to be architecturally pure. You can't just go in and do all these crappy pictures.' So I did the images, and we formed a working group, independent of the Coalition, called the Old Brooklyn Waterfront Alliance [OBWA]. And we were a noisy group, with the mantra: It's not good enough that the LDC is going to build a park on Piers 1 to 5. We want a park between the bridges."[39]

Instead of publishing the images right away, VanderPutten and his fellow OBWA members presented them privately to local politicians, as well as to officials at the Department of City Planning and the New York State Office of Parks, Recreation and Historic Preservation, assuring them that the images would be published only if Walentas's project was allowed to continue: "So I gave [the remaining Coalition board members] this presentation of what OBWA was and what we were up to. And I said, 'This is the only way we can battle this. We don't have any money, but these images tell a story that's pretty bad.' And Maria Favuzzi just grabbed the book with the images and said, 'This is what we're going to do. We're going to be the advocacy group to keep the inter-bridge area in Brooklyn Bridge Park.' "[40]

It was immediately clear to everyone in attendance that the failure to include the inter-bridge property represented a critical flaw in the LDC's plans for the park—and that the Coalition, with its expansive organizational membership and proven commitment to the park movement, had an important role to play in ensuring that the area between the Brooklyn and Manhattan Bridges was included in the final park design.

"As you can imagine, this really did not go well with a lot of these people that had put together the LDC, thinking that that would be the end of the Coalition," says VanderPutten. "After that meeting, we came out and said, 'This is what we're going to do. We're going to re-form the Coalition, and we're going to make sure that the inter-bridge area is put back in the plan. We're going to get a proper, paid executive director. We're going to get our own funding somewhere, by some hook or crook. We're going to keep on going.' "[41]

SIX

CHANGING OF THE GUARD

> Our attitude was that this wasn't the end of the process. It was only the beginning.
>
> **JOANNE WITTY**

OW THAT THE BROOKLYN BRIDGE PARK COALITION had found a new purpose in resisting the plan of David Walentas of Two Trees Management for a high-rise commercial multiplex in Dumbo (Down Under the Manhattan Bridge Overpass) and promoting the inclusion of the inter-bridge area in the overall park design, the next task was to find an executive director with the organizational, community-development, and fund-raising skills that would enable the Coalition to generate broad-based support for its objectives among both the general public and the elected officials who controlled the funding for the park project. The board's original plan was to retain Anthony Manheim as the Coalition chair, to continue in his advocacy work and maintain relationships with representatives of the sixty-one organizations that the Coalition now included among its membership, while also hiring a full-time executive director with the professional skills and experience to take the lead in fund-raising, public relations, and strategic development.

Coalition board member and legal adviser Mark Baker recommended Tensie Whelan, a gifted and highly respected young community organizer with whom he and former Coalition co-chair Tom Fox had worked on the Hudson River Park negotiations. Whelan, who had served as the executive director of the New York League of Conservation Voters and the vice president of the National Audubon Society, had impressed the Coalition board members during a recent consulting assignment that she had undertaken on behalf of the park project, and they soon reached a consensus that she was the best candidate for the position.

At first, Whelan did not share the Coalition's conviction that she was the right person for the job. A resident of nearby Park Slope, Whelan was aware of the ongoing controversy surrounding the waterfront movement and the Coalition's recurring conflicts with local elected officials and community leaders, as well as the internal conflicts within the waterfront movement, and she respectfully declined the offer.

Even after Whelan's refusal, the Coalition board members still felt strongly that she was the best person for the position, and board member John Watts, a skilled negotiator who rarely took no for an answer, offered to make a second appeal. Watts encouraged Whelan to do a thorough investigation of the current situation and to identify the resources and organizational changes that had to be addressed. He assured her that the Coalition would do everything in its power to provide her with whatever she needed to do the job.

After spending several weeks speaking privately with elected officials, community leaders, and others involved in the Brooklyn Bridge Park movement, Whelan finally agreed to accept the Coalition's offer, as long as two conditions were met. First, she would agree to work only half time for the Coalition (on a pro bono basis for the first six to nine months), while continuing her current commitments to the other organizations with which she was already involved. Second, Manheim would have to resign his positions as Coalition chair and board member.

From her conversations with the government leaders and elected officials with whom she talked, Whelan learned that Manheim was regarded as the driving force of the park movement, who "through sheer force of will had galvanized engagement around the idea of having a park on the waterfront."[1] She also learned, however, that through his increasingly strained relations with local elected officials and public authorities, Manheim had become the greatest obstacle to the realization of the dream of a park along the west Brooklyn piers that he, more than anyone else, had inspired.

According to architect Fred Bland, who had been involved in the piers negotiations since the earliest interactions between the Port Authority and the Brooklyn Heights Association (BHA) Waterfront Committee in the mid-1980s and was also a close friend of Manheim, "The politicians, for whatever their reasons, said, 'Get rid of him and we'll go forward. Don't get rid of him, and we don't want to touch it.'"[2]

Faced with the stark choice between continuing under the leadership of Manheim, who (according to Baker) had begun to withdraw from Coalition activities since the lawsuit against the Port Authority over the Strober Organization's use of Pier 3 and the creation of the Local Development Corporation (LDC), and turning to Whelan, who promised to bring desperately needed organizational, strategic planning, and fund-raising skills to the organization, the remaining board members made the painful decision to ask Manheim to step down.

Once the decision to remove Manheim as leader of the Coalition had been made, several board members contacted him individually to inform him of their plans and to try to persuade him to step down voluntarily. "I took Tony for a drink," recalls board member Irene Janner, "and I said, 'I feel terrible, but I would have to vote against you continuing on the board too, because it's hurting the organization.' I said, 'You'll be president emeritus. Your portrait will be on the wall of the Coalition. But you have to get out of the day-to-day stuff, because no one will talk to us.'

"Tony will go down in history as the father of the park," says Janner, "because none of it would have happened without him. But he would not go, and we literally had to vote him out. And it was very, very upsetting."[3]

Manheim repeatedly refused to consider the board members' requests that he resign on his own initiative, and on the night before the next Coalition board meeting, Bland, who had continued to be involved in Coalition activities but was not a member of the board at the time, was enlisted to make one last, desperate plea for him to step down voluntarily. "Someone called me," remembers Bland, "and said, 'You know Tony well. We're not getting through to him. He's going to be fired or unelected or whatever the right term is at tomorrow night's board meeting unless he resigns earlier. And we don't want that to happen. It's not fair for him to be fired. We don't want to do that.'

"So I said, 'I know Tony well, and I like Tony. Let me see what I can do.' So I called him and said, 'Would you have a drink with me?' And we went down to the Knickerbocker [at 33 University Place in Greenwich Village], which is just two blocks away [from Bland's office], and we each had a martini. I think it was probably around the end of the first martini, while we were eating, I said, 'Tony, this isn't right. It's the worst thing that could happen. Can't you just go gracefully and resign?' And he said, 'No. You want another martini?' And we actually each ended up having three martinis. (I don't think I've ever done that.) But he wouldn't agree. He said, 'I'm sorry. If they want to get rid of me, they're going to have to bump me out.' And the next night they did."[4]

The following day, by a vote of 4 to 3, Anthony Manheim was officially "bumped out" of his position as Coalition chair, as well as his membership on the Coalition board. Once the vote was taken and the decision had been finalized, Manheim was civil and polite in accepting the will of his fellow board members. "We talked it over with Tony," Whelan says of Manheim's response to the decision, "and he was really gracious and said, 'I will step down so we can move forward.' "[5]

After Manheim's quarter of a century as a leader, visionary, and provocateur in the west Brooklyn piers movement, it was difficult for everyone who had previously been involved in the Coalition—and even of some of the elected officials and community leaders with whom he had occasionally quarreled—to imagine the park movement without him.

"Tony deserves a tremendous amount of credit," Tom Fox insists. "He was the engine that pulled us behind him. He really was. Maria [Favuzzi] and I were sidecars, stoking the fire. I can see myself in the back car, covered with coal dust, throwing fuel on the fire. But Tony was the locomotive. There wouldn't be a Brooklyn Bridge Park if it wasn't for Tony."[6]

"To my mind," says Bland, "Tony Manheim is the key to the whole early part of the story. And it was a horrible thing that he was dethroned, but it was the only way we were going to move forward."[7]

MANHEIM'S REMOVAL as president of the Coalition immediately strengthened the organization's credibility with Brooklyn Borough President Howard Golden and the other local elected officials with whom he had butted heads in the past as well as the leaders of the LDC, who were apprehensive of future confrontations. For many Brooklyn Heights residents, however, Manheim's sudden and unexpected absence from the movement he had founded and guided for almost fifteen years raised serious questions about the Coalition's priorities and purpose going forward.

"Manheim, the guiding dynamo of the park vision for so long, is evidently out of the picture," wrote Brooklyn journalist Henrik Krogius shortly after the announcement of Manheim's departure, "which may ease relations between the coalition and the LDC, but which also raises the question of the coalition's continuing purpose."[8]

At the Annual Meeting of the BHA in February 1999, several weeks after Manheim was voted off the Coalition board, a crowd of several hundred local residents gathered at Grace Episcopal Church at 254 Hicks Street in Brooklyn Heights to jointly honor Manheim and the Coalition with the BHA's Community Service Award. The entire crowd, including State Senator Martin Connor, Assemblywoman Joan Millman, and City Council member Ken Fisher, rose to applaud as Manheim's old friend Fred Bland presented him with the award, citing the former Coalition leader's "awe-inspiring" dedication, along with his ability to inspire commitment to "a compelling vision that won't go away."[9]

ONCE THE DIFFICULT ISSUE of Manheim's departure had been resolved, Tensie Whelan wasted little time in taking the reins of the Coalition, immediately introducing the board members to a ninety-day strategy that she had formulated for reestablishing the organization's importance and credibility in the park movement. Whelan's strategy focused on three key areas: campaigning, coalition building, and organizational development.

The most pressing task that Whelan faced was working with the Coalition board to redefine the organization's purpose for existing, now that the LDC had been designated as the legal entity in charge of the design and development of Piers 1–5, and identifying the most effective strategy for achieving that purpose. Whelan was immediately impressed by the board's tentative decision before her arrival to focus on the property between the Brooklyn and Manhattan Bridges not covered by the LDC mandate, as well as the work that Gary VanderPutten and others had already done to document the impact of commercial development on the site.

"We led Tensie through the whole history of what we had done up till this point and how the inter-bridge area had been left out of the LDC plan and how we wanted to take it back," remembers VanderPutten. "And she flipped through the book of images that I had done, and she said, 'Who have you shown this to?' I said, 'We've shown it quietly. We haven't gone out there and flooded the neighborhood with leaflets or anything. We've been pretty kind to the politicians.' And she said, 'All right, give me a month. I intend to pursue this. I just need to do some due diligence, and I'll get back to you.'"[10]

A month later, Whelan reported back to the Coalition board with a list of resources that she would need to gain support for the organization's vision of a public park between the bridges, including 1,000 copies of the original images from VanderPutten's book, aerial views of the inter-bridge area, an artist's depiction of a public park in the inter-bridge area, and a professional presentation of the assembled images.

VanderPutten recalls the decisive manner with which Whelan communicated her instructions: "She said, 'Gary, I want pictures of the park area from the air. Rent a helicopter. I don't care how you get it. I'm not paying for it. You figure it out. I need to have about a hundred slides of what the waterfront looks like right now. Just get it done. Don't send me the bill.'"[11]

"The strategy I proposed was around several things," explains Whelan. "The first was on showing the negative impacts of the Walentas development plans for the inter-bridge area. He wanted to cantilever out over the water this huge multiplex and shopping source. And if you did that, it would totally screw up the whole view plane of everything.

"And the other was to create a positive vision in its place," she continues. "So we wouldn't just be *against* something, but would be creating a Coalition *for* something. So we devised these tools of taking aerial photographs and then putting green and all these other positive things to show what the park would actually look like, instead of all the crap that was there at the time. We also commissioned an artist to draw a beautiful watercolor of what it could look like if we achieved our goal of putting a park there."[12]

Whelan's next step was to reestablish and expand the Coalition's connections with organizations within and beyond the communities that would be affected by the proposed commercial development of the inter-bridge area. An experienced community organizer with strong institutional connections, Whelan immediately began reaching out both to the city, state, and national organizations with which she had established relationships and to local community organizations with an interest in the park movement, many of which had interacted with the Coalition in the past but were uncertain of the organization's appropriate role since the LDC had been established. Within a few months, the Coalition had gained—or regained—the support of an impressive roster of local, city, state, and national organizations that were not only enthusiastic about the goal of creating a park on the west Brooklyn piers but also supportive of the role that the Coalition had chosen to play in achieving that goal.

"I designed a whole outreach strategy of bringing in key groups like the Brooklyn Heights Association and all the key neighborhood groups that were going to be affected by all of this," explains Whelan. "Also, because of my work—I had run the New York League of Conservation Voters before and the National Audubon Society—I knew people at the state level that could get involved and some national chapters from the environmental and conservation community. We started to build a constituency for the park."[13]

Finally, Whelan focused her attention on expanding the Coalition's board (which had shrunk to seven members in the wake of the creation of the LDC and the forced departure of Anthony Manheim), while also redefining the skills and responsibilities associated with board membership. "I also wanted to focus on the institutional development of the Coalition itself," says Whelan of her decision to adjust the composition and responsibilities of the board. "It had to be give-get. We needed to be clear about the board giving money. We needed to have a good fund-raising plan. We needed to have a strategic plan. We needed to have a staffing development plan, because there was no staff other than me part-time."[14]

"Tensie told us, 'You've got to change the board,'" remembers VanderPutten. "Forget the local community advocacy. You need people on this board who have experience and purpose. And with her knowledge of the whole political community and the funding community in this area, that's exactly what she did."[15]

The new board recruited by Whelan featured an impressive roster of individuals with extensive experience and connections in New York City politics, waterfront management, and urban-park advocacy and funding. The board members included Albert Butzel, chair of the Hudson River Park Association; Kent Barwick, president of the Municipal Art Society; Claude Shostal, president of the Regional Plan Association; Dick Dadey, managing director and government-affairs specialist with Malkin & Ross Strategic Services; Peter Davidson, publisher of *El Diario* and chairman of the J. M. Kaplan Fund; Marcia Reiss, deputy director of the Parks Council; and photographer and park advocate Lisa Barlow (daughter of Elizabeth Barlow Rogers, founder and president of the Central Park Conservancy). "That these people would agree to be on our board just astonished me," confesses VanderPutten.[16]

In addition to her decision to reform the Coalition's board, Whelan recruited two new full-time staff members. Bianca Lila, with whom Whelan had worked at the New York League of Conservation Voters, was hired as the Coalition's community-outreach director, and Marianna Koval, a Brooklyn attorney who had been consulting with the Coalition to help devise a strategy for the northern section of Brooklyn Bridge Park, was retained as deputy director.

"I had first heard about Brooklyn Bridge Park when I was with the Brooklyn Heights Association in 1995," Koval recalls. "But it seemed like a pie-in-the-sky kind of thing, and people would roll their eyes when they talked about. But then sometime later, probably around 1996, I walked down to the piers and looked at the water and the pier sheds and the whole area, and I realized that the idea was incredibly visionary.

"So I contacted Mark [Baker, with whom she had worked at the law firm Dewey Ballantine], and I said, 'I really think we could do something more with the park project here at the BHA to create a greater constituency for it.' So I offered to create a series of 'park parties.' I didn't really know what I was doing, but I organized a series of 10 'park parties,' asking people to cut into their communities in various ways. Somebody could do a school network, and somebody else could do a church or synagogue network. And I invited different board members from the Brooklyn Bridge Coalition Board to come and give a talk."[17]

Whelan and Koval formed a close personal bond and an extremely productive working relationship from the start, sharing a vision for the inter-bridge property and the park development as a whole, along with a similarly intense commitment to getting things done. "The two of them went off like a house on fire," echoes Gary VanderPutten.[18]

"We were really effective from the start," says Koval of the whirl-wind of activities that characterized her early working relationship with Whelan, "and raised about $400,000 to $500,000 very quickly from both foundations and individuals. We went around citywide, going from of-fice to office, with pictures that Gary had taken of the site. Tensie and I went back and forth about what was possible. Buzzy O'Keefe, who runs the River Café, agreed to host an organizing meeting at the River Café, and we invited representatives of all the major civic organizations from around the city to a breakfast meeting, gave them a tour of the Brooklyn Bridge Park area, but particularly emphasized that we needed to include the inter-bridge area."[19]

As Koval's comments describe, she and Whelan set to work right away, raising public awareness about Two Trees Management's new plan for the private development of the inter-bridge area, along with the Coali-tion's new emphasis on developing and implementing a strategy for inte-grating the area north of Pier 1 into the waterfront park.[20] The May 1999 issue of the Coalition's new newsletter, *Waterfront Matters*, featured a "waterfront alert," informing members and local residents of recent revisions in the Two Trees plan for the commercial development of the inter-bridge area, along with a lengthy profile of Empire–Fulton Ferry State Park, the small waterfront park between the bridges that would be separated from the park to be developed along Piers 1–5 by the proposed private development.[21]

The newsletter's summer issue provided readers with an extensive list of reasons for opposing the Two Trees plan (overwhelming size, lack of open space and unique views, traffic congestion, incompatibility with other plans for the waterfront, absence of community participation, and inappropriateness of privately developing public land), along with Van-derPutten's arresting images of the view of the Brooklyn Bridge from the west Brooklyn shoreline before and after the implementation of Two Trees Management's expansive commercial development.[22]

In addition to its advocacy for the inclusion of the inter-bridge area in the overall park design, the Coalition used its recently acquired financial resources to hire Ray Gindroz of the Pittsburgh-based urban-design firm Urban Design Associates to propose a park design for the area between the Manhattan and Brooklyn Bridges. When the LDC's mandate even-tually expanded to include the inter-bridge area, Gindroz continued to work on the project, leading workshops in public meetings and providing invaluable guidance for the landscaping, use, funding, and public access to the park.[23]

Throughout the summer, Whelan and the Coalition were also in full swing promoting the organization's new message. On June 1, 1999, Whelan and Coalition chair John Watts sent a letter to Mayor Rudolph Giuliani, expressing their concern over the Two Trees plan for the inter-bridge property and their competing vision of a grand public park along the west Brooklyn waterfront. "Brooklyn Bridge Park," the letter explained, "will be the first great new park in the United States in the new millennium. It will be the first destination for Brooklynites, New Yorkers, Americans, and tourists from other countries. It will bring people together in a peaceful and unique waterfront environment to enjoy each other, the open space and world-class views. It is an idea whose time has come—but it needs your help and support."[24]

The letter, which was published in full in the *Brooklyn Heights Press & Cobble Hill News*, was cosigned by all the neighborhood associations on or adjacent to the property, as well as an impressive roster of city, state, and national organizations (including the Natural Resources Defense Council, the Sierra Club, the League of Conservation Voters, the Parks Council, the Neighborhood Open Space Coalition, and Riverkeeper Robert F. Kennedy, Jr.).

"Not only did we still exist," says Gary VanderPutten of the immediate impact of the Coalition's initial media blitz against David Walentas's plan, "we still existed with some pretty remarkable talent. People had to pay attention to us. Politicians were paying attention to us."[25]

Local elected officials were eager to support the Coalition's campaign against the proposed Two Trees development. City Council member Ken Fisher, while clarifying that he was not automatically against any form of commercial development on the property, expressed concerns that the Two Trees proposal was "too much, too soon" and that the large-scale development plan "would overwhelm the neighborhood" if implemented in its present form. Assemblywoman Joan Millman echoed Fisher's concerns about the scale and design of the Two Trees plan, assuring her constituents that "extensive public review" would be required before the project would be allowed to move forward.[26]

In addition to bringing on board elected officials and the media, the Coalition's high-profile campaign for a park on the inter-bridge property gained the attention—and the ire—of David Walentas, whose ambitions for the inter-bridge area had been repeatedly frustrated by the protests and counterproposals of activists from Brooklyn Heights. Without mentioning Whelan or the Coalition by name, Walentas fired back at the organization in an interview with the *New York Times* published on April 11, 1999. The individuals currently opposing his development plans for the inter-bridge area, complained Walentas, were "outsiders" and not residents of Dumbo, who were determined to maintain the state park as a "vacant lot" for their own private use, even if it meant an economic loss to the Dumbo community. "We own the whole neighborhood," Walentas insisted. "Everyone else is from a different neighborhood."[27]

A MORE DIRECT PUBLIC SHOWDOWN with Walentas occurred the following month, when the Dumbo developer announced his decision to hire Jean Nouvel, a celebrated French architect known for his highly modern, technologically innovative designs (including the Arab World Institute, the Cartier Foundation for Contemporary Art in Paris, and the Galeries Lafayette department store in Berlin) to provide an integrated design for the new commercial development on the property between the Brooklyn and Manhattan Bridges.

In a series of interviews and op-ed pieces in the *New York Times* and the local Brooklyn press, Whelan and Koval provided readers with a multipronged critique of Two Trees Management's development plan, questioning the appropriateness of both the selection of Nouvel for the project and the private development of what was rightfully public land, while reminding readers of the role that the inter-bridge property could play as part of a vast waterfront park extending from the inter-bridge area to the southern border of Pier 5.

"The biggest problem is that it completely eviscerates the plan for Brooklyn Bridge Park," explained Whelan to a reporter from the *New York Times*,[28] before finally providing a dramatic summary of the Coalition's position in an op-ed piece the following day: "Hiring a famous architect diverts attention from the real issue. That issue is not who designs this commercial complex. The issue is whether a regional shopping and entertainment complex, with large-scale parking garages, should be built on this publicly owned land—the site of what could be a spectacular waterfront park."[29]

The public dispute with Walentas continued throughout the summer of 1999, with no sign of a compromise or resolution when, suddenly and with no public explanation, the administrations of both Rudolph Giuliani and George Pataki turned their backs on the Two Trees plan. "We were just roaring along," remembers Gary VanderPutten, "and then all of a sudden, the state and the city withdrew their support from Walentas and his proposed development of the inter-bridge sector. Boom! No one knows completely why that happened."[30]

The city's sudden rejection of Two Trees Management's plan may have been the indirect result of the Giuliani administration's desire to correct a perceived imbalance between the state and the city in the control of the future Brooklyn Bridge Park. "There had been grumblings on the part of the city since the formation of the LDC with funding by the state," recalls Joshua Laird, who was working as director of planning at the Department of Parks and Recreation at the time. "Toward the end of the Giuliani administration, we began to have discussions of what the city might do to become a major player in the park. That's when we came up with the idea of the city taking its property at the foot of Main Street under the Brooklyn Bridge, where we already had real estate that we could control, and creating parkland there. By creating something there, we were actually able to get the jump on the state [in the competition to build the park]."[31]

THE END OF 1999 was a period of loss as well as triumph for the Brooklyn Bridge Park Coalition. In October, Tensie Whelan announced publicly that she would be resigning her half-time position as executive director of the Coalition at the end of the year to become the executive director of the Rainforest Alliance, with Deputy Director Marianna Koval assuming the leadership of the organization. Whelan had privately informed Coalition chair John Watts and other board members of her plans several months earlier. "Tensie has played an effective advocacy role in the inter-bridge area of the park," said Watts when the decision was announced publicly, "expanded the Coalition's membership to sixty organizations, recruited a board and advisory committee of park and civic leaders who will advocate for the park, and raised substantial funds to implement our programs."[32]

Concurrent with the notification of Whelan's departure, Watts announced that environmental attorney Albert Butzel had been elected president of the Coalition at the board meeting on October 12. As chair of the Hudson River Park Alliance, Butzel had recently led the effort to jump start the stalled construction plans for Hudson River Park in Manhattan and had been responsible for drafting the Environmental Impact Statement for the Forty-second Street Development Project.

"Tensie actually left the position in August 1999," explains Koval of the decision to bring Butzel on board, "and she asked me if I wanted to be executive director. I was really nervous and didn't think that I had the political skills to do it, so I suggested that Al Butzel come on as president and then I would be executive director. Al was already on our board, and he was a very smart land-use lawyer who had worked very hard helping to draft the legislation for Hudson River Park. He understood the legal aspects of creating a self-sustaining park and the importance of making sure that all the land that was supposed to remain parkland be actually titled and transferred to the Parks Department in perpetuity."[33]

"By the end of 1998, we [in the Hudson River Park movement] had gotten the city and the state to commit a couple of hundred million dollars to Hudson River Park and had also enacted legislation to create a public trust to manage the park," recalls Butzel. "I wanted to be the head of the public trust but was not successful, so I was sitting around continuing to do advocacy on behalf of the park, when [Coalition board members] David Offensend and John Watts invited me to lunch and explained that they'd like me to join the Coalition as its president. They said, 'You'll be the president and will handle all the political and financial stuff, and Marianna will be the executive director and do all the community organizing and public events.' It was one of those times when opportunity and need crossed paths, and I said I'd be happy to do it."[34]

TENSION BETWEEN THE COALITION and the LDC was perhaps inevitable, given the two groups' conflicting governance structures and organizational mandates, along with the fact that they were competing with each other to establish their legitimacy as the leader in the planning process. The conflicts between them were also exacerbated by negative public and private statements by representatives of each organization about its counterpart in the park movement.

Since the creation of the LDC in 1997, Coalition members had repeatedly questioned the LDC's legitimacy on the grounds that the exclusion of the inter-bridge area from its mandate violated Guiding Principle 1.c (which stipulated that "the Plan shall encompass the waterfront area between Manhattan Bridge and Atlantic Avenue including Empire–Fulton Ferry State Park, the Brooklyn Bridge area and the upland of Pier 6"). The Coalition also maintained that the LDC's limited governance structure violated Guiding Principle 2 (which stated that the Coalition would be involved in the review process for the development of the piers).[35]

Still struggling to rally both the local community and the public authorities in charge of the piers behind the planning process for the park, newly elected LDC president Joanne Witty and the other members of the LDC board bristled at the Coalition's public questioning of the newly formed organization's authority and legitimacy.

Witty (who had worked as an attorney for both the city and state governments, as well as with the League of Conservation Voters) was appointed to the LDC board by State Senator Martin Connor, whom she knew from Saint Ann's School in Brooklyn Heights, where both had children attending classes. "Marty wanted to appoint someone from the community who had the credentials," she recalls, "but who was neutral [on the subject of the park]."[36]

Connor explained to Witty that the formation of the LDC was "a last-ditch effort to work with the Port Authority to get something done with the piers." Connor, Howard Golden, and the other elected officials who had formed the LDC had persuaded the Port Authority to postpone its latest plan to distribute a Request for Proposals (RFP) to potential commercial developers for the piers in favor of a Request for Expression of Interest (RFEI), which would allow the agency to take the pulse of the development community without actually committing any of the property for development.

The LDC's ultimate goal, as Connor described it to Witty, was to persuade the Port Authority to open the development process to the construction of a public park on the property conforming to the "13 Guiding Principles." The more immediate and urgent task, however, was to work with the agency to ensure that the current RFEI and the plans for development that it generated did "as little damage" as possible to the local community and its interests.

As to how the newly formed LDC was to reach an agreement with the Port Authority, when all past attempts had failed, Witty and her fourteen fellow board members were left to their own devices. "We were starting at ground zero," she explains, "with no rules or directions as to how we were supposed to do this." In this context, Witty and her fellow board members naturally viewed the Coalition's recent challenges to the LDC's legitimacy as a serious threat to its already fragile relationship with the Port Authority and its ability to ensure the development of a park on the piers. "It seemed at the time," recalls Witty, "that their [the Coalition's] allegiance was to the Coalition—and nothing else."[37]

ON THE OPPOSITE SIDE OF THE CONFLICT, Whelan and the other Coalition board members were understandably sensitive to public and private statements by Witty that the Coalition "was desperate to reinvent itself" and had "taken the park as far as it could," as well as the LDC president's criticism of the Coalition's advocacy on behalf of the inter-bridge area. "The Coalition has been very successful," Witty acknowledged before questioning the necessity of the organization's existence now that the LDC had been formed. "They kept the idea of the park alive, but the LDC can take it to the next level."[38]

"We were told [by the LDC], 'Don't rock the boat,'" Koval recalls of the Coalition's early conflicts with the LDC over planning for the inter-bridge area. "'We already have a deal to develop the piers. Go away. You don't know what you're talking about.'"[39]

Witty also questioned the Coalition's call for the inclusion of the inter-bridge area in the park plan, which she warned could inadvertently result in disagreements among community residents, weakening the public consensus for a park along the piers, alienating officials at the Port Authority, and causing further delays in (if not the complete disruption of) the development process.[40]

THE CONFLICTS AND CONTROVERSIES faced by newly elected LDC president Joanne Witty were not limited to an occasional run-in with the Coalition. With a membership that included representatives of Community Boards 2 and 6, the Brooklyn business community, and each of the neighborhood associations, the LDC was faced with the daunting task of developing a consensual plan for the park through a process that included groups with differing, at times competing, interests and priorities for the proposed park. "The biggest challenge," recalls Witty of her early days at the LDC, "was to figure out how you pull together many, many disparate community groups who didn't want development here but wanted a park, but what that meant to everybody was very different."

"There were fifteen of us [on the LDC board]," she continues. "We didn't know each other. We weren't sure what it was we were supposed to do. There were some of us who clearly didn't want to be there at all. We met regularly in a small conference room at Borough Hall, and we talked and talked and talked. Everybody raised their fears about all the ways that this could go wrong and how we could be manipulated by the Port Authority, which in the end could just go off and do its own thing. The question was: How could we operate in this space in a constructive way that would be acceptable to the Port Authority and would also be true to the community's goals for the park?"[41]

"There are a few things I'm known for arguing for," remembers original LDC board member Franklin Stone of the organization's early discussions about the park. "One is for year-round uses for the park, because I didn't want it to be desolate in the winter months. Two, I wanted a place to have a drink on the waterfront, because there was no place for us to have drinks. And three, I wanted a place that we wouldn't be snaking our way up to [the recreational complex at] Chelsea Piers. I wanted something that would let our kids play right here."[42]

One of the Witty's first and most important decisions was to hire the Manhattan consulting firm Hamilton, Rabinovitz & Alschuler (HR&A) to assist the LDC with the planning, political, real-estate, and economic-development skills needed to negotiate with the Port Authority and oversee the planning of the park. In the months and years that followed, Witty would work closely with HR&A chairman John Alschuler and team members Josh Sirefman and Candace Damon on every aspect of the planning and negotiations for the park.

"Essentially, the LDC at that point was an organization without a staff, and we became the staff," remembers Sirefman. "There were three people who were most involved in the project from HR&A: John Alschuler, Candace Damon, and myself. At that time I was relatively junior, so I literally became the staff of the LDC, managing outreach, relationships with the board, and keeping them organized, doing the financial analysis for the park.

"Since then I've been involved in many, many projects of scale that have included all kinds of public outreach," says Sirefman, "but my work with the LDC remains the most extraordinary public process I've ever been a part of. There were fifteen people on the board, and they literally had fifteen different opinions. It wasn't like you'd go out and interact with the world and then decide if you're going to listen or not listen. It was like the debate with the world just continued within the board itself. That really gave the process a dimension that I don't think you see very often."[43]

IN THE MIDST OF THE ONGOING CONFLICTS within Brooklyn Heights and the adjacent communities, as well as within the LDC itself, the official planning and negotiations for the park continued to progress behind the scenes. In spite of her initial worries about the capacity of the LDC to negotiate effectively with the public authorities, Witty and her partners at HR&A were eventually able, with the assistance and support of Lillian C. Borrone, director of the Port Commerce Department at the Port Authority, to reach a "standstill agreement" with the agency in charge of the piers. As a result of the negotiations, the Port Authority agreed to suspend the disposition process for three years while the LDC worked on a Master Plan for the creation of a public park on the site. The Master Plan, if approved by the Port Authority, would then be used to guide a renewed RFP process that would devote as much of the property as possible for development as public parkland.

"What we didn't understand at the time," confides Witty, "is that the Port Authority needed us as much as we needed them. They wanted the same things that we did."[44]

As a part of the methodology for the Master Plan, Witty and the other LDC board members decided to face the debates and disagreements within the community head on, proposing a series of borough-wide public planning sessions (or "charrettes") that would allow everyone with an opinion about the park and its relationship to the adjacent neighborhoods to contribute feedback to be used in the creation of the Master Plan.

"We really had to figure out how to create a plan that all these different people could support," says Witty, "that was viable and not some pie-in-the-sky daydream, something that could actually be built and that was financially possible. Our challenge was, 'How do you do that?' And the idea that we came up with and executed was the idea of a unique public planning process for the park that really brought in people from every walk of life, from every neighborhood and the business community, the community boards, everyone who cared about this, with hundreds and hundreds of people sitting around."[45]

The public charrettes, which were conducted over a two-year period in dozens of neighborhoods throughout the borough, became the first cooperative activity between the Coalition and the LDC. "The LDC and the Coalition worked collaboratively together to bring the community out," Coalition board member Dick Dadey recalls of the early interactions between the two groups. "And, you know, there were differences of opinion, but I think you just needed to mention the park, and people showed up. And what was interesting was that when the initial meetings were taking place and people would go back into the neighborhood and talk about what had happened, it would excite others, and others then would come and want to be a part of it. Others would come to see what was happening. And so it grew through word of mouth."[46]

"When parks had been built in the past, there really wasn't a public dialogue to determine what people wanted. It was just something that happened," says architect Matt Urbanski, a member of the Michael Van Valkenburgh design team that led landscape design for the HR&A design team. "But this park from the beginning was going to be about a public dialogue, based on the public interest in making this space. The challenge was in creating a forum and a means of talking to everyone, bringing people together, conveying what are the possibilities and also trying to find out from people what they thought were the possibilities. That was a big challenge."

According to Urbanski, one of the biggest problems the team faced was the public's lack of knowledge about the role of landscapes in the park's design (figure 19). "It wasn't understood at the time that landscaping actually had uses," says Urbanski, "that it wasn't just direction. We made up four types of landscapes (civic, boundless, natural, and urban)

MAIN STREET
PARK

JOHN STREET
PARK

EMPIRE FULTON
FERRY

BROOKLYN BRIDGE
PLAZA

PIER 1

PIER 2

PIER 3

PIER 4

PIER 5

PIER 6

that we used to illustrate the different uses. It turned out to be a very fruitful way of talking."[47]

Another problem the design team encountered was the strong resistance to the park concept from some people in Brooklyn. "There was a lot of acrimony in the beginning at these meetings," remembers park designer Michael Van Valkenburgh, "probably more than at any park that I've ever made in my life—and we've built them all over the country. But there's never been the level of acrimony that this one started out from.

"You have to remember," continues Van Valkenburgh, "that it hadn't been that long since Elizabeth Barlow Rogers founded the Central Park Conservancy in 1980. She had completely dragged that park back from the total brink of disaster. It was just ruined. So the idea that a public space could be accessible and beautiful and calming was not a part of public consciousness. By culling out and isolating the different types of landscapes, we were able to allow people to talk about what they liked, rather than just venting about things that were frightening or worrisome."[48]

According to HR&A partner Candace Damon, who assisted in the organization and facilitation of the early charrettes, the public meetings were conducted in phases, a process that allowed park advocates to build consensus for the general idea of the park among the broader community before soliciting feedback on more specific and, in some cases, controversial features of the park design. The earliest meetings consisted of large public gatherings that were designed to introduce the entire Brooklyn community to the general concept and essential features of the proposed park. "After having completed some due diligence on our own [during the early meetings and negotiations of the LDC board]," explains Damon, "we went to the community and said, 'Here's what the land looks like. Here's what we're hoping to do. Here are some of the initial design issues.' And then we gave them an opportunity to respond."[49]

Following the general presentations and discussions at the large public meetings, smaller meetings were held with disparate groups throughout Brooklyn as the discussions became more focused on the needs and concerns of particular neighborhoods and community residents. It was during this second phase that the park team began to reach out to specific groups and to focus on issues that were particularly controversial or about which it was difficult to build consensus, such as access, financing, and the appropriate balance between active and passive space.

According to Damon, the Coalition played a particularly important role in expanding the reach of the planning process for the park into neighborhoods beyond Brooklyn Heights and Cobble Hill and in recruiting individuals from various age groups, ethnic groups, and socioeconomic positions to attend the charrettes. "I remember one of the charrettes that we co-organized with the Coalition," recalls Damon, "with the specific intent of bringing in eighteen-year-olds, and we somehow managed to attract 150 kids. They were mostly from St. Ann's, of course, but some Caribbean kids from Canarsie also somehow made it to the meeting. Leaving aside the obvious racial aspect [of a group of ethnic children visiting a park in Brooklyn Heights], there was also the whole issue of what was the best way for these kids to gain access to what was for them a strange site. I remember that we were debating the viability of building a bridge from Montague Street to the center of the site, an idea that had already ignited resistance from some elements of the community, and this Caribbean girl from Canarsie suddenly interjected, 'If you build it, we'll come. Regardless of the access. There are no other parks for us to go to. Just build it, and we'll come.'"[50]

Along with the hundreds of local residents who flocked to the meetings, the charrettes also quickly gained the attention of the elected officials and public authorities that would soon play an important role in the planning and construction of the park. "It wasn't just about local neighborhood activists," recalls Dick Dadey. "There were elected officials coming to these community-planning charrettes and seeing hundreds and hundreds of people excited about the prospect of Brooklyn Bridge Park and spending not just one night but several nights over the course of several months and really offering some great ideas. And seeing all this come together showed our public officials how serious the community was about making this happen and how committed we were to doing whatever was necessary to get government to act to build this park."[51]

"By the time we were done, we had thousands of people involved," recalls Witty of the yearlong charrettes process. "You name it, we had it. People expressed concerns about everything imaginable. So, of course, we left issues open and weren't able to satisfy everyone. And there finally came a point where we had to shut it down. Our attitude was that this wasn't the end of the process. This was only the beginning."[52]

SEVEN

TEARING DOWN THE BARBED WIRE

> "If you come, we will build it.
>
> **MARIANNA KOVAL**

WITH THE LOCAL DEVELOPMENT CORPORATION (LDC) in charge of the design and construction of Brooklyn Bridge Park, the Brooklyn Bridge Park Coalition, having just led a successful citizens' campaign for the inclusion in the park of the area between the Brooklyn and Manhattan Bridges, decided to focus its attention on building enthusiasm and support for the park, both among residents of Brooklyn and the rest of New York City and among the elected officials and public authorities whose ongoing financial support was essential for the park's realization. The best way to build support for the park, Marianna Koval, executive director of the Brooklyn Bridge Park Coalition, increasingly realized, was to get people onto the site where they could witness for themselves the spectacular views of New York Harbor and the Manhattan skyline, the natural beauty of the landscape (the decaying piers and warehouses notwithstanding), and the invigorating experience of reclaiming a waterfront that had been virtually inaccessible to most of the borough's residents for generations.

Motivating local residents to experience the waterfront firsthand would be far easier said than done, however. The piers and the inter-bridge area, which were a lengthy walk from any of the adjoining neighborhoods or bus and subway stops, were generally viewed as dark,

PLATES **3** (OPPOSITE, FIGURE 19) / **4** (TOP, FIGURE 27) / **5** (BOTTOM, FIGURE 28)

PLATE 10 (FIGURE 39)

PLATE 11 (FIGURE 41)

PLATE 20 (FIGURE 48)

threatening places where residents rarely, if ever, ventured, with barricades or barbed-wire fences blocking the entrance of those who did.

"When I came to the city in the 1970s to go to college," explains Mark Baker of the borough's residents' simultaneous fascination with and aversion to the East River piers, "you didn't go down to the waterfront. Right here [the current headquarters of the Brooklyn Bridge Park Corporation (BBP Corporation) and Conservancy at 334 Furman Street, near Pier 6] was an abandoned building. But I lived four blocks away. It was barbed wire. So this was about tearing down the barbed wire."[1]

To overcome the public's lack of knowledge about and fear of the waterfront, Koval recommended that the Coalition host a series of programmed activities that would motivate residents to visit the park site. "The way to get people [onto the park property]," she explains, "was to begin acting as if the park was already there—through programming and creating activities. It was cultural, recreational, educational, stewardship. How did you get people to feel ownership? Well, you get them down there doing something that's for them."[2]

Koval and the other Coalition members viewed the organization's new strategy to gain support for the park by bringing people to the site as supportive of and complementary to the LDC's official mandate as the designer and developer of the park. "The Coalition is actively involved in the LDC planning effort," explained Koval in the spring 2000 issue of the Coalition's newsletter, *Waterfront Matters*. "Our goal is to help shape a plan that reflects the wishes of our constituent groups and possesses the benefits and economic reality that will enable us to convince public officials that it is a park worth funding. *And that is the key*. Brooklyn Bridge Park will become reality only if we obtain the political buy-in of the governor and the mayor, because only they have access to the funding—some $100 million—needed to create the basic infrastructure."[3]

MARIANNA KOVAL'S STRATEGY of building support for the park by bringing people to the waterfront proved to be enormously successful from the beginning. On June 7, 2000, the Coalition hosted a highly publicized event to open the park property to the public. Sunset Samba, as the event was advertised, was an organizational fund-raiser in the guise of a Brazilian carnival. More than 800 people crowded into and danced outside an enormous covered tent on Fulton Ferry Landing, directly opposite lower Manhattan across the East River.[4]

"We put together a fund-raiser that Brooklyn had never seen before," says Koval. "Up until this time, the Coalition had had little tiny benefits, but this was 'big city.' We put a tent up on Fulton Ferry pier, and [set designer] Mary Howard took all these ropes and stanchions, and then she created a grass walkway with sod. My dad got napkins, and [board member] Dick Dadey was rushing around doing things with the sod. We had Brazilian dancers with pasties. We got [River Café owner] Buzzy O'Keefe to do the caipirinhas. And it was fabulous."[5]

In addition to its success as a fund-raiser and publicity event, Sunset Samba served as a "victory party" for the Coalition, the LDC, and the entire waterfront movement, which had just received word of substantial financial commitments to park planning and development by both the borough and city governments. While the $72,000 raised from ticket sales and individual and corporate donations paled in comparison with the $14 million committed by Brooklyn Borough President Howard Golden and the additional $50 million pledged by Mayor Rudolph Giuliani (both contributions to be paid over four years), it marked the continuing commitment of the community to contribute to the park's success.[6]

"It is no longer a dream: Brooklyn Bridge Park will be built," proclaimed Koval to those in attendance, expressing the gratitude of all those in the park movement to the elected officials who had helped make the funding possible, including City Council members Ken Fisher and Herb Berman, Mayor Giuliani, City Council Speaker Peter Vallone, Deputy Mayor Tony Coles, and Borough President Golden.[7]

Among those in attendance, the "hero of the hour" was Fisher, who had skillfully masterminded the negotiations for the funding from city government and who received a lengthy ovation from his fellow revelers.[8] "I get a call from Joe Lhota," remembers Fisher, reconstructing the interactions with city government that precipitated the significant financial commitment from Giuliani, "who was then the first deputy mayor. He was the former budget director. He lived on Pierrepont Street [in Brooklyn Heights], and his wife, Tamara, was the president of the Pierrepont Playground.

"I said, 'Joe, you're not gonna believe this, but that son-of-a-bitch Howie Golden (because I knew the mayor and Golden hated each other, and by that point, I had had my own falling out with Howie) has put $14 million in the budget for Brooklyn Bridge Park. They're gonna call this the frigging "Golden" Gate Park. You can't let him get away with that.'

"So he takes some time and then calls me back and says, 'Do you need the $50 million all in one year?' And I say, 'No, I'll take it over four years.' And then he calls me back about a week later, maybe it was a little longer, and he says, 'Okay, you got it.' "[9]

One local hero was noticeably absent from Sunset Samba: Howard Golden, who had secured the $14 million of borough funds that Fisher was able to leverage in his informal negotiations with Lhota and Giuliani. Since the deliberate exclusion of the Coalition from the LDC at the time of its formation in 1998, little love had been lost between the borough president and the Coalition, whose members believed the organization had continued to exist in spite of Golden's efforts to the contrary. In spite of his initial concerns about the proper use and security of the waterfront property during the early years of the park movement, however, Golden had become firmly committed to the park over time, and the dedication of $14 million of the borough's money to the project was a crucial factor in the park's realization.

"If there's anybody that deserves the statue [for the realization of the park]," insists Tom Montvel-Cohen, a political consultant who worked with the city government on the piers development during the late 1980s and later conducted a transportation study on behalf of the LDC, "it's Howard Golden. At first, he wasn't convinced about the importance of [Brooklyn Bridge Park] the way he was about the development projects at MetroTech and Atlantic Avenue, but once he was on board, he made it happen. The man was relentless in pursuing the difference-making projects that he felt were game changers."[10]

In addition to Golden's undeniable importance to the funding and realization of the park, the Coalition played a critical role in ensuring that city funding was available for the project, both in its public activities and in its private negotiations with public officials behind the scenes. According to Koval, the funding that Fisher secured from the city would never have been available in the first place without the Coalition's public campaign to halt the development of Two Trees Management's multiplex in Dumbo (Down Under the Manhattan Bridge Overpass) and to include the inter-bridge area, which was owned by the city, as a part of the park. "There had been a deal made with [David] Walentas that Brooklyn Bridge Park would stop at Pier 1 and not continue beyond the Brooklyn Bridge," she explains. "And everyone was supposed to understand and toe that line, and the Development Corporation was only going to plan for Piers 1 to 5. The reason why [our success in undermining Walentas's proposal] was so critically important is that, if the deal with Walentas had held, then there would have been no city land and the city would not have been a partner in the development of the park. And, of course, it was the city that put the first $50 million in."[11]

Coalition president Albert Butzel had also been working diligently behind the scenes, lobbying officials in state and city government to secure the necessary funding for the project. "The central effort was to try to get the state and the city to commit money to the park. I had a couple of advantages in that I had gotten to be quite close with Brad Race, who was

Pataki's chief of staff, and Charles Gargano, who was the chairman of the Empire State Development Corporation [ESDC]. And over at the city, I had a pretty close friend, Tony Coles, who became the Deputy Mayor for Planning, Education and Cultural Affairs, and I spent a lot of time lobbying them for the money.

"I'm sure that there are a lot of people who were involved in what happened," Butzel acknowledges, "but [Coles] was the point person, and it was under his pressure that Giuliani finally came through."[12]

WHILE THE COALITION WAS WORKING to build support for the park by sponsoring activities to bring people to the site and advocating with local elected officials, LDC president Joanne Witty had her hands full trying to build consensus among the representatives of the communities and business groups included in the LDC. According to Greg Brooks, Borough President Howard Golden's chief of staff and the first vice president of the LDC, the early meetings of the corporation were highly contentious affairs. "I led the first two or three meetings, before Joanne Witty became president," says Brooks. "It was a really important process because the leadership came from the community and not from government—but it was also extremely challenging. Joanne took a tremendous amount of flack in those early meetings, but she stood her ground and did what she had to do."[13]

After a year negotiating privately with the Port Authority and conducting the charrettes throughout the local community, the LDC held its first formal public meeting on November 7, 1999, with 350 organizational leaders and local residents assembling at the Marriott Hotel in downtown Brooklyn for workshops in "Urban Connections," "Funding Structure," and "Regulations, Landscape and Environment," followed by an open-house gathering for leaders of community organizations the following day. LDC president Joanne Witty, Assemblywoman Joan Millman, and landscape architect Michael Van Valkenburgh, whose firm had recently been hired by the LDC to develop a Master Plan for the park, were on hand to address the crowd, respond to questions about the LDC's plans for the piers, and listen to the concerns of local residents.

LDC and Coalition board member John Watts was at the meetings as well, representing the Coalition's insistence that the design of the park include as much "soft and green" open space as possible. "So often in the planning of parks," Watts insisted, "the concern for green space comes at the end of the process. And then as it is built up, that green space becomes smaller and smaller until there is hardly any park left. The question is, at what point is it not a park?"[14]

WHILE SUNSET SAMBA WAS A SUCCESS, both as a fund-raiser and as a publicity event for the waterfront, Koval recognized that the Coalition would have to reach far beyond the wealthy residents of Brooklyn Heights and the city's other social and political elites if the park had any real hope of success. "I've always felt that the focus on creating a citywide park was crucial," says Koval. "In this neighborhood in particular, with all the income inequality in the city, it's damn important that we attracted everyone in the city. And I think one of the really important things that we did was to reach out to organizations all over the city and make it a citywide issue. We were never going to get the money we needed for a park that would serve as the front yard for a wealthy neighborhood. We were only going to get it for a park that would be for everyone. And how do you do that? Well, you ask them what they want and give them a platform to create activities."[15]

During the spring and summer of 2000, Koval and the Coalition took a variety of steps to reach out to the public beyond Brooklyn Heights and the other communities immediately adjacent to the 1.3 miles of waterfront property on which the park would be located. The Coalition formed the Education Advisory Council (which included the presidents of Pratt Institute, New York City College of Technology, Medgar Evers College, and Community School Board 13), while Koval also met with religious leaders and representatives of neighborhood associations and other community groups from across the borough. In addition to including non-waterfront communities in its plans for the park, the Coalition reached out to the borough's children, organizing a series of educational workshops involving 100 students from five public and private high schools in the neighborhoods adjacent to the park.

The summer of 2000 also witnessed the debut of the Brooklyn Bridge Park Summer Film Festival, with more than 500 visitors gathering at Empire–Fulton Ferry State Park for an outdoor screening of *On the Waterfront*. The film series, which was organized by Coalition Film Committee co-chairs Nell Archer and Kate Crane, would become one of the Coalition's most popular activities and would serve over the next few years as many New Yorkers' initial exposure to the park site.

WHILE THE COALITION'S AGGRESSIVE EFFORTS to include visitors from beyond Brooklyn Heights and the adjacent neighborhoods were vitally important to securing the ongoing support of elected officials and public authorities, Koval's vision of a citywide park, welcoming a diverse mosaic of visitors from throughout the city and around the world, was not popular with everyone.

The summer 2000 issue of the Coalition's newsletter alerted its readers to the threat posed to the park by the recently formed Waterfront Development Watch, which was described as a "small group" of Joralemon Street residents living on the three blocks west of Hicks Street, just up the hill from the Coalition and the LDC's shared headquarters on 334 Furman Street, who were concerned that their quiet, tree-lined street would eventually be overrun by people pouring into and out of the park.

Throughout the summer, members of the Waterfront Development Watch and other disgruntled Brooklyn Heights residents went public with their concerns about the potential impact of the proposed park on their neighborhood, speaking out at community meetings and in interviews with local journalists. In August, the brewing neighborhood controversy surfaced in the *New York Times*, where reporter Julian E. Barnes fueled the conflict and animosity within the neighborhood by presenting what many Brooklyn Heights residents viewed as an unfair caricature of the debate and the people involved in it.

In his article, Barnes quoted a number of park opponents from the Heights who openly worried that the opening of the park would precipitate a sudden barrage of graffiti, rowdy teens plaguing the neighborhood, and "muggings up and down the street." "I'd rather see a Target or a Costco down there," complained one local resident, "than see this neighborhood overwhelmed by people who come from someplace else." Turning his attention to park advocates from the neighborhood, Barnes observed that "some [albeit unnamed] park supporters have argued that concerns over traffic, quality of life, crime, and litter are code words that betray a fear of blacks and Hispanics from poorer sections of the borough."[16]

The *Times* article represented precisely the type of negative publicity and internal debate that park advocates had been working tirelessly over the previous year and a half to avoid, conducting planning charrettes and other public meetings to achieve public consensus about the park by ensuring that opinions and interests of all residents were recognized and addressed. Brooklyn journalist and park advocate Dennis Holt was particularly incensed by the harsh caricatures of those who opposed specific features of the park's design. Describing the *Times* piece as "lamentable" and "irresponsible journalism," Holt observed that, in focusing on the xenophobic and potentially racists comments of a few isolated individuals, the article essentially ignored park opponents' substantive concerns about the financial model for the park, which would lean heavily on the private sector for its ongoing maintenance, and the dramatic increase in vehicular traffic that would inevitably result from the opening of a public park on the piers.

"We can, as people have," Holt maintained, "disagree on what kind of park we ought to have, or any park at all for that matter, without issuing innuendos about race and color. The tragedy of the *Times* story is that people all across the city and the country who know nothing about what is going on will read this and probably believe it."[17]

With each step toward the park's realization, the internal debates would intensify, along with the tendency to question in the media the motivations of both park opponents and park advocates. Even with the heated disagreements in some sectors of the waterfront community, the ability of the Coalition and the LDC to rally local residents behind Brooklyn Bridge Park maintained the support for the project among elected officials.

IN SEPTEMBER 2000, after having participated in more than fifty public meetings involving more than 2,000 participants expressing their preferences regarding both the general design and specific features of the park, LDC president Joanne Witty announced the long-awaited publication of the Brooklyn Bridge Park Illustrative Master Plan (figures 20–23). The Master Plan, which was prepared by Hamilton, Rabinovitz & Alschuler, was approved by a unanimous vote of the LDC board of directors.

In the midst of the private achievements and public celebrations, Witty still had serious concerns about the future of the project. "You have to understand that the park was still in peril at this point," she confides. "It was never a done deal. The Master Plan quickly received the endorsement of various groups, including the *Times*, and that was important. But it was only a concept plan at this point. Our job was to keep it together [while it received the funding and public endorsements that would allow it to continue]. We were the 'keepers of the Plan.'"[18]

At the time, the LDC's ability to proceed with the planning of the park was repeatedly frustrated by the failure of the Pataki and Giuliani administrations to formally endorse the Master Plan and follow up with their financial commitments to the park. According to Witty, the delayed endorsement of the Master Plan was exacerbated by the lack of cooperation and communication between the state and city governments. "That was when the rubber really hit the road," says Witty. "And getting there was really hard, because there had to be an agreement between these two parties before we could do anything. And the state and the city were not talking to each other. Meanwhile, the Port Authority was pulling its hair out."[19]

While the LDC's negotiations with the city and the state remained stalled, Witty continued to negotiate successfully behind the scenes with the Port Authority. In November, after taking several months to review

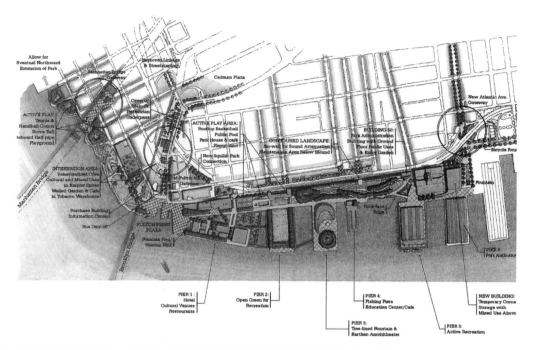

FIGURE 20 (TOP)

Brooklyn Bridge Park Illustrative Master Plan, 2000.

© URBAN STRATEGIES, INC.

FIGURE 21 (BOTTOM)

Illustrative Master Plan: rendering of the walkway across Dumbo.

COURTESY OF MICHAEL McCANN

FIGURE 22 (TOP)
Illustrative Master Plan: rendering of the view from the Brooklyn Bridge.
COURTESY OF MICHAEL McCANN

FIGURE 23 (BOTTOM)
Illustrative Master Plan: rendering of the promenade on Pier 1.
COURTESY OF MICHAEL McCANN

the Master Plan, the agency appropriated $200,000 to refine the plan, begin environmental-impact studies for the property, and plan the transfer of control of the seventy-one-acre tract from the Port Authority to the a public entity in charge of the park's construction.[20]

AT THE END OF 2000, Al Butzel, whose leadership had been instrumental in securing funding commitments from the borough, city, and state governments, resigned his position as president of the Coalition. With Koval serving as the public face of the Coalition, expanding the organization's relationships with community leaders and interacting with the media, Butzel had been hard at work behind the scenes, using the connections he had established at Hudson River Park to broaden the Coalition's base of environmental and public-advocacy groups and lobbying his contacts in state and city government to provide funding for the planning and construction of Brooklyn Bridge Park.

With the transfer of the park property from the Port Authority finally under way, state and city funding for the park nominally secured, and Koval's outreach and programming emphasis for the park now in full swing, the Coalition's president and executive director found themselves disagreeing about the most effective strategy for advancing the interests of both the organization and the park movement. "Al and I had different views," explains Koval. "He knew the inside game on how to get to Pataki and Giuliani, and I didn't. But I was very convinced that the only way we were going to move the park forward in the long term was to build a citywide constituency and the only way to build a citywide constituency was to bring people to the park and let them see the beauty of the site and become advocates."[21]

With the two leaders at a stalemate, Koval submitted her resignation at the end of the year, explaining to the board the reasons why she was leaving. "I was shocked that they all came around and asked me to stay, and Al [left his position as president and] went on the board. He was very decent and good about it. Because of that, I think, the board increasingly shared my vision that we would bring people to the park through programming. The mantra that we developed in 2001 and going forward was 'If you come, we [the LDC and the Coalition] will build it.'"[22]

"Marianna and I had a strained relationship," acknowledges Butzel, "and not surprisingly, since we're both people who want to do big things. She had a much better feel for the community, but I had a much better feel for the politics. It wasn't easy for her, and it wasn't easy for me. I came to respect her a lot."[23]

ON JANUARY 8, 2001, six months after the combined $64 million pledge to the park from Mayor Giuliani and Borough President Golden, Giuliani formally authorized $65 million in city funding for the park (a substantial increase from his earlier commitment of $50 million) in his annual State of the City Address. The mayor's announcement followed awkwardly on the heels of a similar announcement by Governor George Pataki, who authorized $85 million of Port Authority money for the construction of the park in his State of the State Address two days earlier. "The transformation of the downtown Brooklyn waterfront from an obsolete maritime area into a vibrant community asset begins today," said Pataki. "All New Yorkers deserve world-class waterfront parks. Today, we embark on the revival of the Brooklyn waterfront for the twenty-first century."[24]

According to reports from local media at the time, Pataki's conspicuous failure in his address to credit Giuliani for his earlier commitment to the project was deliberately intended to embarrass the mayor, who had angered the governor by publicly criticizing the Port Authority's delays in clearing snow from Kennedy International Airport following a storm the previous week.[25]

State Senator Martin Connor recalls a series of conversations before the State of the State Address with Pataki and his staff that resulted in the governor's pledge to support the park. "I said, 'You know, a little birdie told me that Rudy Giuliani in the State of the City Address next Monday morning is leading off with Brooklyn Bridge Park,'" Connor informed Pataki in a telephone conversation at the end of the week before Giuliani's planned announcement, "'about how he's building Brooklyn Bridge Park and how the city did this little playground on city-owned land. The visuals have already been prepared.' And he said, 'Yeah, I know about it!' And I said, 'Governor, you control 95 percent of the land involved here and the piers. That's yours. But you're going to end up building the park, and Rudy's going to proclaim it the Rudy Giuliani Brooklyn Bridge Park.' And he said, 'No, he's not! I'll get back to you!' And he hung up."[26]

That evening, Connor met privately with Pataki's chief counsel, James McGuire, and chief of staff, Brad Race, at Justin's on Lark, a popular Albany restaurant frequented by members of the New York State Assembly and the governor's staff. "It was around 9:30 that night, and I'd gone out to get a beer and something to eat. In comes Jim McGuire and then Brad Race, and Brad says, 'Hey, Marty. What's up with this park and the governor? You've got him barking orders at everyone. He's going to do this park! It's going to happen!'"[27]

The following morning, Connor met with the governor's communications director, Zenia Mucha, to iron out some additional details about the park, and the following week, the decision was announced. "That Thursday, they had the press releases circulated," Connor recalls, "and it dropped Friday morning. I still have the press release. And it said, 'The state's giving all the land with the Port Authority. And there'll be $85 million. And basically the state's going to build this park.'"[28]

ALTHOUGH THE STATE AND CITY FUNDING would not be officially authorized until December 30, 2003, and February 24, 2004, respectively, the combined commitments by Governor Pataki, Mayor Giuliani, and Borough President Golden virtually ensured that Brooklyn Bridge Park would be constructed. The leaders of the park movement were understandably ecstatic in their response to Pataki's long-anticipated announcement.

"Finally!" said Koval in response to a *New York Times* reporter. "People coming over the Brooklyn Bridge into Brooklyn will have something beautiful to look down onto instead of abandoned piers and parking lots."

"The commitment of money from the governor makes this entire project real," echoed Joanne Witty in the same article.[29]

Even among members of the anti-park movement, Pataki's decision was seen as significant. "It validates what we still believe is a flawed plan for the waterfront," acknowledged Donald Rattner of the Waterfront Development Watch.[30]

Not to be upstaged by Pataki, Giuliani proclaimed in his State of the City Address on January 8 that the city would immediately begin the conversion of the Main Street parking lot in the inter-bridge area into parkland and link it to Empire–Fulton Ferry State Park "to create an uninterrupted expanse of parkland between the Brooklyn and Manhattan Bridges."[31]

ON THE MORNING OF SEPTEMBER 11, 2001, the future of Brooklyn Bridge Park—and of New York City—suddenly became uncertain with the destruction of the Twin Towers of the World Trade Center in lower Manhattan, just opposite the Brooklyn Heights Promenade across the East River. In the wake of the disaster, Mayor Giuliani and the city's other elected officials were faced with far more immediate concerns than the funding and construction of a public park.

Koval's first reaction was that the city and state governments would be forced to abandon their commitment to the park as the mayor and the governor turned their attention and directed their financial appropriations to more urgent needs, but a call from board member Mark Baker quickly convinced her of the importance of the waterfront in the city's recovery.

"There was one piece of land on Pier 4 that wasn't owned by the Port Authority," remembers Koval. "It had been owned by a private developer and had gone into foreclosure, but no one had ever foreclosed on it. I had done some research, and I actually thought the Coalition should buy it, because it was right in the middle of the park and would give us leverage as a community organization. And then Mark called me [right after September 11] and said, 'Marianna, the Dutch are giving a million daffodil bulbs to the city of New York to commemorate all the loss of life. Let's get some and go onto Pier 4 and plant a memorial.'"

Koval continues: "So Mark and I went down—I think we finally got some kind of permission from whomever had been the owners—and were given 25,000 bulbs. The trash was probably ten feet high. We cleared that lot over six to eight weeks. And we did a memorial with thousands of thousands of people who came from all over the city to help us plant the bulbs. And then they came up in the spring, and they were gorgeous. And [volunteer] Nancy Webster designed a big sign, 'After Winter, Spring,' and we put the sign where the World Trade Center had been."[32]

With Coalition staff organizing a team of volunteers, the 25,000 daffodils were planted over five weekends beginning on October 21, as part of a citywide campaign to plant the 1 million daffodils that had been donated by the Dutch government to honor the victims of the attack on the World Trade Center. When they finally blossomed in the spring of 2002, the flowers covered a 1.2-acre site on Pier 4, filling two beds measuring 20 feet by 180 feet and re-creating the approximate shape of the World Trade Center towers. Koval recalls: "All my firemen, from the firehouse across the street from my house, were down training here when we came down to water the flowers one day, and I asked them to come down and be photographed standing in front of [the flower garden] with us. And it was all by accident."[33]

"I think that 9/11 was an incredible moment for the park," explains Baker, "because attitudes in New York City changed so dramatically. Parks and open spaces were places where people congregated. There were scenes on the Promenade looking out over the World Trade Center. The Promenade became an important place for coming together and for holding candle memorials. I think New Yorkers began to feel more strongly that parks were important for them. Particularly that sense that this area has been wounded and we need to do something to make it better became a very compelling force at the governmental level for the park. [Planting the daffodils] was part of the healing process that was really important for the community and the city. It was also our first time getting out on the piers."[34]

MAYOR MICHAEL BLOOMBERG and the city's other public officials also recognized the importance of waterfronts and public parks in the city's rebirth and recovery. On January 30, 2002, Bloomberg pledged his support to "bring new life" to the city's waterfronts, and Daniel Doctoroff, Deputy Mayor for Economic Development, focused his statements specifically on the west Brooklyn waterfront: "Brooklyn Bridge Park is a major priority, and we'll do everything we can to move it forward."[35]

"The Bloomberg administration's interest in parks and open space was apparent from the beginning," says Joshua Laird, who served as Assistant Commissioner for Planning and Natural Resources in the Department of Parks and Recreation under Bloomberg. "Brooklyn Bridge Park wasn't priority number one, but [Bloomberg] saw early on that it was a potential win for the city and an opportunity to build an important regional park. And there was definitely a change in attitude about working with the state."[36]

On May 2, 2002, Mayor Bloomberg made good on his earlier commitment, when he and Governor Pataki signed a Memorandum of Understanding (MOU), declaring the shared commitment of the state and city governments to the construction of Brooklyn Bridge Park and outlining guidelines for the creation, development, and operation of the park (figure 24). The guidelines for the park included

1   The Park will be a unified park, developed by a single entity.
2   The Park's open space will be legally protected and commercial development limited.
3   Commercial revenues will pay for the Park's maintenance and operation.
4   The community will continue to be directly involved in the Park's development.
5   The Park's development will be guided by the Master Plan developed by the LDC.
6   The Park's development will be funded with $150 million.[37]

The MOU stipulated that the park would be designed and constructed by the newly formed Brooklyn Bridge Park Development Corporation, using the Illustrative Master Plan developed by the LDC as the guide. In contrast to the LDC, whose board members included appointees from the local neighborhood associations, community boards, and Chamber of Commerce, the Development Corporation's eleven directors were

FIGURE 24

Mayor Michael Bloomberg announces the city and state's commitment of $150 million to design and construct Brooklyn Bridge Park and to form the Brooklyn Bridge Park Development Corporation, May 2, 2002. Among those pictured are (*left to right*) Governor George Pataki, Empire State Development Corporation chairman Charles Gargano, Local Development Corporation president Joanne Witty, Assemblywoman Joan Millman, City Council member David Yassky, Deputy Mayor for Economic Development Dan Doctoroff, State Senator Martin Connor, Brooklyn Bridge Park Coalition chair John Watts, and Brooklyn Borough President Marty Markowitz.

COURTESY OF TOM FOX

appointed exclusively by the elected officials, with six appointments by Governor Pataki and five appointments by Mayor Bloomberg.[38]

"The MOU was the first clear sign that the park was going forward," says Coalition board member Dick Dadey about the significance of the event. "After 9/11, everyone thought this was over. And then so soon after that, Pataki and Bloomberg signed the MOU. The ceremony was packed. People were cramming onto the pier. I was stunned by the number of people that were there. Now the park was no longer just an idea of the community, but it had the backing and the interest of the chief executives of the state and the city."[39]

"There was a lot of work behind the scenes," recalls Koval of the extensive discussions with city and state officials regarding the principles that would guide the park's construction, "trying to reach the governor's people, and negotiate the different pieces of the Memorandum of Understanding. We wanted to make sure that the '13 Guiding Principles' were reflected in it."[40]

The guidelines for the MOU fell short of the "13 Guiding Principles" developed by the Coalition and the administration of Borough President Howard Golden in 1992, but the critical principles of community involvement, limited commercial development, and comprehensive planning of a unified park were prominently featured in the agreement. While critics of the plan could (and inevitably would) complain about the omission of specific provisions from the original "13 Guiding Principles" (for example, restrictions on housing or invasive public corridors) in the language of the memorandum, the plan endorsed by the state and city administrations was based on the community's original vision for the waterfront.

"What was unique about this process," City Council member Ken Fisher commented at the time the borough, city, and state money was committed, "is that it started at the grassroots level. It was always driven by the community and supported by the elected officials, not the other way around. It's very disingenuous for anyone to say, 'The developers imposed a plan on the community,' because in this case, the developer is us—the community."[41]

ON SEPTEMBER 22, 2003, Governor Pataki and Mayor Bloomberg appeared together at a ribbon-cutting ceremony to mark the official opening of the property between the Brooklyn and Manhattan Bridges previously known as the "Main Street lot." The governor and mayor were joined at the ceremony by Brooklyn Borough President Marty Markowitz, Parks Commissioner Adrian Benepe, Empire State Development Corporation chairman Charles Gargano, State Senator Martin Connor, Assemblywoman Joan Millman, and City Council member David Yassky.

What had been an underused parking lot leased to Two Trees Management by the Department of Parks and Recreation was converted into 1.5 acres of native grasses, wildflowers, and public benches, directly connected to Empire–Fulton Ferry State Park and providing visitors with an uninterrupted strip of public parkland along the inter-bridge waterfront. A small slice of the property had been opened the previous December as the Main Street Playground and had already become a popular destination for neighborhood children.

"Reclaiming the waterfront is a right of all New Yorkers," proclaimed Bloomberg, reiterating his commitment to the city's waterfront parks after September 11, "and opening this section of Brooklyn Bridge Park underscores our commitment to opening up our waterfronts for scores of New Yorkers."[42]

"I predict that Brooklyn Bridge Park will become one of the major tourist attractions in the world," said Markowitz. "When people come to New York, the first stop will be Brooklyn and Brooklyn Bridge Park."[43]

For seasoned Coalition board members such as Mark Baker and John Watts, who had labored for so long for the park's realization, often with little external assistance, the sudden outpouring of support from elected officials at every level was a powerful vindication. "All at once, it seemed like everyone out there, every single elected official, wanted to be associated with the park," says Baker. "We went from almost everyone saying, 'no,' to everyone saying, 'yes.'"[44]

For Koval, the most moving part of the ribbon cutting was seeing the Parks Department sign at the Main Street entrance identifying Brooklyn Bridge Park. "That said it all," says Koval.

KEEPING WITH ITS STRATEGY to bring people to the park, the Coalition continued to sponsor interim uses and programmed activities for the park site throughout the following year. In addition to the popular outdoor film series, other activities included the public garden at Pier 4; children's programming at the Main Street Playground and new park area at Main Street in the inter-bridge area; regular walking tours of the park area; and numerous dances, concerts, art exhibitions, and other cultural events presented in cooperation with other Brooklyn organizations.

ON FEBRUARY 26, 2004, the Brooklyn Bridge Park Coalition's board made the decision to rename the organization the Brooklyn Bridge Park Conservancy. With the funding for the park's realization in place and the initial construction in the inter-bridge area under way, Executive Director Marianna Koval acknowledged that the organization's original mission to serve as an advocate and a catalyst for the park concept was "ready for re-tooling to reflect new realities" and that a new name and organizational identity were needed to signal the change. The newly defined "job description" for the Conservancy included supporting the work of the Brooklyn Bridge Park Development Corporation in designing and constructing Brooklyn Bridge Park, building a broad-based constituency for the park through interim uses and public events and activities, and raising private funds to support its ongoing activities and public programming. The emphasis on interim uses and programmed activities came as little surprise to anyone who had been following the organization during the first three years of Koval's tenure. More than anything else, the name change represented a formal, public declaration of what had already become the defining feature of Koval's term as the organization's executive director: the importance of programmed activities in making the park a reality in the life of the borough and the city. "The change to the Conservancy," says Koval of the decision to formalize the shift in organizational objectives and priorities that had already begun to take place, "that was when we outlined what we wanted to do as part of the park. We wanted to be the programming partner, and that's what we became."[45]

Since the formation of the LDC in 1998 and the intense negotiations for public funding for the park's planning and construction, Koval and the other Coalition members had increasingly grown to believe that the vision of a pure park championed by Anthony Manheim, John Watts, Benjamin Crane, and other early park advocates was, whatever its virtues, simply not viable for the Brooklyn waterfront, particularly with the constraint of self-sustainability imposed by the "13 Guiding Principles" and the Memorandum of Understanding signed by Governor Pataki and Mayor Bloomberg. Nor was the concept of a pure park consistent with the feedback generated by the public charrettes, in which Brooklyn residents had repeatedly expressed the desire for active recreational space to be included in the park. If Brooklyn Bridge Park was to become a reality, the Development Corporation and the Conservancy would have no choice but to confront the difficult political and economic realities around them head-on and create a park that the public would use and the elected officials would support.

"This was the part that was crucial," insists Koval, "finding a way to actually get the park funded and built—and getting people on the site to support it. You can stop projects; that's easy enough. The hard part is in taking the steps and making the compromises that it takes to get something done."[46]

"Nobody was buying the idea of a passive park in the front yard of Brooklyn Heights," explains LDC consultant Tom Montvel-Cohen. "That just wasn't selling. If the park was going to happen, it would have to be big, and it would have to be for everyone, a grand mosaic that the public would support and that all the elected officials could get behind."[47]

The shift in emphasis from a passive park (with extended sections of undisturbed meadows, wooded areas, and shoreline) to an active park (with playgrounds, recreational facilities, and planned activities to attract visitors) was far more than a reasoned compromise to secure funding from elected officials, however. Since the daffodil display following the attack on the World Trade Center on September 11, 2001, had symbolically "torn down the barbed wire" that alienated the city's residents from the Brooklyn waterfront, Koval and the Conservancy board realized that they cared much less about featuring landscape and design than about creating a public open space for all New Yorkers to enjoy as they wanted.

EIGHT

THE PERFECT IS THE ENEMY OF THE GOOD

> The mantra that Al Butzel taught me early on, that "the perfect is the enemy of the good," is right. The hard thing is to figure out what the good is.
>
> **MARIANNA KOVAL**

WHILE THE BROOKLYN BRIDGE PARK CONSERVANCY was focusing its energies on bringing people onto the park site, the Development Corporation (as the newly formed Brooklyn Bridge Park Development Corporation was popularly known) was making slow but steady progress toward the design and construction of Brooklyn Bridge Park. With the funding for the park's planning and construction secured and the Memorandum of Understanding (MOU) formally endorsed by the state and city governments, the Development Corporation hired the landscape-architecture firm Michael Van Valkenburgh Associates, which had contributed to the Illustrative Master Plan for the park.

Van Valkenburgh and his associate Matt Urbanski had served as consultants in the initial public discussions of the park's design following the formation of the Local Development Corporation (LDC) in 1998, participating in dozens of planning charrettes with more than 2,000 community leaders and other residents throughout the borough, and the design firm was already intimately familiar with the physical features of the waterfront property; the interests and expectations of local residents; and the social, political, and financial challenges that would inevitably be involved in the park's realization.

The firm's first assignment was to develop a preliminary project plan in consultation with representatives from the local community, followed by the formulation of a maintenance and operations budget for the park (including an analysis of the budgetary requirements of other New York parks) and the preparation of a revenue analysis to determine the type and scale of commercial development necessary to support the park over time.[1]

As lead designer Michael Van Valkenburgh recalls, the assignment proved to be a daunting but ultimately an extremely rewarding challenge. "The original RFP [Request for Proposals] described a role for the team leader that I don't think has ever been matched," explains Van Valkenburgh. "It included designing the landscape, figuring out the urban parcels, balancing the maintenance budget, and then balancing the yield from the potential development from the potential cost that would allow the park to exist. It required the lead consultant to become part of a massive team—including engineers, architects, ecologists, and economic consultants—that morphed and changed as the project evolved. I have not heard of a job description like that before or after Brooklyn Bridge Park. It was very hard, but I think it made it a better park."[2]

IN MARCH 2004, following repeated public complaints about delays in the park's development and the lack of updates from the Development Corporation to the community regarding the project's progress, Development Corporation president James Moogan was "quietly replaced" by Wendy Leventer, the former president of the Forty-second Street Development Corporation.[3]

Moogan, who had developed a reputation as a consensus-builder during his earlier tenure at New York State Office of Parks, Recreation and Historic Preservation, had difficulty educating the public about the laborious, time-consuming activities that were required to keep the massive project in motion, and community residents had become impatient with the lack of visible progress on the site. The momentum of the project had recently been stalled by Moogan's negotiations with the Port Authority regarding the inclusion of Pier 6 in Brooklyn Bridge Park, which, although representing a tremendous addition to the overall park design, had resulted in extensive delays in an already lengthy environmental-impact study that had to be completed before the plans for the park could move forward.

"James Moogan was an earnest, thoughtful, and well-intentioned man," says Coalition board member Dick Dadey, "but he was not effective at saying to the community, 'This is what's happening, and this is how long it's going to take. There are necessary infrastructure activities that need to take place before the park gets built.' Instead he would raise expectations, which led to this feeling that things were stalled, which ultimately led to his departure."[4]

At the time of her hiring, Leventer did her best to temper public expectations regarding the timing of the park's completion. "Because we're government, we don't do anything in under a year," said Leventer, cautioning that construction could take an additional three to four years after the completion of the stalled environmental-impact study. "We're thinking that if we're lucky, there's not going to be a shovel in the ground until '08, just because that's the way the timing goes."[5]

FOLLOWING THE PRESENTATION and public discussions of the completed Master Plan in the fall of 2005, the document was modified and expanded into the General Project Plan for the park, which was adopted by the Empire State Development Corporation (ESDC) on December 18, 2006. The General Project Plan included a detailed description of the overall physical design and individual features of Brooklyn Bridge Park, along with specific recommendations for the location, size, and capacity of the revenue-generating commercial developments that the park would need to include to fulfill the mandate for self-sustainability included in the MOU of May 2, 2002.

The General Project Plan featured a vast, sprawling landscape of passive open space and active recreational facilities, including a broad waterfront greenway, floating walkways connecting the piers, and rolling hills and expansive pockets of natural habitat on the upland areas above the piers. Winding pedestrian pathways and bicycle lanes provided visitors with uninterrupted links to the rich variety of recreational features scattered throughout the park, including playgrounds; multipurpose playing fields; open lawns; soccer fields; a pier devoted to court sports, including basketball, volleyball, and handball; twelve acres of calm paddling water; and a beach for launching human-powered boats. Visitors would be able to enter the park through large gateways at Atlantic Avenue, Old Fulton Street, and John Street in Dumbo (Down Under the Manhattan Bridge Overpass); a pedestrian bridge linking Squibb Park to Pier 1; and additional entrances crossing Furman Street at Joralemon, Dock, Main, Washington, Adams, Pearl, and Jay Streets.

The preliminary financial analysis from the Master Plan estimated that the construction costs for the entire park would be approximately

$130 million. As the MOU had already prescribed, the cost of the park's construction would be funded by state and city governments, the Port Authority, and additional private investments.

To honor the mandate for self-sustainability included in the "13 Guiding Principles" and the MOU, the Master Plan stipulated that the cost of the ongoing maintenance and operation of the park would be covered by revenues generated by private development within the project area. Private developments proposed by the General Project Plan included a hotel, a restaurant, a marina, office and retail space, and—the feature of the plan that would generate the most controversy among residents of the neighborhoods adjacent to the site—housing, including 500 residential units in a converted manufacturing facility at 360 Furman Street, 150 to 180 residential units in a mixed-use hotel/residential development to be built on the upland area above Pier 1, up to 430 residential units in two newly constructed buildings on Pier 6, and 130 residential units in a building on John Street in the area between the Brooklyn and Manhattan Bridges.

Anticipating the groundswell of public resistance that would inevitably result from Van Valkenburgh's proposal for housing on the park property, the Conservancy decided to go on the offensive, immediately announcing that the organization strongly endorsed "the basic elements of the Plan." "The Plan advances the vision of a great park on the Brooklyn waterfront," wrote Koval in the Conservancy's newsletter, "while it accommodates the financial realities of the existing construction budget and incorporates the precondition of self-sustainability in the long-term operations of the park. Importantly, the Plan allows less land than ever contemplated to be committed to commercial development to support the park—only eight acres in exchange for seventy-two acres of dedicated parkland directly on New York Harbor."[6]

According to Daniel Doctoroff, former Deputy Mayor for Economic Development, the proposal to use housing as a revenue source for the park had been an open part of the park design for a number of years. "One of the things that we did from the start," remembers Doctoroff, "was to establish that the park was going to pay for itself. I had always pushed for the park to be self-sustaining, using Pier 1 in particular and the proceeds from that to pay for the operating expenses and capital that it would defray. Payments in lieu of taxes would support the park going forward, as well as some of the development rights. I always thought that the alternative between a partial park and no park would be appealing for everyone."[7]

"They [the public authorities] could not have been more explicit," agrees John Alschuler of Hamilton, Rabinovitz & Alschuler, the Manhattan consulting firm in charge of the initial planning for the park. "They said, 'We're going to give you the funds you need to build it and then don't come back. You're on your own.' "[8]

Not everyone was enthusiastic about the provision in the Master Plan, however. The decision to support the inclusion of housing on the park property, which many local residents viewed as a "Faustian bargain" with the public authorities, was a radical departure from the position of many of the early leaders of the west Brooklyn waterfront movement, who had proposed the creation of a public park as an alternative to the prospect of housing and other commercial developments on the piers. Based on the analysis provided in the Master Plan (which determined that the presence of housing would not result in the privatization of the park) and ongoing negotiations with elected officials, even the more anti-housing members of the Conservancy board had gradually come to believe that the realization of the park was simply not possible without the inclusion of at least some residential housing on the property.

"The mantra that Al Butzel taught me early on, that 'the perfect is the enemy of the good,' is right," explains Koval. "The hard thing is to figure out what the good is." By the time the Master Plan and General Project Plan were released, Koval and the Conservancy board had begun to regard housing less as a necessary evil than as a potential asset to the overall park experience.

"In 2005, when the Master Plan came out," remembers Conservancy board member Gary VanderPutten, "the response from the community was ballistic, particularly among the Cobble Hill group and from some of the people in Brooklyn Heights. People were enraged. The LDC, of course, had no real choice but to support it. At the Conservancy, we carefully examined it and determined that this really might be the only viable way to do this. The whole idea behind this was that if you're going to have a park, then it has to be self-sustaining, and if it's going to be self-sustaining, then you have to some level of commercial development to handle the maintenance cost.

"Look at what's happened to Hudson River Park," VanderPutten continues. "It's really in trouble. It needs $37 million just to repair what's under Chelsea Piers. They don't have any to money fix it, and that's because their Guiding Principles say that absolutely no public housing can be built on this park. That's a killer. In contrast, our Guiding Principles say that housing is allowable but not preferred. It's not preferred, but it is allowable. And that sentence is the only reason we're here."[9]

THE EARLIER CONTROVERSIES between the leadership of the park movement and a small but highly vocal minority of local residents over the placement of pedestrian corridors for the park were minor skirmishes compared with the firestorm of public debate that erupted once the recommendations from the Master Plan and the General Project Plan were made available to the public.

Local housing opponents Judi Francis, Roy Sloane, and the Brooklyn Bridge Park Defense Fund, formed in response to the park plan, were at the head of the opposition, joining the Sierra Club to file a lawsuit against the ESDC, claiming that the development plan for the park violated the state's "public trust doctrine" by handing over parkland to developers and seeking to block the use of housing as a revenue-generating source for the park. "There's mischief afoot here with developers taking over the shoreline," insisted Francis, openly questioning the motivations of the authorities in charge of the park's development.[10]

"The Brooklyn Bridge Park Conservancy thinks it's a sad day for the people of Brooklyn who've worked twenty years to create a park on the waterfront," said Koval in response to the announced litigation. "Friends of parks don't sue to stop them," insisted Conservancy and LDC board member Hank Gutman. "Litigation cannot possibly cause a park to be built, and litigation cannot improve a park plan. All litigation can accomplish is to delay, or even prevent, the park becoming a reality."[11]

The lawsuit to stop housing on the park was dismissed in November 2006 by Judge Lawrence Knipel of the New York State Supreme Court in Brooklyn. He ruled that the "public trust doctrine" did not hold in the current case because the parcels to be sold or leased to developers "are not parkland, have never been parkland, and were never designated to become parkland."[12]

"They were taking land that was never a park to begin with," explains former Parks Commissioner Adrian Benepe, defending the reasoning behind the revenue plan, "and that was in commercial use, income-producing commercial property owned by the state of New York, and they were rededicating it and saying some small portions would be set aside for the development of revenues to support a public park."[13]

Judge Knipel's ruling did little to discourage the Brooklyn Bridge Park Defense Fund's Judi Francis, who announced that she would appeal the decision. "If it acts like a park, and has been talked about as a park," reasoned Francis, "then it is a park in every sense of the word."[14]

The local opposition to the use of housing as an income source for the park also included former Coalition executive director Anthony Manheim, who went public with his long-standing concern over the potential of residential housing to privatize the park. "When you have private, residential uses," cautioned Manheim, "they're in direct conflict with the public use."[15]

In addition to opposing housing as a revenue-generating source for the park, Francis called for the following for the park's management and design: enact legislation designating all land within the site as "parkland under the ownership of the city or state parks agencies"; put park management in the hands of "park professionals," rather than business leaders from the ESDC; conduct "an independent fiscal analysis of the alleged costs and revenues" of the park; replace the existing environmental-impact study with an independent study of the impact of the park on the local environment and the communities around the park; and include swimming pools and other indoor recreational facilities currently lacking in Brooklyn.

Koval worked diligently to diffuse the anger and suspicions of local residents by directly addressing the major concerns of those who opposed the Master Plan through local print media and the Conservancy newsletter, in which she explained the rationale for the selection of sites where housing would be located (view protection, urban access), posted a time line illustrating the reduction in the percentage of property dedicated to housing, and provided information regarding the potential benefits of housing (care, advocacy, security, increased activity) on or adjacent to the park property. The Conservancy also believed that creating and encouraging early patterns of use in the growing park—before any housing was built—would be essential to creating public ownership and countering concerns of privatization.[16]

"This is where we knew we were going to have a lot of pushback," recalls Koval, "and I wrote these FAQs. Why is housing included? Will housing privatize the park? What other revenue-generating developments were suggested? I felt that it was something that had to be dealt with directly."[17]

As the controversy raged in community meetings and through the local and city media, the Development Corporation, in spite of its public endorsement of the Master Plan and General Project Plan, remained silent regarding the issue of housing. "It was just very bad politics," insists Koval. "All of this resistance, this opposition, would never have happened if the Development Corporation had had a more open and less secretive approach and had walked people through the process that they walked through to come to those conclusions.

"I'd say, 'We should pick off the people who are persuaded by the opposition but who might be willing to listen to us and focus on them, so we can isolate the ones who aren't willing to listen or compromise, no matter what we say.' It's all basic stuff. If you sit down and treat people seriously and listen to what they have to say, you'll have a much better chance of being effective. But they seemed to have the idea that, 'We're the government. Get out of our way.'"[18]

An outgrowth of this initiative to find common ground among local residents was the Park Community Council, which included representatives of various neighborhood groups as well as local boating and biking groups. "We started the Park Community Council in 2006," recalls long-time park advocate and Conservancy board member Nancy Bowe, "after the General Project Plan had been announced. It was composed of the neighborhood groups that generally supported the park plan—not that we supported everything, but we were trying to form a counterbalance to what we called the 'anti-park movement.' There was such an anti-housing movement at the time that the neighborhood groups that supported the park felt that it was important to band together, even though we weren't all uniformly happy with everything, in support of the basic tenets of the plan, including housing."[19]

While the reluctance of Development Corporation president Wendy Leventer to respond to the public's concerns about housing generated mistrust and suspicion among some local residents, her single-minded focus on pushing the project through, regardless of public dissent, may ultimately have played a vital role in the park's realization.

"Wendy Leventer never wavered from doing what she believed was right for the park," insists Josh Sirefman, chief of staff to the Deputy Mayor for Economic Development in the Bloomberg administration. "Frankly at that moment of time, I think it would have been really, really difficult to move [the project] along if there was somebody in that role who was easily pulled this way or that by the different constituencies. I'm not saying it wasn't painful, and I'm not saying there weren't other issues to consider. I get that. But I also think in the grand scheme of things, if we didn't at that moment have somebody who just put their head down and just pushed forward, I'm not sure we would have ended up where we did."[20]

At the time, however, the editorial writers of the *New York Times* echoed Koval's assessment of the continuing controversy between local residents and the Development Corporation. "The Brooklyn Bridge Park Development Corporation needs to make a more intense effort to show these plans around and explain them, listen to questions and respond to both praise and complaints," they wrote, shortly after the release of the Master Plan. "This park has been too many decades on the drawing boards. The last thing it needs is another full stall, which it risks if its planners fail to solicit and hear the voice of Brooklyn's army of activists."[21]

WHILE THE PUBLIC DEBATE OVER HOUSING in the park continued, the Conservancy intensified its emphasis on interim uses and programmed activities for the park, all with the goal of increasing the use of and the stakeholders' support for the park. Working through a license with the New York State Office of Parks, Recreation and Historic Preservation, the Conservancy's program schedule for the summer of 2006 included, in addition to the popular film series and annual fund-raising event, a bike tour, culinary events, drama and dance productions, outdoor presentations of ballet and modern dance in the Tobacco Warehouse, a puppet theater, a sculpture exhibit, and a harbor camp program for children.

In the summer of 2007, the Conservancy teamed up with New York City waterfront historian Ann Buttenwieser and the Neptune Foundation to organize the most popular—and most challenging—event of the park's preconstruction era: a massive floating pool anchored in the East River. Designed by Buttenwieser, the "Floating Pool Lady" was an 80- by 260-foot cargo barge converted into a seven-lane, 25-meter swimming pool (figure 25). The "pool," which had been temporarily anchored on Pier 2, was moved to the area between Piers 4 and 5, where it attracted more than 71,000 visitors from July 4 to September 3, 2007. The lively crowds that came to swim and lounge represented the first time in more than 200 years that the public had access to the waterfront in that section of the property.[22]

More than 10,000 visitors were transported to the pool by a free shuttle bus that ran every ten minutes between the pool area and the Borough Hall and High Street subway stations. The LDC, under the leadership of Henry Gutman, provided the bus. The funding for the shuttle service was part of $1 million grant secured from the Department of Transportation by Congresswoman Nydia Velázquez the previous year to identify ways of accessing the park that would reduce reliance on vehicular traffic.[23]

"The floating pool was so incredibly important for letting people see how we could get tens of thousands of people to this site," recalls Koval. "And it also was amazing to see kids, Latinos, African Americans, walking down in their bathing suits, and church ladies coming for the water-exercise classes."[24]

"The floating pool," says Conservancy board member David Kramer, "was the first moment in 'If you build it, they will come.' If we weren't going to have a park yet, we were at least going to have something. We could at least have this pool. We had tremendous crowds, and it didn't affect the quality of life of people in the neighborhood at all. And it was a hugely diverse constituency. And there were so many people of color who came, all these people from Bedford-Stuyvesant and East New York to be at this park. And it wasn't just for Brooklyn Heights, or just for rich

people, or even just for Brooklyn. It was truly going to a regional park that drew people from all over."[25]

"That was the hardest thing I ever did in my whole life," says Koval of the legal and logistical challenges involved in opening the floating pool to the public. "No one wanted to approve the permitting necessary to let the pool be moored anywhere in the city. And we were just unrelenting. We drove it and drove it. That was the key thing. I decided that, damn it, we should have the floating pool and there was no better site in the city of New York. It was so complicated, and government was so difficult. And we had no money. I persuaded the ESDC to allow me to take money for capital funds and to swap it out for expense money, and that had never done that before in the history of the organization."[26]

WHILE THE CONSERVANCY continued to expand its schedule of programmed activities and interim uses to draw people to the waterfront, the Development Corporation and the public authorities reached a major milestone on May 31, 2006, when Mayor Michael Bloomberg and Governor George Pataki announced that the Port Authority had officially authorized transfer of control of Piers 1, 2, and 3, along with parts of Pier 5, to the Development Corporation.

"This is an important milestone in the creation of what is set to become one of New York City's most magnificent public spaces," proclaimed Bloomberg at a ceremony held in the park's inter-bridge area. "Brooklyn Bridge Park will become the quintessential example of our

Administration's commitment to return the city's waterfront to its residents and improve the quality of life in all five boroughs."[27]

"At the beginning of the 1900s, the wrong decisions were made. It was decided to cut people off from the waterfront," said Pataki, reassuring citizens that the both the state and the city were now firmly committed to restoring access to the shoreline.[28]

"I feel that Pataki and Bloomberg both deserve tremendous credit for the creation of Brooklyn Bridge Park," says former Parks Commissioner Adrian Benepe. "Pataki saw himself as a part of a Republican tradition that goes back to Roosevelt and values parks and conservation. He and his administration were willing to go out on a limb [for the city's parks], and I got the sense that he took genuine joy in helping to make it happen.

"And Bloomberg viewed parks as an important part of the city's economic development," continues Benepe. "For the first time in the history of New York, there was a very definite view that parks were worth investing in."[29]

"I don't think it's been fully appreciated the degree to which all these initiatives, including the parks, were linked together into a coherent strategy," says Josh Sirefman of the city government's commitment to parks at the time. "In the early months [of the Bloomberg administration], we came up with this strategy to foster New York's competitive edge. We had an underlying philosophy that we can't just sit still and let things happen. Before that, it was like, New York is New York, and it will always be the center of the universe. And you have to remember that this was all happening post-9/11 and everything had been shaken to its core. But under Bloomberg, there was always a mandate to think big—and also a liberation to think new—and the waterfront was a really big component of that."[30]

The primary responsibility for realizing the Bloomberg administration's plans for Brooklyn Bridge Park was assumed by First Deputy Mayor Patricia Harris and her chief of staff, Nanette Smith, who also served as special assistant to the mayor. A former assistant to the deputy mayor in the administration of Ed Koch, Harris was responsible for the oversight of all the city's efforts on behalf of the park, including securing the annual budget, arranging the hiring of Regina Myer as president of the Development Corporation, and facilitating the negotiations between the city and the state over the funding and governance of the park. Smith, who had served in the New York City Art Commission during the Koch administration, was responsible for executing the administration's vision on the ground: meeting daily with representatives of the Development Corporation and reaching out to the Conservancy and others involved in the realization of the park.

THE IMPLEMENTATION of the General Project Plan began in earnest in December 2007 when the Development Corporation authorized the demolition of all the remaining pier sheds on the property, a number of upland structures, and the Purchase Building between the piers at the Dumbo waterfront.[31] The Development Corporation's decision to demolish the 1930s-era Purchase Building, to provide a direct connection between the southern and northern sections of the park, proved to be a controversial one, even among some of the park's strongest supporters.

Since 2002, the 300-foot-long, 30-foot-high warehouse had been used as the temporary headquarters of the city's Office of Emergency Management. On February 21, 2006, the New York City Landmarks Preservation Commission had ruled by a vote of 7 to 2 that the Purchase Building was a part of but not a "contributing building" to the Brooklyn Heights Historic District and thus could be demolished to clear a view plane of the Manhattan shoreline from the inter-bridge area.[32]

While a number of local community groups opposed the demolition, the Conservancy lent its support to the decision to remove the building from the site. "While we are supporters of preservation," explained Koval after the decision of the Landmarks Commission was announced, "we viewed this particular instance as one where the public interest was better served to remove the building to create the Brooklyn Bridge Park."[33]

IN MARCH 2007, the ESDC announced that Wendy Leventer had been dismissed from her position as president of the Brooklyn Bridge Park Development Corporation. Throughout her tenure, Leventer had exhibited singular skill in addressing the institutional and financial challenges involved in the project. However, her failure to meet regularly with and listen to the concerns of community leaders about the park's progress had led to a gradual loss of confidence among many local residents that the plan for the park would be realized. In addition, her unwillingness to hold public discussions regarding the ongoing adjustments to the park design had been greeted by open resistance by some Brooklyn residents. After taking the job in 2004, she had immediately encountered opposition from Brooklyn anti-housing activists, who were angered to learn that the maintenance of the park would be paid for with revenue generated by housing and other commercial developments on the site. The lawsuit over housing initiated by the Brooklyn Bridge Park Defense Fund in 2006 had resulted in even further delays to the process and growing unrest in the community.

While many park advocates faulted Leventer for her lack of responsiveness to the concerns of local residents, others who were involved in the park's planning and construction credited her for her tenacity and stubborn commitment to the project. "Wendy had a lot of headaches to deal with," explains LDC president Joanne Witty. "She came in when the rubber hit the road. She had to take the project through the environmental-impact study, and in order to do that you had to have the next level of design, which was being done simultaneously. But she took us through the EIS very rapidly. She knew how to do it. She knew how to build a project."[34] "It's my opinion," says park designer Michael Van Valkenburgh, "that BBP [Brooklyn Bridge Park] is as good as it is because of Wendy Leventer's spine and unwillingness to bend in the political wind."[35] "Wendy demanded that the park be great," agrees Van Valkenburgh's fellow designer, Matt Urbanski. "Period. That's the spirit that she brought to the foundation of the design of the park. The fact that it was public sector was not an excuse for settling for anything less than great."[36]

IN NOVEMBER 2007, the Development Corporation announced that Regina Myer had been hired as its new president. Myer had served for twenty years in the New York City Department of City Planning, the last eight as the director of the Brooklyn office, before becoming the Senior Vice President for Planning and Design at the Hudson Yards Development Corporation.[37] Based on her previous experience, Myer had deep knowledge of land-use issues. During her tenure at the Department of City Planning, Myer had overseen the rezoning of downtown Brooklyn and Dumbo, as well as the comprehensive rezoning of Williamsburg–Greenpoint, one of the first major waterfront-development initiatives in the borough, and was familiar with the planning process at Brooklyn Bridge Park.

"Regina Myer is someone who could not only build the park," asserts Patricia Harris regarding the positive impact that Myers would have on the project, "but was also effective in working with creative partners like the Conservancy, the Public Art Fund, and others to bring innovative programming to the park. We needed someone for this role who could be bold, innovative and forward looking. Sometimes in government, you need to really think outside the box in order to make big, lasting projects like this one happen. Regina is that person and Brooklyn Bridge Park, and New York, are better off because of it."[38]

Encouraged by the commitment of the city and state governments to the construction of the park, Myer was eager to bring momentum to what many in the community perceived as a stalled endeavor. The official groundbreaking on Pier 1 began on February 13, 2008, with demolition in full swing by March (figure 26) and potential contractors bidding on park

construction throughout the summer and beginning work on Piers 1 and 6 in January 2009.

"The approvals were in place for the park," remembers Myer of the sudden burst of activity that accompanied her arrival at the Development Corporation, "and we already had a good deal of the park design. We were ready to finally build the park. Our attitude was to get this thing started. Money was allocated, and the pressure was from both the government and the community to show results or the money would be pulled. That to me was the wonderful challenge. Everybody was done talking about whether we should have a park. We should just build the park."[39]

WHILE THE CHALLENGES AHEAD OF HER were formidable, given the obstacles that her predecessors had encountered, Myer was energized by the project from the beginning, both by the nature of the assignment and by the level of support she received from her partners in city government and the team of professionals she began to assemble around her at the Development Corporation. "As a planner," explains Myer, "having the ability to implement this vision is the coolest thing that could ever have happened to me. It is the job of a lifetime.

"What was exciting to me about this project," she recalls, "was that, while there was obviously an evolution of community support for the park, the government was really interested in making the park and understood that it was of value for the city.

"The importance of what Bloomberg people like Josh Sirefman [chief of staff to Daniel Doctoroff] and [Deputy Mayor for Economic Development] Dan Doctoroff did for the park just can't be overstated," says Myer. "They had the guts to put Pier 6 in the project. They just made it happen. They also had the guts to put 1 Brooklyn Bridge Park in. We would not have been able to open and have the government maintain it, had we not had 1 Brooklyn Bridge Park. They also signed onto the pilot legislation, which meant that they signed away taxes to the general fund for this park. So that was a decision that they made, and that they don't make very often.

"They were willing to take risks because they were willing to be innovative," continues Myer. "They were completely comfortable with the park's public–private model, and they were willing to be creative to build the park. They didn't say, 'We're not doing that. We only do it this way.' They just weren't that kind of people."[40]

Myer's original phasing plan for the park was given a boost by a substantial financial contribution from the Bloomberg administration shortly after she assumed the leadership of the Development Corporation. "When I first came in," recalls Myer, "we had a budget of $150 million, but within the first few months, the city had increased its contribution by $75 million. That gave us the ability to develop a phasing plan, which we announced in June 2008, showing an additional $75 million from the city."

Another challenge facing Myer was to develop a budget plan for the park. "It's what makes the whole thing tick," says Myer. "We had the revenue coming forward from day one from 1 Brooklyn Bridge Park. It was pretty exciting when we got the first check from them."[41]

IN THE SUMMER OF 2008, the Development Corporation and the Conservancy decided to take advantage of the gap in time between the demolition and construction on Pier 1 and the installation by the Public Art Fund of Olafur Eliasson's *Waterfalls* beneath the Brooklyn Bridge to provide visitors with a taste of what the finished park would be like. The "Pop-Up Park" was a 26,000-square-foot site on Pier 1 near Fulton Ferry Landing designed by Brooklyn resident and landscape architect Susannah Drake's dlandstudio. Opening on June 26, "Pop-Up Park" featured a café, landscaping with trees and grass mounds, benches and picnic tables, a large sandbox, and a spectacular view of New York Harbor and the

Manhattan skyline. For local families, many of whom were making their first visit to the park site, the main attraction was the opportunity for children to play together in the large sandbox while parents enjoyed a glass of wine on the waterfront.

By the time the site closed on September 28, it had attracted more than 120,000 visitors to the west Brooklyn waterfront, representing a remarkably diverse group of people, including 21 percent from the adjoining neighborhoods, 23 percent from elsewhere in Brooklyn, 14 percent from elsewhere in New York City, 17 percent from the rest of the United States, and 25 percent from fifty-two foreign countries. While the site itself was modest in size—little more than a strip of walkway along part of the pier—the size and diversity of the crowds that it attracted clearly demonstrated the future park's potential as a popular regional destination.

With the initial construction of Brooklyn Bridge Park now fully under way, Myer was outspoken in her support of the Conservancy's latest creative activity to generate interest in and support for the park. "We are so pleased with the success of Summer '08 at Pier 1," said Myer at the time. "Pier 1 proved to be a magnificent destination for Brooklynites. New Yorkers and tourists, and allowed people to experience the beauty and incredible views of New York Harbor."[42]

Not everyone in the Brooklyn community was impressed with the features of the temporary installation. Judi Francis, president of the Brooklyn Bridge Park Defense Fund, who had led the local protests against housing on the park site, described "Pop-Up Park" and the other interim uses sponsored by the Conservancy as a "bait-and-switch," contending that essential but expensive park features such as swimming pools, skating rinks, ball fields, and food and drink concession stands (which had been featured in one or more of the interim projects) would not be included in the park's final design. While the Development Corporation insisted that Brooklyn Bridge Park would, in fact, ultimately include all those amenities and more, a spokesperson from the organization did concede that the ice-skating rink proposed in the General Project Plan had been delayed by at least five years due to an interagency battle between the city and state governments.[43]

IN FEBRUARY 2009, ten years after she assumed the leadership of the Brooklyn Bridge Park Coalition, Marianna Koval announced her resignation as the president of the Brooklyn Bridge Park Conservancy. As a widow and single parent, Koval was no longer able to sustain the eighty-hour work weeks necessary to navigate the external challenges and internal conflicts of the park movement. Renewed after two years of distance and perspective from her role leading the Conservancy, Koval enrolled at the Kennedy School of Government at Harvard University, where she modeled the lessons she had learned at the Conservancy for use by other parks around the nation and the world.

ON MARCH 12, 2009, a month after Koval's resignation, Nancy Webster was tapped to be the Conservancy's acting executive director. A former creative director at Marsteller Advertising, a division of the large public-relations firm Burson Marsteller, Webster had become tangentially involved in the Coalition's activities during the summer of 2000 when her partner, Nell Archer, organized the Coalition's popular outdoor film series and she was enlisted to help promote the event. A few months later, she joined the Coalition staff as director of marketing and communications and was promoted to deputy director the following year.

Webster had been drawn into the controversies on the Brooklyn waterfront in the late 1990s, when she was persuaded by her friend Michael Crane (son of Benjamin Crane, who had called for a park on the piers more than a decade earlier) to take the reins of the Dumbo Neighborhood Association (DNA). Dumbo was an emerging neighborhood of artists and young professionals in the inter-bridge area just north of the west Brooklyn piers, and Webster soon found herself at the forefront of a series of public protests over development projects in the quiet, formerly industrial district. Working in conjunction with Nancy Bowe at the Brooklyn Heights Association and Gary VanderPutten at the Fulton Ferry Landing Association, Webster led a successful effort in the spring of 2002 to halt a sixteen-story apartment building at 38 Water Street, at the base of the Brooklyn Bridge.

A few months later, Webster and the DNA also opposed the Watchtower's plans to rezone a large parking lot at 85 Jay Street, on the northern side of the Brooklyn Bridge, in order to construct a 1,000-occupant apartment building and underground parking garage. After failing to gain the support of the City Council, Webster decided that it was smarter to take a more pragmatic approach to the conflict and work to secure improvements to Bridge Park 2, a long-neglected city park on York Street across from the Jay Street site and adjacent to the Farragut Houses.

The same pragmatism would inform her advocacy efforts for Brooklyn Bridge Park. "I was president of the Dumbo Neighborhood Association in 2005 when the park's master plan was released. Some members of the steering committee were upset that the plan included housing as a way to generate revenue. But the Coalition's support of the plan and the

explanation that a limited amount of housing had the potential to generate the most revenue to support the park and take up the least amount of
park space made a lot of sense to me."[44]

Webster's support for the plan, however, was not shared by others on
the steering committee who voted to oppose the park's General Project
Plan. With that, Webster decided to step aside and devote her time to fur-
thering Brooklyn Bridge Park. "I could not support a position opposed to
the park that I viewed as short-sighted and parochial," said Webster. "I
didn't want to just oppose things. I wanted to help make positive change
happen in my neighborhood, and for me there was nothing more exciting
than Brooklyn Bridge Park."[45]

NINE

A PARK AT LAST

> We've engaged a huge number of people who appreciate how beautiful these shoreline parks can be. That's the future. It's so many people. It's not this small group. It's an army now.
>
> **DAVID OFFENSEND**

WITH CONSTRUCTION ON PIERS 1 AND 6 FINALLY UNDER WAY, supporters of Brooklyn Bridge Park encountered a major obstacle to the park's realization during the Wall Street collapse of October 2008. The stock market crash and the resulting national and global financial crisis had a devastating impact on the economy and administrative budget of New York State, with massive job losses (more than 17,000 in New York City alone in the twelve months following the crash), plunging tax revenues (which were reduced by more than one-third during the same period), and a virtual standstill in real-estate transactions and commercial development.

Even before the crisis, newly elected governor Eliot Spitzer had assumed a wait-and-see attitude toward Brooklyn Bridge Park and the state's financial commitment to its construction, repeatedly voicing his general support for the park but questioning whether the state possessed the financial resources to honor the previous administration's $85 million commitment to the project. In a public hearing shortly after Spitzer's election, Empire State Development Corporation (ESDC) spokeswoman Jessica Copin was less than reassuring to park supporters in stating the governor's position on the park and other outstanding public development projects. "We can't give any information as the new Administration is reviewing and accessing all the projects," Copin explained.[1] Later in the year, Spitzer suggested that proceeds from the sale of state-owned land adjacent to the Jacob K. Javits Convention Center in Manhattan might be used to cover the state's commitments to Brooklyn Bridge Park and other public development projects, but a proposal for the sale of property and transfer of funds was never formally enacted, and the park's future remained uncertain.[2]

Following Spitzer's resignation in March 2008, his successor, former state senator and lieutenant governor David Paterson, quickly reassured Brooklyn residents that, in spite of the state's ongoing financial difficulties, his administration remained firmly committed to the park's realization. Speaking at the Brooklyn Bridge Conservancy's annual "Sunset" fund-raising gala on June 3, Governor Paterson, who had never addressed the issue of the park during his earlier term in the New York State Senate, proclaimed to those in attendance, "Brooklyn Bridge Park is a New York treasure. I am pleased to be here and to celebrate the upcoming construction of the larger piers area, which will enhance this already outstanding park."[3]

The state's balance sheet told a different story, however, and one that held far less promise for the timely realization of Brooklyn Bridge Park. Between the 2008/2009 and 2009/2010 fiscal years, the gap between the state's incoming revenues and anticipated spending mushroomed from $1.7 billion to $13.7 billion, with projections for increasing budget deficits for several more years. It was clear, based on these figures, that it would be years, at best, before the state could make good on Governor George Pataki's $85 million pledge to the park and that a different financial plan would have to emerge if construction on the park was to continue as planned.

In January 2009, Mayor Michael Bloomberg proposed that the city assume sole control of Brooklyn Bridge Park, along with Governor's Island in New York Harbor, for which the state had covered the operating costs. According to Bloomberg's plan, the city would cover the expenses for the two projects using a $300 million fund originally allocated for the expansion of the Javits Center on Manhattan's West Side.

"We would use that money to continue to develop these two things which are great parts of the city," explained Bloomberg during a press conference in March. "The city has more of an interest. I think the state government has their [sic] own problems. It's a good deal for the state. If not, they can take them over or close them down."[4]

Even in the midst of such crippling financial shortfalls, it was understandably difficult for the governor's office and ESDC to relinquish control of—and future credit for—a project that had captivated the public for more than a decade and that had finally come so near to realization. An entire year would pass—with city officials openly worrying that the state's fiscal problems could undermine the project and the park's future remaining in limbo—while state and city authorities negotiated behind the scenes to resolve the problem in a way that would both cover the expenses required for the park's construction and ensure that the state had a continuing, if limited, role in the park's ongoing development.[5]

The arduous, behind-the-scenes task of restructuring the control of the park fell heavily on two recently appointed public officials with no previous governmental experience. Peter Davidson, a native of Brooklyn Heights and relative of former Brooklyn Bridge Park Coalition leader Anthony Manheim, assumed his position as executive director of the ESDC after a successful career as an entrepreneur, an investment banker, and the chairman of the J. M. Kaplan Fund. Robert Lieber, a former managing director at Lehman Brothers, joined the Bloomberg administration as Deputy Mayor for Economic Development after a year of service as the president of the New York City Economic Development Corporation.

Davidson and Lieber shared an impatience with the inefficiencies of large government bureaucracies, a problem that was compounded by the competing political interests of the state and the city over the ownership of the park. "I was immediately stupefied by the insanity of the entire process," recalls Lieber, "where every decision was based on politics, instead of merit. A 50–50 balance of responsibilities between city and state governments is a disaster model."[6]

Both men were determined to find a way to resolve the problem, however, and for months before the announcement, they worked quietly together behind the scenes to produce an arrangement that would be acceptable to both the state and city governments.

A variety of factors converged to enable the state to gracefully relinquish control of the project to the city. First, Davidson had determined, in consultation with Governor David Paterson and Deputy Secretary for Economic Development and Infrastructure Timothy Gilchrist, that the ESDC should assume "a lighter touch" in its oversight of the city's infrastructure, restricting its involvement to subway systems, taxing policies, and roads. "From a strictly philosophical point of view," explains Davidson, "there was no longer any reason for the state to be involved in the construction of the park."[7]

Second, New York was facing a financial shortfall that, combined with the complex legislative process to which state appropriations were routinely subjected, made it virtually impossible for the administration in Albany to honor its earlier commitments to the park. In addition to the city's stronger financial position at the time, the mayor enjoyed far greater flexibility in committing and securing project funds, even during a period of financial instability.

"The state has to go through an elaborate legislative process before anything can be approved," explains Daniel Doctoroff. "The city has a strong-mayor form of government where the mayor proposes a budget and the city council negotiates around the edges. So when the mayor stands up and says I'm going to commit $150 million to this and we're going to need another $50 million, then you can rely on that commitment."[8]

Finally, both Davidson and Paterson were relative newcomers to their positions in state government and were consequently not nearly as identified with or invested in the ambitions and commitments of their predecessors. While there were still many people in state government who argued that the governor and the ESDC were bound "to see the project through to completion," Paterson and Davidson reached the conclusion that releasing the major responsibilities for the project to the city's control was the right thing to do.[9]

Both Davidson and Lieber give particular credit to newly installed Governor David Paterson for publicly endorsing their plans. "Paterson totally understood what we were doing and the reasons we were doing it," Davidson insists, "and he was very supportive from the beginning."[10] "Governor Paterson got it done," agrees Lieber. "If he had said 'no,' then none of this would have happened."[11]

FINALLY, ON MARCH 10, 2010, Mayor Bloomberg, Governor Paterson, State Senator Daniel Squadron, and Assemblywoman Joan Millman announced a plan by which the state pledged to relinquish to the city responsibility for and control of Brooklyn Bridge Park, in exchange for which the city committed an additional $55 million ($36 million of which was earmarked for the construction of the Pier 2 and John Street sections of the park), in addition to the $139 million it had already committed to the project, for the next phases of construction.[12] According to the terms of the agreement, the ongoing planning, construction, maintenance, and operations of the park would be administered by a newly created operating entity, to be known as the Brooklyn Bridge Park Corporation (BBP Corporation), which would be governed by a seventeen-member board. The Development Corporation's Regina Myer was selected as the president of the new entity.[13]

To ensure that the community's interests were adequately represented in the future planning for and development of the park, the agreement also authorized the creation of the Community Advisory Council, through which local residents could continue to voice their concerns regarding the park's development, and the Committee on Alternatives to Housing (CAH), with State Senator Squadron and Assemblywoman Millman retaining the right to veto plans for residential housing at Pier 6 and John Street if the planned developments failed to address the concerns of the adjacent communities.

"New York State has been unmatched over the past several years in jumpstarting transformative projects that spur economic development and create jobs," said ESDC executive director Peter Davidson at the time. "And when a development is successfully underway, we find the right partners and systems to help us achieve the best long-term outcomes for our projects. That time has now come with Brooklyn Bridge Park, and this new structure is a win for the state, a win for the city, and a win for the local community in making this shared long-term vision a reality."[14]

In addition to the shortfall in the state budget, the BBP Corporation was confronted with a dramatic expansion in the anticipated budget for the construction of Brooklyn Bridge Park, with the projected cost having doubled from the $150 million cited in the Illustrative Master Plan, presented in 2000, and the Memorandum of Understanding (MOU), signed in 2002, to more than $300 million by 2010. "Peter Davidson at ESDC really felt strongly that the city was the right steward for the park," recalls Myer of the rationale behind the state's willingness to cede control of the park to the city. "The outstanding problem was that, although $150 million had initially been allocated, our cost estimates projected that the park was actually going to cost at least $300 million to build. It became clear to ESDC that the state couldn't commit the resources that were necessary to fully build out the park, since the New York State budget for the entire state park system was about $100 million. It was very unlikely that the state would commit that level of resources in the city."[15]

According to Robert Lieber, the mushrooming construction and maintenance expenses for the park were the inevitable result of ongoing underestimations of the real cost of completing the project, including the cost of refurbishing the decaying piers on which much of the park would be built. "Piers rot," explains Lieber, "and it's expensive to repair them." The practice of ignoring essential expenses until the last minute, says Lieber, "goes back to the days of Robert Moses, when you estimated the cost of a project at $50 million, even though you knew it would really be $100 million. Then once you got started, it was impossible to stop."[16]

In the case of Brooklyn Bridge Park, the underestimations were more often a reflection of wishful thinking on the part of park advocates, determined to devise an affordable and self-sustainable model for the park's realization, than of deliberate miscalculation. The revised financial projections for the project were real, however, and it would be left to the city, the community, and the BBP Corporation to agree on a plan for funding and maintaining the park.

ON MARCH 22, 2010, less than two weeks after the announcement of the agreement by which the state ceded primary control of Brooklyn Bridge Park to the city, Mayor Bloomberg and Governor Paterson announced the opening of the nine-acre Pier 1—the first section of the piers to be officially opened to the public (figures 27 and 28). More than twenty-five years had passed since Anthony Manheim's initial conversations, in 1983, with the Port Authority over the disposition of the Brooklyn piers; sixteen years since the Brooklyn Bridge Park Coalition and the borough's elected officials had endorsed the "13 Guiding Principles" for the park's development; and twelve years since the formation of the Local Development Corporation (LDC).

The highly publicized ceremony was held at the top of the Granite Prospect, a set of granite steps built into the landscaped lawns of Pier 1 above the promenade and native salt marsh that sprawled along the waterfront (figure 29). "The piers along the Brooklyn waterfront south of the Brooklyn Bridge have for years sat vacant or underutilized," said Mayor Bloomberg, "acting as a barrier between Brooklyn residents and their waterfront. Today we're removing that barrier and reclaiming this waterfront for Brooklynites and New Yorkers."[17] "All of our hard work has clearly paid off," continued Bloomberg, "There are few places in the city, even in the world, where you'll find a setting like this one on Pier 1."[18]

"It was such a pivotal moment for the park," recalls Jennifer Klein, director of capital operations for Brooklyn Bridge Park. "You didn't see the rain; all you saw was greenery. It was a feeling of pride and accomplishment and excitement about what we'd done and what we were going to continue to be doing. Being a part of that from the moment of taking down those sheds to the earth rising up to thirty feet, it was such an incredible high, a feeling of elation and satisfaction that we finally did it. And not only that—it came out so beautifully."[19]

IN ADDITION TO INCREASING SUPPORT for the park in the media and among the public, the opening of Pier 1 had a positive effect on the relationship

FIGURE 27 (TOP)

Looking toward Pier 1 from the Brooklyn Bridge, ca. 1980.

COURTESY OF BROOKLYN BRIDGE PARK CONSERVANCY

FIGURE 28 (BOTTOM)

Looking toward Pier 1 from the Brooklyn Bridge, 2010.

© ETIENNE FROSSARD, NEW YORK, N.Y.

FIGURE 29

Opening day of Pier 1, March 22, 2010. Pictured are (*left to right*) City Council member Brad Lander, State Senator Daniel Squadron, Public Advocate Bill de Blasio, Assemblywoman Joan Millman, Deputy Mayor for Economic Development Robert Lieber, Mayor Michael Bloomberg, Parks Commissioner Adrian Benepe, Governor David Paterson, Empire State Development Corporation executive director Peter Davidson, Brooklyn Bridge Park Conservancy chairman David Kramer, Brooklyn Bridge Park Development Corporation president Regina Myer, Brooklyn Bridge Park Conservancy executive director Nancy Webster, Brooklyn Borough President Marty Markowitz.

between the Conservancy and the BBP Corporation, the leaders of which gradually assumed a more collaborative and less competitive approach to supporting the park's development.

"It was so important to have [the Conservancy and the BBP Corporation] working together," says former Parks Commissioner Adrian Benepe. "The board members and the staff leadership of both organizations were crucial. One always had a sense that the neighborhood was there to back you up when you were dealing with certain elected officials. And that was essential. I was extremely impressed by the loyalty and the decency that they all displayed. They were able to marginalize some of the opposition to the park through their patient and persistent decency. It was the same polite stubbornness that stopped Robert Moses from ramming the BQE [Brooklyn–Queens Expressway] down Brooklyn Heights."[20]

WHILE THE BBP CORPORATION and the Conservancy were focused on the construction and programming of Brooklyn Bridge Park, and as the public was discovering and flocking to the newly opened Pier 1, the debate over housing in the park continued among the leadership of the Cobble Hill, Willowtown, and Dumbo (Down Under the Manhattan Bridge Overpass) neighborhood associations.

On November 30, 2010, the Committee on Alternatives to Housing held the first of two public hearings. Convened by BBP Corporation president Regina Myer, the hearings held by the CAH were open to the public and designed to provide greater opportunities for the local community in decisions about the role of residential development in the financial model for the park. State Senator Daniel Squadron and Assemblywoman Joan Millman had opposed housing in the park in their election campaigns of 2008 and were instrumental in the creation of the committee. In addition to their pivotal roles on the committee, the two state legislators had each been granted veto power over the proposed residential developments for John Street and Pier 6 by the MOU. Along with many of the local residents in attendance, Squadron and Millman were joined in their opposition to housing by City Council members Brad Lander and Steve Levin, both of whom spoke out forcefully against the existing plans for residential development in the park.[21]

Based on the public input from the hearings and the guidance of Bay Area Economics, a consulting firm, the CAH released the "Draft Report on Alternatives to Housing" the following February, which, after months of deliberations and private negotiations with the Bloomberg administration, eventually resulted in a modification of the revenue-generation plan for the park's capital maintenance (a projected $16 million a year by the time of the agreement).

Under the revised plan, publicly endorsed by Mayor Bloomberg on August 1, 2011, the city reaffirmed $55 million in capital funding in fiscal year 2013 for the construction of Pier 2 and the John Street site. According to the revised MOU, the size of the John Street development would be reduced based on the identification of $750,000 in new, annual revenues by the CAH. It also stipulated that the additional planned housing on Pier 6 would be potentially reduced or eliminated through a possible future rezoning and sale of other sites currently owned by the Watchtower Bible and Tract Society of New York. In the event that alternative funds were not secured by the end of 2013, the BBP Corporation would be allowed to issue requests for proposals for the residential development of the two Pier 6 properties.[22]

The revised MOU relieved State Senator Daniel Squadron from the ominous prospect of exercising the veto of residential housing that he had been granted by the agreement of March 2010 between the city and the state. Without an alternative plan, the sudden removal of either the Pier 6 or the John Street residential project from the park financing plan would have undermined the ability to cover the cost of the park's maintenance. With no revenue-generation proposal for the park's maintenance in place, the city would almost certainly have shelved its plan for the construction of Pier 2, placing the realization of the entire park in jeopardy. Vetoing housing at the time would have ultimately resulted in

the depiction of Squadron and his fellow state legislator Joan Millman
(in the event that she also chose to veto the proposed housing) as ob-
structionists to the park. "What this agreement does," explained Squadron at the time, "is propose a new, broader-base model—not as extreme
as the plan that we're changing, but a way to build a great new park in
tough times."[23]

The revised MOU represented a win–win scenario for the Bloomberg
administration, since it stipulated that either alternative funds for the
park's maintenance would be in place by the two-year deadline or that
the BBP Corporation would be allowed to proceed with the Request for
Proposals (RFP) process for the Pier 6 properties as originally planned.
In a statement released to the press following the signing of the revised
MOU, Mayor Bloomberg praised the agreement. "Our goal when we took
control of the piers was to transform them into one of the world's great
waterfront parks," he said, "and this agreement will enable us to realize
that vision in its entirety."[24]

In addition to the potential reductions in the size of the residential
developments, the deadline of January 1, 2014, represented a symbolic
victory for housing opponents, as December 31, 2013, was the final day of
the final term of Mayor Michael Bloomberg. Activists in the anti-housing
movement regarded the Bloomberg administration as the driving force
behind the proposed residential development in the park. Many local
housing opponents reasoned that, even if the Watchtower Society failed
to sell enough real estate before 2014 to substantially reduce the proposed developments at Pier 6, the newly elected mayor, whatever his or
her party affiliation or development policies, would inevitably be more
sympathetic to their concerns than had Bloomberg.

"Judi [Francis, of the Brooklyn Bridge Park Defense Fund] disagrees,"
acknowledged Cobble Hill anti-housing activist Dorothy Siegel, "but I'll
take my chances with the next mayor. Will the next mayor want to build
housing at [Pier 6]?"

"Daniel Squadron and Joan Millman were able to potentially eliminate three-quarters of the housing in the park," Siegel continued. "If
Squadron had vetoed the plan, we would have lost the recreation and
the $11 million that the mayor cut [which is now restored because of the
deal]. The city would not have been obligated to do any more work in the
park."[25]

Consistent with her uncompromising response to earlier negotiations and decisions on the role of housing in the park, Francis was unimpressed with the agreement that Squadron and Millman had achieved
with the Bloomberg administration. "In today's secret, back-room deal,

Mayor Bloomberg exacted a high ransom from Brooklynites," she said. "We urge Senator Squadron to use his veto over housing. Period."[26]

ON AUGUST 24, 2010, the BBP Corporation issued an RFP for "adaptive use" of the Tobacco Warehouse in the area between the Brooklyn and Manhattan Bridges. On November 17, it announced that it had entered into a provisional sublease agreement with St. Ann's Warehouse, a Dumbo-based theater and performance group that occupied a space across Water Street from the Tobacco Warehouse that was scheduled for immediate demolition and redevelopment by Two Trees Management Company, to redevelop the property. The announcement provoked an immediate rift between local neighborhood activists, who questioned the appropriateness of locating an art and performance space in the midst of the park, and the Brooklyn Academy of Music and other representatives of the local arts community, which welcomed the use of the historic structure to support the arts and theatrical performance.

In addition to the public's concern about the appropriate use of the space, some residents voiced suspicion that the selection of St. Ann's Warehouse had been determined in advance by the Bloomberg administration. In a public hearing in November, City Council member Steve Levin, Assemblywoman Joan Millman, and Congresswoman Nydia Velázquez questioned the fairness of the process through which the RFPs had been developed and issued and the lack of public participation in the proceedings.[27]

The controversy intensified on March 21, 2011, when the Brooklyn Heights Association (BHA), the Fulton Ferry Landing Association, the New York Landmarks Conservancy, and the Preservation League of New York State filed a federal lawsuit against the National Park Service, Secretary of the Interior Kenneth Salazar, and the BBP Corporation, asserting that the public authorities had illegally "de-mapped" the property from federally protected parkland (based on the spurious claim that both the Tobacco Warehouse and the Empire Stores had been "inadvertently overlooked" in the original federal map of the parkland) and requesting an injunction against the proposed development until the matter could be resolved by the court.[28]

On April 8, 2011, District Court Judge Eric Vitaliano ruled that the Tobacco Warehouse could not be converted or renovated for use by St. Ann's Warehouse. The project would remain on hold for an entire year, while the Bloomberg administration and the BBP Corporation negotiated a deal with several of the plaintiffs in the lawsuit, with the assistance of State Senator Daniel Squadron and Assemblywoman Joan Millman. According to the terms of the agreement, the city donated a one-acre parcel beneath the Manhattan Bridge to be used as parkland, in exchange for which St. Ann's Warehouse, which had signed a three-year lease with another location following the ruling of 2011, was allowed to proceed with its plans for construction on the site.

As a part of that settlement," explains BBP Corporation president Regina Myer, "the city designated two out-parcels from the city inventory, the Department of Environmental Protection Building and the Department of Transportation paint-storage building, as replacement parcels. This brings the Dumbo waterfront into park use, which was always a dream, and we're finally going to achieve that."[29]

"The agreement does two things," explained Squadron, who also ensured that the agreement included the creation of a special citizens committee to monitor the development of the site. "It's a sign that process and community involvement are critical as we build open space, and it's an expansion of a park that is transforming the city."[30]

WITH THE FUNDING AND GOVERNANCE ISSUES that had stalled the park's progress in the past finally resolved, the task facing Regina Myer and the BBP Corporation was to maintain the momentum provided by the gala ribbon cutting at Pier 1.

One of the biggest challenges facing Myer and the BBP Corporation during the early years of construction and site openings involved the need to establish site control on Pier 6 and the inter-bridge area. "Piers 1 to 5 were all pretty clean in terms of site control," Myer recalls, "but Pier 6 was not in our control. We had approvals [to develop the site], but we didn't have site control until the summer of 2009. American Stevedoring was still here. We entered into contracts before we actually had site control, which is a little risky. The underlying property is owned by the city of New York and was under a lease through the Port Authority to American Stevedoring. We had to convince the Port Authority to tell its tenant to vacate."[31]

Even though Empire–Fulton Ferry State Park had been included in the master plan for Brooklyn Bridge Park, the acquisition of the nine-acre park in the inter-bridge area on June 20, 2009, was also a major challenge.[32] According to Myer, "The state Parks Department didn't give Empire–Fulton Ferry to the Brooklyn Bridge Park Development Corporation until 2010. I worked on that with [New York State Office of Parks, Recreation and Historic Preservation commissioner] Carol Ash. We

worked together, with the understanding that BBP Corporation would build this park and move ahead with a great design that was funded."[33]

As Myer explains, developer David Walentas, who during the previous three decades had orchestrated the conversion of Dumbo into a thriving commercial and residential center while frequently finding his plans at odds with those of park advocates, provided the funding to upgrade the Empire–Fulton Ferry section of the park (figure 30). "This was at the same time that David and Jane [Walentas] were talking about their decision to build the carousel [the $9 million, twenty-six-foot glass pavilion that would later be erected near the shoreline at the Empire–Fulton Ferry section of the park]," recalls Myer, "and we made it as a condition to accept the donation of the carousel as long as the park would be upgraded. The Empire–Fulton Ferry State Park had been nominally upgraded for community use—and it was beloved, I should add—but it was never really designed. It had a boardwalk and a shoreline and a lot of scraggly grass and bushes. We convinced David and Jane to give us the money [approximately $4.5 million] to upgrade this park, which was wonderful, because it was not in our budget.

"The last little thing we achieved under site control was at the foot of Old Fulton Street [in the inter-bridge area]," remembers Myer. "When I started at BBP, the plan included parking right in front of Fulton Landing pier. So I convinced all my friends in city government to move the street line, which improved the Water Street and the Old Fulton Street connection."[34]

In addition to the site-control negotiations, another important piece of the puzzle for Myer and the BPP Corporation involved the purchase of a 1.5-acre site on John Street in Dumbo from Consolidated Edison. "Before my time," says Myer, "there had been a promise from Con Edison that they would donate the site to the park, and that promise went away for reasons unbeknownst to me. Because we have a development site in that part of the park as well, we were able to simultaneously put the development site out to bid while we had an option with Con Edison. So once we had a happy bidder [Alloy Development/Monadnock Development Partnership], we were able to pay Con Edison."[35] The combined purchase agreement and development contract, which was announced by Mayor Bloomberg on July 21, 2013, resulted in a forty-two-unit building, along with ground-floor retail space and the Brooklyn Children's Museum annex, that will generate revenue for the ongoing operation and maintenance of the park.[36]

WITH SITE CONTROL FINALLY ESTABLISHED throughout the park property by the summer of 2010 and much of the funding for development in place, the construction of the park continued to proceed unabated. "There was no doubt in my mind when we started the project that we did not have time to rethink the overall design," explains Myer of her urgency to push the project forward. "We had to start building. People would come up to me and say, 'What about this?' and 'What about that?' But if we opened up one area for discussions, then something else would be opened and then something else and then something else. And then the whole thing would unravel, and it would take another four years to get started again. We had a very strong sense of urgency that we just had to build it. We had a beautiful design; we should just build it."[37]

The opening of Pier 1 was followed in June 2010 by the partial opening of Pier 6—which features beach-volleyball courts, concessionaires, a dog run, a marsh garden and other native plantings, four themed playgrounds, and the landing for the Governor's Island Ferry—with additional sections of Pier 1 (3.5 acres) (figures 31–33) and Pier 2 (1.4 acres) following later in the year. Pier 5, which opened on December 13, 2012, features three athletic fields, two playgrounds, and a picnic area. The opening of the upland landscape and greenway of Piers 3 and 4 on November 13, 2013, provided the final connection in the park's continuous greenway, along with the Granite Terrace and the first of the park's "sound-attenuating" hills. Pier 2, which opened in the spring of 2014, features a

FIGURE 31 (TOP)
Snowy evening on Pier 1, 2014.
© JULIENNE SCHAER

FIGURE 32 (BOTTOM)
View of the Brooklyn Bridge from the lawn on Pier 1, 2014.
© JULIENNE SCHAER

wide variety of athletic and recreational facilities, including five full-size basketball courts, a roller rink, six handball courts, three shuffleboard courts, two bocce courts, a workout area, and a half-acre of open turf (figures 34 and 35). The northern end of the park was completed in the fall of 2015 with the opening of the John Street section, which features a 13,000-square-foot lawn and tidal pathways and a bouldering wall, and 99 Plymouth Street, home of the Conservancy's Environmental Education Center, as well as an art gallery and a community space. At the park's southern border, the remaining section of Pier 6 opened in October 2015 and features a central wildflower meadow and large lawns.

Each phase of construction, explains Myer, proceeded almost exactly according to the design in the General Project Plan of 2005. "There were so many aspects of the design that were just about perfect," says Myer. "We have made improvements and refinements in certain areas such as the Pier 3 Greenway Terrace and the Pier 5 uplands, and we eliminated the water-garden system and hedged in the lawns on Pier 6, making it a much more open meadow instead, and we're still working on the Squibb Bridge. But Pier 2 changed only very, very slightly, and the playgrounds on Pier 6 and Pier 5 are exactly as designed in 2005."[38]

FIGURE 34 (TOP)
Pier 2 and uplands, ca. 1980.
COURTESY OF BROOKLYN BRIDGE PARK CONSERVANCY

FIGURE 35 (BOTTOM)
Basketball court on Pier 2, 2014.
© JULIENNE SCHAER

FIGURE 36
Main Street Playground, 2012.
© JULIENNE SCHAER

LIKE SEPTEMBER 11 and the financial crash of 2008, a catastrophic event would soon potentially threaten the park: on October 28 and 29, 2012, Hurricane Sandy pounded the southern shoreline of New York City and Long Island, causing extensive flooding and wind damage to the entire area and resulting in the closing of bridges and tunnels and the suspension of subway service between Manhattan and Brooklyn. Brooklyn Heights and the other upland areas in Brooklyn were spared the brunt of the storm, but the Dumbo neighborhood in the inter-bridge area and the entire west Brooklyn waterfront were overwhelmed by flooding and violent winds, with major sections of the park immersed beneath several feet of saltwater.

A few days after the storm, Regina Myer reported that the park had suffered "some flood damage," including the lawns, the Swing Valley Playground on Pier 6, and the Main Street and Pier 1 playgrounds (figure 36), along with substantial damage to the electrical and irrigation equipment throughout the park. Although all the park's lawns were temporarily closed while the water subsided, the rest of the park was reopened within days, including the greenways, the dog runs, the picnic areas, and the ferry to Governor's Island.[39]

As the storm raged across the city, Jane's Carousel, built in 1922 and housed in a $9 million, twenty-six-foot glass pavilion that had been erected on a three-foot platform thirty feet from the shoreline, was soon engulfed by the huge waves that pounded the waterfront. "Soon, with the constant waves crashing against the building, I could see the floor getting wet and the water rising," said David Walentas, owner of Two Trees Management, who watched the storm's progress with his wife and fellow donor, Jane, from the fifteenth-story window of their Dumbo apartment. "The only lights were in the carousel building. Then at 10:30 they started to flicker. And I said, 'oh no.' That's when it was over."[40]

All told, Jane's Carousel suffered $300,000 worth of damage from the storm, requiring the replacement of the structure's electrical system and warped floors. Remarkably, the carousel and its irreplaceable wooden horses, along with the glass pavilion designed by Jean Nouvel, were left completely unscathed (figure 37). After having successfully endured Hurricane Sandy, however, the Walentases decided to be better prepared for the next storm. The following year, the pavilion was equipped with an "Aqua Fence" system, consisting of forty-four four-foot-high watertight panels that can be deployed to protect the property within three hours of a storm prediction.[41]

The reopening of the park was expedited by the park's maintenance team, as well as the rapid response of the Conservancy, which quickly mobilized and delivered 100 volunteer workers to clean and remove debris from the perimeter of the park and along the sidewalks.

The good news for the BBP Corporation, the Conservancy, and other supporters and users of Brooklyn Bridge Park was how minimal the damage to the park had been. When the floodwaters finally subsided, the

FIGURE 37
Jane's Carousel, 2014.
© JULIENNE SCHAER

shoreline and most of the structures on the piers and the upland area were still intact, and the wide variety of plant life along the waterfront, in the words of park designer Michael Van Valkenburgh, "never missed a beat."

"All the while that we were starting to work on Brooklyn Bridge Park," explains Van Valkenburgh, "we were a year or two further along in a major park on the West Side of Manhattan, Segment 5 of Hudson River Park. We were keenly aware through that project the assured likelihood that there would be a saline inundation and there would be consequences around it. So a year or two earlier, we had kind of moved through all these issues in the Hudson River project."[42]

According to Van Valkenburgh, the resilience of the shoreline in the midst of the powerful winds and violent floodwaters was attributable to the original park design, the planning of which had anticipated the inevitability of strong winds and saltwater flooding. "We replaced the existing vertical concrete walls and relieving platforms with riprap," explains Van Valkenburgh, "which is basically just very large loose rocks, like you might see all along the New England coastline.... The new edges are more porous, they let the seawater pass right through, and they move slightly to absorb impacts, rather than cracking and falling apart, even with unusually high volumes of water" (figure 38).

The resilience of the plant life after prolonged exposure to saltwater, Van Valkenburgh explains, "can be attributed to prior research both in plant studies we conducted and in visits to sites we knew had experi-

enced flooding. In elevated areas we used species that are proven toler-
ant of salt on their stems and leaves, but, interestingly, saline tolerance
on those parts of plants is different than the impacts of saltwater soaking
the root zone."[43]

DURING THIS INTENSIVE PERIOD of construction and openings throughout
Brooklyn Bridge Park, the Conservancy and the BBP Corporation maintained a shared commitment to active programming in the park, sponsoring regular activities and events designed to draw people to the site.
With major sections of the park now open to the public, the "interim
activities" of the past, which were designed to give visitors a preview of
the park before its construction, have been replaced by official activities
and events, with the benefit of facilities, displays, continuous walkways,
and landscaped open spaces that dramatically enrich the beauty and the
accessibility of the park.

In the summer of 2015 alone, the Conservancy, working in partnership with the BBP Corporation and other organizations, facilitated
hundreds of individual activities and events, many of them on a weekly
basis, in the areas of arts and entertainment, recreation, fitness, and education and environmental awareness, along with regular opportunities
for volunteer service. Highlights in the area of entertainment and arts
programming included the ongoing outdoor film series (figure 39), the
Metropolitan Opera and Jazzmobile concerts, music and dance parties,

FIGURE 39
**Thursday-night movies
on Pier 1, 2012.**
© ETIENNE FROSSARD,
NEW YORK, N.Y.

FIGURE 40 (TOP)

Public kayaking at Pier 2, 2014.

© ETIENNE FROSSARD, NEW YORK, N.Y.

FIGURE 41 (BOTTOM)

Pilates at Empire-Fulton Ferry Park, 2012.

© ETIENNE FROSSARD, NEW YORK, N.Y.

literary events and book readings, family festivals, theater, and art installations.

Recreational and fitness activities included family field days, volleyball leagues and workshops, free public kayaking (figure 40), soccer leagues, a Pop-Up Pool on the uplands of Pier 2, and regular classes in yoga (figure 41), hip-hop aerobics, and senior fitness, along with regular access to the park's soccer fields, basketball and handball courts, roller rink, children's playgrounds, and bike paths.

Educational and environmental activities included walking tours and lectures on various aspects of the waterfront's history (profiles of the original Native American population and early settlers, historical battles, the Underground Railroad, and the Golden Age of Brooklyn), on-site examinations of the flora and fauna on the site (native plants, wildflowers, and pollinators), seining workshops focusing on the marine life of the East River (figure 42), and on-site presentations of the design and construction of the park. The Conservancy's extensive school-based education program, awarded start-up funding by Congresswoman Nydia Velázquez in 2008, utilizes the park as a living classroom. More than 12,000 students in 2015, two-thirds of them from Title I schools, attended classes for hands-on learning about the park's design and environment.

IN THE SIX YEARS since the opening of Pier 1, Brooklyn Bridge Park has continued to expand, with the gradual addition of the remaining waterfront and upland regions stretching for 1.3 miles and including 65 acres along the shore of the East River. In 2015, the park featured expansive lawns, waterfront promenades, a greenway, innovative playgrounds, playing fields, basketball and handball courts, natural habitats, and direct access to the water. In 2015, approximately 150,000 people visited the park each weekend, including visitors from the adjacent neighborhoods, the rest of the borough and the city, and the United States and the world. From 2011 to the present, Brooklyn Bridge Park and the design team of Michael Van Valkenburgh Associates have received numerous awards and formal recognitions, including the Municipal Art Society's MASterworks Award for Best Urban Landscape, the American Planning Association's National Planning Excellence Award for Urban Design, the American Institute of Architects' New York State Community Development Award, and the Silver Medal of the Rudy Bruner Award for Urban Excellence.

The park's design and use as a source of waterfront recreation are informed by both its past and its future. Plying a route similar to that of the eighteenth- and nineteenth-century Catherine Ferry, the East River Ferry began service to lower Manhattan from the foot of Old Fulton Street in June 2011. The Empire Stores, long abandoned, are seeing new life as a retail and commercial center. Vestiges of the pier sheds from the 1950s were left intact to define play areas and provide shelter for park visitors. Re-created areas of marshland and coastal forest that informed the landscape of the original Lenape settlers provide a natural habitat for the bird and marine life that flourished in the preindustrial waterfront. And the park's natural edges allow access to the East River, creating the city's sixth borough—New York Harbor—and providing a new recreation source for a citizenry beginning to discover and embrace the fact that they live on islands.

Although the park wins accolades from urban-planning and architectural organizations, while also attracting enthusiastic visitors from across the city and country, the main revenue stream for its maintenance and operations—housing—continues to be a source of controversy.

In May 2014, the BBP Corporation released an RFP for the park's final two residential-development sites at Pier 6. Contrary to anti-housing activists' hopes that Mayor Michael Bloomberg's successor would be more sympathetic to their point of view and scale back the developments at the southern end of the park, the administration of Mayor Bill de Blasio, a longtime park supporter dating from his tenure in the New York City Council, instead announced that not only would the properties go forward, but they would be reworked to include up to one-third of their square footage as affordable housing. "We want neighborhoods that reflect the diversity of this borough and meet the needs of its working people. This is a unique opportunity to see this world-class park built and sustained for decades to come, while at the same time providing opportunities for middle-income workers who increasingly cannot afford to live in Brooklyn. It's a win–win for the community and the borough," said Deputy Mayor for Housing and Economic Development Alicia Glen.[44] The Pier 6 RFP revitalized the debate about the inclusion of housing in the park's financial model, with a newly formed group, People for Green Space Foundation, arguing that the park was overfunded and filing an Article 78 suit against the project. As part of the suit's settlement in 2015, the BBP Corporation was required to seek a modification to the park's General Project Plan from the Empire State Development Corporation (ESDC) to accommodate the affordable housing.[45]

At Pier 1, another newly formed group, Save the View Now (STVN), filed a lawsuit to halt the construction of the hotel and the residential building at the northern end of the park, with an accompanying affidavit from Otis Pearsall, one of the original vice chairs of the Piers Committee of the Brooklyn Heights Association (BHA), claiming that the two buildings' heights violated the park's planning documents. Following the dismissal of the suit, STVN, joined by the BHA, filed a subsequent suit alleging that a portion of the Pier 1 building intrudes into the Brooklyn Heights Promenade's legally protected Scenic View District and is awaiting final judgment.

In spite of the resistance of some community members to Brooklyn Bridge Park's financial model, the project's commitment to self-sustainability is representative of a growing and successful trend among urban parks. Faced with tightened city budgets, an increasing number of parks—including the Presidio in San Francisco, Millennium Park in Chicago, and Hudson River Park and Battery Park City Park in New York—strive to be self-sustaining from revenue derived on the park footprint. Others, notably Central Park and Prospect Park, rely on private philanthropy for their maintenance and operations funding.

With the self-sustaining principle enshrined in the "13 Guiding Principles," Brooklyn Bridge Park's limited housing plan will provide the park's maintenance and operations funding, including the refurbishment of the more than 17,000 wooden piles that support the park's massive piers. While the Port Authority's original proposal, from 1988, for the piers included 3 million square feet of housing and commercial development spread across the piers, with only five acres of open space, the park's current plan calls for only four acres of new construction to support and sustain eighty-five acres of open space, including an estimated $250 million to $300 million in marine infrastructure repair over the next fifty years.

Before leaving office, Mayor Bloomberg increased the city's capital commitment to Brooklyn Bridge Park by an additional $45 million to fund Pier 3, bringing New York City's total contribution to the park to $150 million, along with New York State's initial contribution of $65 million. Currently, uncommitted capital funding to complete the park stands at $31.5 million—$9 million for Brooklyn Bridge Park Plaza (the namesake of the park) and $22.5 million for the innovative floating walkways, which have not yet been approved by the New York State Department of Environmental Conservation. As a sign of his own commitment to the project, Mayor Bill de Blasio (a longtime park supporter but with different priorities from his predecessor) retained in his first budget the $40 million allocated by Bloomberg for the park.

Brooklyn Bridge Park was formed by a multitude of voices, each creating and responding to different challenges and pressure points along the way. There was the small group of dedicated activists who originally pushed the city government to adapt its vision for the waterfront. There were the government leaders who worked cooperatively with the growing citizens' movement over time, providing crucial funding and a plan to pay for the park's maintenance and operations through future years. There were the engineers, architects, and planners who synthesized the hopes of different communities and melded that vision with the physical and financial realities of the park's waterfront location. And, finally, the Brooklyn Bridge Park Corporation and the Brooklyn Bridge Park Conservancy have worked together in recent years to manage, respectively, the construction, financing, and public programming of the park. Over three decades, the collective contributions of each of different groups have coalesced into a spectacular, beloved, extraordinary public space enjoyed by more than 1 million visitors each year.

ENTERING THE PARK AT JAY STREET, just north of the Manhattan Bridge, visitors stroll by a gently sloping lawn and cross pedestrian bridges over newly created salt-marsh areas on their way to the Manhattan Bridge Anchorage and the Conservancy's Environmental Education Center, which features an interactive park model and a 250-gallon East River aquarium.

Empire–Fulton Ferry at Water Street, between the towering columns of the Brooklyn and Manhattan Bridges, features a graceful lawn and a winding boardwalk along the waterfront that includes the original Fulton Ferry Landing, where Robert Fulton once launched his steam-powered ferry boat. The twenty-six-foot pavilion housing Jane's Carousel stands just a short walk inland from the waterfront, its almost century-old horses constantly occupied by both children and adults. To the north of the park are the impressive Empire Stores and the Tobacco Warehouse, new home to noted theater company St. Ann's Warehouse. Near the entrance to the south are an ice cream parlor and a cluster of outdoor eateries, where visitors can sit and enjoy refreshments while taking in the spectacular views of the bridges, New York Harbor, and the Manhattan skyline.

Walking south to the 9.5-acre Pier 1, the largest of the park's piers, visitors pass beneath the shadows of the Brooklyn Bridge and along the section of the park that will eventually be Brooklyn Bridge Plaza, the public courtyard that will connect the southern and northern ends of the park. Pier 1 includes a playground at the northern edge, three spacious lawns, a maze of tree-lined pathways, a water garden beside the walkway, and a salt marsh at its southern border. Just upland from the pier, the Granite Prospect, a staircase built from slabs of granite salvaged from the reconstructed Roosevelt Island Bridge, rises above the shoreline.

Pier 2, one of the main centers of active recreation for the park, features five acres of courts for basketball, bocce, and handball and pulses with young athletes playing pick-up games and enjoying the pier's inline-skating rink.

A short walk south of the Pier 2 recreational complex, the Pier 3 upland features the sweeping Granite Terrace, with dozens of four- to five-foot granite blocks rising out of a shady cluster of evergreens and flowering trees, and the large "sound-attenuating hill" that runs along the length of the pier area and separates the parkland from the busy traffic of Furman Street and the Brooklyn–Queens Expressway, reducing noise levels by up to 75 percent. A great lawn just south of the Granite Terrace provides visitors with direct views of Governor's Island and the Statue of Liberty in New York Harbor, while a smaller lawn to the north provides a clear view of the Manhattan skyline.

Gazing toward Pier 3 itself, visitors will notice that the last of the park's five-acre piers is undergoing construction. Next to the construction barges lining the pier's northern side, a red-and-white dive flag signals that divers are underwater, conducting the yearlong repair of the pier's aging wooden piles.

FIGURE 43
**Kayaking from the beach
on Pier 4, 2014.**
© ETIENNE FROSSARD,
NEW YORK, N.Y.

Pier 4 is the site of the park's only sunken pier, the abandoned posts and platforms crumbling into the East River. The upland area has been converted into a sand beach, where visitors can either take a barefoot stroll or launch nonmotorized boats into the East River's still waters (figure 43). Just to the south, a marina is located in the open water between Piers 4 and 5.

Pier 5, another of the park's main recreational areas, is devoted to large, multi-purpose playing fields, which can be adapted for soccer, rugby, lacrosse, flag football, and ultimate Frisbee, along with two playground areas for children. The pier's playing fields are flanked by bleachers and benches that are lined by shade sails on the pier's northern and southern sides, providing a comfortable and relaxing spot for diners, spectators, and visitors in need of a rest from the long stroll along the waterfront (figure 44). In addition to the playing fields, Pier 5 features the Picnic Peninsula, the park's largest picnic area, with tables made from salvaged wood and shaded by large, weather-resistant umbrellas (figure 45). At the far end of the pier, a thirty-foot-wide promenade offers a panoramic view of the skyline and the river, from New York Harbor to the south to the Brooklyn and Manhattan Bridges to the north.

Looking east, toward the Brooklyn–Queens Expressway, visitors will note the construction of Pier 5's uplands, which will feature a small boathouse, the park's maintenance and operations building,

FIGURE 44
Playing fields on Pier 5, 2013.
© JULIENNE SCHAER

FIGURE 45
Picnic Peninsula on
Pier 5, 2014.
© ETIENNE FROSSARD,
NEW YORK, N.Y.

additional lawns and picnic areas, and the continuation of the park's sound-attenuating berm.

At the end of the 1.3-mile stroll along the waterfront, Pier 6 features several large destination playgrounds, beach-volleyball courts (figures 46 and 47), a rooftop café, a dog run, large lawns, a flower field, and a ferry dock with regular service to nearby Governor's Island.

NOT SURPRISINGLY, the early leaders of the movement to create Brooklyn Bridge Park take pride in its ultimate realization, though, given the controversies and compromises that have accompanied the site's development over the past thirty years, some express disappointment with specific features of the park's design and the time it has taken to complete.

"It's the most marvelous thing that ever happened for Brooklyn Heights," insists Benjamin Crane, whose passionate speech at a BHA meeting in 1987 in the undercroft of the First Unitarian Church inspired many local residents to rally around the notion of a park on the piers. "I had my brief cameo and then I moved on, but people like Otis Pearsall, John Watts, and Tony Manheim—they were the ones who hung in there and made it happen. It was Tony, I would say, who kept the flag waving until the governor and the mayor finally decided to fund it. And now you have this marvelous park that's used by everyone."[46]

FIGURE 46 (TOP)

Playground on Pier 6, 2013.

COURTESY OF NANCY WEBSTER

FIGURE 47 (BOTTOM)

Beach-volleyball court on Pier 6, 2014.

© ALEXA HOYER

While still an enthusiastic supporter of the park, Otis Pearsall worries that years may have been wasted because of the "doctrinaire mind-set of the 'pure park' advocates" in the early park movement. In their detailed monograph on the early years of the Piers Committee, "The Origins of Brooklyn Bridge Park: 1986–1988," Pearsall and original committee chair Scott Hand observe the striking similarities in the balance between housing and open space in Scheme D (Intensive Mixed-Use Development), illustrated in Buckhurst Fish Hutton Katz's report *The Future of the Piers* in 1987, and the current design of Brooklyn Bridge Park, openly wondering if the park might have been constructed a decade earlier if the Piers Committee and Community Board 2 had not "flatly rejected any notion of compromise" with the Port Authority on the issue of housing.

A decade and a half after his forced departure from the leadership of the park movement, former Brooklyn Bridge Coalition executive director Anthony Manheim is far more sanguine about the extensive time line for the park's creation. "I do take comfort," explains Manheim, "from learning from Morrison Heckscher's recent book on the history of Central Park that it took more than thirty years, start to finish, to complete. We're only in thirty years at this point. So we're still a little ahead of the game."[47]

For Manheim—who served on the Community Advisory Council for the park and who continues to lend his sympathy and advice, though not his direct support, to the anti-housing movement—the park's realization is a vital example of the impact that ordinary citizens can have on their communities. "What keeps me going," explains Manheim, "is what has always kept me going—the illusion that an individual or a group of individuals from the community can make a difference. Certainly in retrospect, a lot of what's good about Brooklyn Bridge Park—and most of it *is* good—is the result of what the community has done. There are still opportunities for improvement and change in the park, which I would love to see, but there's still time for that."[48]

"A lot of people thought that this was just a bunch of white guys trying to protect their views [of the Manhattan skyline]," agrees former Coalition co-chair Tom Fox. "In fact, people actually said that. But it wasn't that at all. These were people who saw a tremendous opportunity to do something special for the entire city and who came up with a vision of how to do it. It took a few years to define that opportunity and to clarify the vision, but it has pretty much stayed together for the past twenty-five years, and I think that's a testament to the public participation that went into it and all of the tribulations that this thing has been through and with all the good things and the bad things that people have said about it. It's continued to change and adapt over time in response to the changing economic, social, physical parameters around it. That's what's made it work. And I'm proud to have been a part of that."[49]

For Adrian Benepe, who served as New York City Parks Commissioner from 2002 to 2012 and now promotes the public–private partnership model for park development nationwide on behalf of the Trust for Public Land, Brooklyn Bridge Park is one of the crowning achievements of contemporary urban design, not simply for Brooklyn and New York City but also for the entire nation. "I have a personal deep love and affection for this park," acknowledges Benepe. "It feels like one of my kids, and I'm delighted with how well it's done. As I travel around the country, people are goo-goo eyed about Brooklyn Bridge Park. You can literally hear an audible gasp when you show them pictures of the site. It's already inspiring other cities around the country not to try to top it but simply to equal it."[50]

"Brooklyn Bridge Park is a great example of what's possible when government works with committed members of the community toward a common goal," explains former mayor Michael Bloomberg, "and Regina Myer and everyone at the Conservancy deserve a lot of credit. The park transformed a neglected piece of our city's past into a beautiful space for all New Yorkers to share, and brought new life and energy to the waterfront. It gave people a new way to experience our historical harbor and skyline, and reconnected people with our natural heritage. It also brought new investment to the neighborhood, and millions of visitors who support local businesses. Innovative parks make cities stronger, better places to live and work—and that's why cities around the world are looking to Brooklyn Bridge Park for inspiration."[51]

For Candace Damon, a partner at Hamilton, Rabinovitz & Alschuler (HR&A), the realization of Brooklyn Bridge Park serves an instructive model for community input in urban-development policy. "Brooklyn Bridge Park is looked to across the country as an example of what community-based planning led by civic groups can accomplish," insists Damon, who played an integral role in both the initial LDC board meetings and the public charrettes for the park. "There may have been more acrimony than one usually experiences in the planning and design of this park, but there has also been far more success. Yeah, we yelled at each other a lot, and most people don't yell at each other. But most people don't get their parks built. I truly believe that this is among the most successful and earliest examples of community-based park planning and creation."[52]

"When Olmsted built Central Park and Prospect Park, the city was overwhelming," explains John Alschuler, chairman of HR&A. "Horses

were everywhere. The streets were mud. We desperately needed parks as places of self-conscious pastoral repose where we could get away from the city. But we have a very different city now. It's much more garden-like. And that allows parks to be much more urban and active. I think what's really striking about Brooklyn Bridge Park is how instructive it has been in its integration of those two elements: the pastoral and the urban (figure 48). That to me is one of the great contributions of the park to the great wave of park making that we're experiencing today."[53]

For Conservancy and LDC board member David Offensend, Brooklyn Bridge Park not only is an important achievement for the residents of Brooklyn but also represents the beginning of a citywide and nationwide movement to reclaim urban waterfronts for the public. "In the long term," says Offensend, "I really hope that this is a step along the way to recapturing more of New York's shoreline for parks. We've got Hudson River Park. We've got Brooklyn Bridge Park. There are other park-type things going up in Greenpoint and other parts of the city. I would love to see the entire shoreline of New York be park.

"I think the success of this park," continues Offensend, "will absolutely inspire others to pick up the tools to make other parts of the shoreline of New York into parks. They'll be encouraged by our success and Hudson River Park's success. And the third one will be easier. And the fourth one will be easier than that. We've engaged a huge number of people who appreciate how beautiful these shoreline parks can be. That's the future. It's so many people. It's not this small group. It's an army now."[54]

"Brooklyn Bridge Park is a true democratic park for all New Yorkers," echoes former Conservancy executive director Marianna Koval, "in both the process of its creation and the product itself. People responded to our call, 'If you come, we will build it,' and came by the tens of thousands throughout the first decade of the twenty-first century. Many, many people invested themselves; gave their money; volunteered their services; talked in their churches, synagogues, and schools; and never stopped talking to elected officials who had to deliver and build the park. This is how you bring change in the city of New York."[55]

WITH THE CITIZENS OF NEW YORK CITY awakening to the recreational benefits of its harbor, the competing interests of open space, development, industry, and shipping continue to vie for space along the shoreline beyond the confines of Brooklyn Bridge Park. Residents of northern Brooklyn are urging the city to fulfill its commitment to build Bushwick Inlet Park, a promise made during the residential rezoning of Williamsburg in 2005. At Sunset Park in southern Brooklyn, the city is investing more than $100 million in the Brooklyn Army Terminal, and the privately owned Industry City hopes to replicate the success of the Brooklyn Navy Yard as a hub for light manufacturing. Nearby, the city is seeking to revive the adjacent South Brooklyn Marine Terminal for shipping and marine cargo, while just to the south visitors enjoy the sports fields, restored wetlands, and harbor views of Bush Terminal Piers Park. In no-longer-sleepy Red Hook, an Italian development company, Estate Four, has announced plans for a 12-acre, 1.2-million-square-foot mixed-use project on the waterfront called the Red Hook Innovation District, which will include offices, shops, performance spaces, and a promenade.

In the autumn of 2014, thirty years after the Port Authority of New York and New Jersey announced its development plans for Piers 1–6, the Citizens Budget Commission, a well-regarded nonprofit organization that researches and advocates for sound city and state budget and management practices, released a report on Piers 7–12, immediately south of Brooklyn Bridge Park. The report recommended that the Port Authority, which is losing $30 million a year on the underused marine terminals, close and sell the piers, repurposing them as a combination of open space with residential and commercial development. While the Port Authority has not commented publicly on its plans or the report, the stage is almost certainly set for a reprisal of the public-advocacy movement—with all the negotiations, conflicts, compromises, and, hopefully, promise—that resulted in Brooklyn Bridge Park.

NOTES

INTRODUCTION

1 Anthony Manheim, interview by David Shirley, February 25, 2014.

2 Ken Fisher, interview by David Shirley and Nancy Webster, August 25, 2014.

3 Adrian Benepe, interview by David Shirley and Nancy Webster, September 22, 2014.

4 Herbert C. Kraft, *The Lenape or Delaware Indians: The Original People of New Jersey, Southeastern New York State, Eastern Pennsylvania, Northern Delaware and Parts of Western Connecticut* (South Orange, N.J.: Seton Hall University Museum, 1996), 22.

5 Ibid.

6 Russell Shorto, *The Island at the Center of the World: The Epic Story of Dutch Manhattan and the Forgotten Colony That Shaped America* (New York: Vintage, 2004), 10.

7 William Everdell, *Rowboats to Rapid Transit: A History of Brooklyn Heights* (New York: Brooklyn Heights Association, 1973), 24.

8 Walt Whitman, "Crossing Brooklyn Ferry," in *The Complete Poems*, ed. Francis Murphy (New York: Penguin, 1986), 190.

9 Landmark's Preservation Commission, *Dumbo Historic District Designation Report* (New York: Landmark's Preservation Commission, December 18, 2007), 4–19.

10 Thomas Dongan, The Dongan Charter of the City of New York, April 27, 1686, University of California Digital Library, 3.

11 "To Extend the Piers: New York Dock Company Begins Work in the East River," *Brooklyn Eagle*, June 15, 1902.

12 "Tracks, Piers, Factories and Warehouses Make the Wheels of Industry Go 'Round," *Brooklyn Eagle*, May 30, 1936.

13 Sherill Tippins, *The February House: The Story of W. H. Auden, Carson McCullers, Paul and Jane Bowles, Benjamin Britten and Gypsy Rose Lee, Under One Roof in Wartime America* (New York: Houghton Mifflin, 2005).

14 Truman Capote, *A House on the Heights* (New York: Little Bookroom, 2001), 15.

15 Hart Crane, *The Letters of Hart Crane, 1916–1932*, ed. Brom Weber (Berkeley: University of California Press, 1965), 183.

16 Hart Crane, "Poem to the Bridge," in *The Collected Poems*, ed. Waldo Frank (New York: Liveright, 1966), 46.

17 "Heights Demand Rights: Dr. Hillis Speaks Plainly Before New Association for Transit Benefits," *New York Times*, February 6, 1910.

18 Empire State Development Corporation, "Historical Resources," in *Final Environmental Impact Statement* (New York: Empire State Development Corporation, December 9, 2010).

19 Port Authority of New York and New Jersey, "Port Authority Marks 50th Anniversary of Containerization at Port of New York and New Jersey," press release, April 25, 2006.

20 Beatrice Pineda Revilla, "History of the Fulton Ferry Landing," The Sixth Borough: Redefining Brooklyn's Waterfront: Brooklyn Heights, http://thesixthborough.weebly.com/history-of-fulton-ferry-landing.html.

21 New York City, Office of Downtown Brooklyn Development, *Fulton Ferry* (New York, April 1972), 6–7.

22 Deborah Hoffman, "The Revitalization of Fulton Ferry: A Prototype of Waterfront Development in New York City" (New York University, Graduate School of Public Administration, July 1979), 21.

23 Edward C. Burks, "A Touch of Frisco in Brooklyn Is Proposed," *New York Times*, December 19, 1971.

24 Hoffman, "Revitalization of Fulton Ferry," 39.

25 Landmarks Preservation Commission, *Fulton Ferry Historic District Designation Report* (New York: Landmarks Preservation Commission, 1977), 18.

26 "The River Café Celebrates Its 30th Birthday," *Brooklyn Daily Eagle*, July 5, 2006.

27 Allan Kozinn, "Bargemusic: Brooklyn's Floating Concert Site," *New York Times*, August 31, 1990.

28 Hoffman, "Revitalization of Fulton Ferry," 41–45.

ONE. WHAT SHALL WE DO WITH THE PIERS?

1 Peter Hall, *Cities of Tomorrow: An Intellectual History of Urban Planning and Design Since 1880* (New York: Wiley, 2014), 419.

2 Robert F. Wagner, Jr., "New York City Waterfront: Changing Land Use and Prospects for Urban Development," in *Urban Waterfront Lands*, ed. Committee on Urban Waterfront Lands (Washington, D.C.: National Academy of Sciences, 1980), 81.

3 Edward A. Gargan, "City Will Revamp Ports Department," *New York Times,* July 9, 1981.

4 Quoted in ibid.

5 Quoted in William G. Blair, "No. 1 No More, New York Port Seeks to Strengthen Its Role," *New York Times*, September 24, 1982.

6   Quoted in ibid.

7   Martin Gottlieb, "City's First Major Fish Plant Set for Brooklyn Waterfront," *New York Times*, December 10, 1983.

8   Eric Lipton, "New York Port Hums Again, with Asian Trade," *New York Times*, November 22, 2004.

9   Gottlieb, "City's First Major Fish Plant."

10 Anthony Manheim, interview by David Shirley, February 25, 2014.

11 Ibid.

12 Ibid.

13 William G. Blair, "Brooklyn Heights Plan Is Disputed," *New York Times*, July 9, 1984.

14 Manheim, interview.

15 Brooklyn Heights Association, board of governors, Annual Meeting minutes, May 10, 1984.

16 Manheim, interview.

17 Fred Bland, interview by David Shirley, May 1, 2014.

18 Manheim, interview.

19 Bland, interview.

20 Robert Parsekian, interview by David Shirley and Nancy Webster, September 17, 2014.

21 New York City Public Development Corporation, *New York City's Waterfront: A Plan for Development: A Report to the Mayor by the New York City Public Development Corporation* (New York: Public Development Corporation, July 1986), 1.

22 Ibid.

23 Brooklyn Heights Association, board of governors, Annual Meeting minutes, February 5, 1985.

24 Manheim, interview.

25 Brooklyn Heights Association, board of governors, Annual Meeting minutes, Spring 1985.

26 Richard D. Lyons, "In Brooklyn Heights, a Spotlight on 87 Neglected Acres," *New York Times,* October 27, 1985.

27 In 1981, New York governor Hugh Carey announced plans for the construction of a six-lane, 4.2-mile highway along the Hudson River in Manhattan to replace the crumbling West Side Highway. "Westway," as the proposed project was called, would run underground through a landfill extension into the Hudson River, with high-rise residential towers and a state park constructed on the land above. The $1.7 billion project encountered opposition from various quarters, however, including New York City mayor Edward Koch, who suggested that the money be used to upgrade the city's subway system, and U.S. District Judge Thomas P. Griesa, who ruled that the proposed construction would threaten the Hudson River's native aquatic species. By 1984, the project had been abandoned.

28 "Mammoth Waterfront Development Might Connect Montague Street with the Piers," *Brooklyn Heights Paper*, October 19–25, 1985.

29 "A Hotel on the Piers? Not a Good Idea; Access to the Piers: The Next Controversy," *Brooklyn Heights Press & Cobble Hill News*, October 31, 1985.

30 George Winslow, "Will Watchtower Development Block Our Promenade View?" *Brooklyn Heights Press & Cobble Hill News*, October 31, 1985.

31 Scott M. Hand and Otis Pratt Pearsall, "The Origins of Brooklyn Bridge Park, 1986–1988," 2014, 14, published on the Brooklyn Historical Society catablog, http://brooklynhistory.org/docs/OriginsBrooklynBridgePark.pdf.

32 Brooklyn Heights Association, board of governors, Annual Meeting minutes, February 5, 1985.

33 Halcyon Ltd., *Development Concepts for the Brooklyn Piers* [Halcyon Report] (Hartford, Conn.: Halcyon, 1985), 3.

34 Philip LaRocco and Alair Townsend, press release, February 18, 1986.

35 Hand and Pearsall, "Origins of Brooklyn Bridge Park," 29.

36 Brooklyn Heights Association, newsletter, Spring 1986.

37 Brooklyn Heights Association, board of governors, Annual Meeting minutes, February 25, 1986.

38 Quoted in Tracy Garrity, "Piers Panel Throws Cold Water on Halcyon Port Authority Study, and Opts for Housing," *Phoenix*, February 25, 1986.

39 Ibid.

40 Brooklyn Heights Association, newsletter, Fall 1986.

41 New York City Public Development Corporation, *New York City's Waterfront.*

TWO. FIGHTING BACK

1 Scott M. Hand and Otis Pratt Pearsall, "The Origins of Brooklyn Bridge Park, 1986–1988," 2014, published on the Brooklyn Historical Society catablog, http://brooklynhistory.org/docs/OriginsBrooklynBridgePark.pdf

2 Anthony Manheim to Scott Hand and Otis Pearsall, July 28, 1986.

3 Anthony Manheim, interview by David Shirley, February 25, 2014.

4 New York City Public Development Corporation, *New York City's Waterfront: A Plan for Development: A Report to the Mayor by the New York City Public Development Corporation* (New York: Public Development Corporation, July 1986), 4.

5 Henrik Krogius, "Will Brooklyn Heights Lose Sight of Manhattan's Skyline?" [editorial], *New York Times*, August 30, 1986.

6 Quoted in Brooklyn Heights Association, newsletter, Fall 1986.

7 Scott M. Hand to Earl Weiner, May 16, 1986.

8 Brooklyn Heights Association, newsletter, Fall 1986.

9 Otis Pratt Pearsall, memorandum, July 14, 1986.

10 Scott M. Hand to Philip LaRocco, August 25, 1986.

11 Benjamin Crane, interview by David Shirley, February 28, 2014.

12 Ibid.

13 Judy Stanton to Scott M. Hand, February 6, 1987.

14 Quoted in Brooklyn Heights Association, board of governors, Annual Meeting minutes, February 24, 1987.

15 "Brooklyn Heights Association Pier Study Revealed Before Audience of 400," *Brooklyn Heights Press & Cobble Hill News,* February 26, 1987.

16 Quoted in ibid.

17 Ibid.

18 Buckhurst Fish Hutton Katz, *The Future of the Piers: Planning and Design Criteria for Brooklyn Piers 1–6* (New York: Bruckhurst Fish Hutton Katz, 1987), 37–38.

19 Irene Janner, interview by David Shirley and Nancy Webster, August 26, 2014.

20 Richard D. Lyons, "In Brooklyn Heights, a Spotlight on 87 Neglected Acres," *New York Times*, October 27, 1985; Anthony Manheim to Scott Hand and Otis Pearsall, July 22, 1986.

21 Quoted in June Rogoznica, "Power Players of the Waterfront," *Round-Up*, May 1987.

22 Thomas J. Lueck, "Office Growth Slows in Boroughs Outside of Manhattan," *New York Times*, February 15, 1988.

23 Quoted in Alan S. Oser, "Perspectives: Downtown Brooklyn; Coming Attractions for Office Tenants," *New York Times*, June 28, 1987.

24 Quoted in Richard D. Lyons, "Fair Winds Building for East River Plans," *New York Times*, August 8, 1987.

25 Buckhurst Fish Hutton Katz, *Future of the Piers*.

26 James Nolan, "New York Legislators Charge Agency Is Partial to New Jersey Piers," *Journal of Commerce*, September 21, 1987.

27 Quoted in ibid.

28 Quoted in ibid.

29 Hand and Pearsall, "Origins of Brooklyn Bridge Park," 56.

30 Quoted in "Hearing Debates Waterfront Planning." *Brooklyn Publication*, October 3–9, 1987.

31 Hand and Pearsall, "Origins of Brooklyn Bridge Park," 58.

32 Ibid., 59.

33 New York City Charter, "City Planning," section 197-c: Uniform Land Use Review Procedure (New York, July 2004); Thomas L. Waite, "Pier Redevelopment Plans Stir Concern," *New York Times*, May 1, 1998.

34 Manheim, interview.

35 Quoted in "Port Authority Pier Planning Action Angers Heights Group," *Brooklyn Paper*, October 24–30, 1987.

36 Quoted in ibid.

37 Quoted in Oser, "Perspectives: Downtown Brooklyn."

38 Quoted in "Port Authority Moves to Open Pier Area for Development," *Phoenix*, January 11, 1988.

39 Community Board 2, Planning and District Development Committee, meeting minutes, November, 11, 1988, in Hand and Pearsall, "Origins of Brooklyn Bridge Park," 61.

40 Ibid.

41 Quoted in "Port Authority in Port Biz for Bucks, Pier Panel Quizzes Agency Reps on 'Profit' Motive," *Brooklyn Paper*, January 23–29, 1988.

42 Hand and Pearsall, "Origins of Brooklyn Bridge Park," 63.

43 Anthony Manheim to Scott Hand, Otis Pratt Pearsall, et al., November 10, 1986.

44 Manheim, interview.

45 Hand and Pearsall, "Origins of Brooklyn Bridge Park," 65.

46 Quoted in Brooklyn Heights Association, board of governors, Annual Meeting minutes, February 9, 1988.

47 Janner, interview.

48 Hand and Pearsall, "Origins of Brooklyn Bridge Park," 78.

49 David W. Dunlap, "Brooklyn's Waterfront: Two Visions of a Compelling Vista," *New York Times*, August 19, 1988.

50 Henrik Krogius, "Port Authority Plan Would Turn Heights into 'Thoroughfare'; No Vision, Only Profit Motive; Port Authority Serves Its Ledgers More Faithfully Than It Serves the Public," *City Express*, July 28, 1988.

51 Hand and Pearsall, "Origins of Brooklyn Bridge Park," 78.

52 David Offensend, interview by David Shirley, May 2, 2014.

53 Dunlap, "Brooklyn's Waterfront."

54 Hand and Pearsall, "Origins of Brooklyn Bridge Park," 82.

55 Ibid., 85.

56 Community Board 2, Planning and District Development Committee, meeting minutes, November, 28, 1988, in ibid., 88.

THREE. THE COALITION

1 Scott M. Hand and Otis Pratt Pearsall, "The Origins of Brooklyn Bridge Park, 1986–1988," 2014, 89, published on the Brooklyn Historical Society catablog, http://brooklynhistory.org/docs/OriginsBrooklynBridgePark.pdf.

2 Ibid.

3 Oliver E. Allen, *The Tiger: The Rise and Fall of Tammany Hall* (Cambridge, Mass.: Da Capo Press, 1963), 29.

4 Robert Caro, *The Power Broker: Robert Moses and the Fall of New York* (New York: Vintage , 1974), 18–19.

5 Ibid.

6 Ibid.

7 Max Frankel, "Moses Fences Off Park Area at Night," *New York Times*, April 24, 1956.

8 "Moses Yields to Mothers; Drops Tavern Parking Lot," *New York Times*, July 18, 1956.

9 Martin L. Schneider, *Battling for Brooklyn Heights: The Fight for New York's First Historic District* (New York: Brooklyn Heights Association, 2009), 30–37.

10 Marianne Moore, "The Camperdown Elm," in *The Poems of Marianne Moore*, ed. Grace Shulman (New York: Penguin, 2005), 354.

11 Maria Favuzzi, interview by David Shirley, February 25, 2014.

12 Quoted in Hand and Pearsall, "Origins of Brooklyn Bridge Park," 20.

13 Favuzzi, interview.

14 Ibid.

15 Tom Fox, interview by David Shirley, February 27, 2014.

16 Ibid.

17 Ibid.

18 Ibid.

19   Ibid.

20   Favuzzi, interview.

21   Mark Baker, interview by David Shirley, February 26, 2014.

22   Brooklyn Heights Coalition, board of governors, Annual Meeting minutes, April 8, 1990.

23   Quoted in David W. Dunlap, "Port Authority Endorses Plan for Pier," *New York Times*, December 4, 1989.

24   Quoted in ibid.

25   Quoted in ibid.

26   Quoted in ibid.

27   Howard Golden to Mario Cuomo, December 4, 1989.

28   Ibid.

29   Mary B. W. Tabor, "Despite Opposition, Agency Plans to Sell Brooklyn Piers to Private Developer," *New York Times*, April 3, 1992.

FOUR. THE "13 GUIDING PRINCIPLES"

1   Brooklyn Heights Association, newsletter, Winter 1989.

2   Tom Fox, interview by David Shirley, February 27, 2014.

3   Mark Baker, interview by David Shirley, February 26, 2014

4   Maria Favuzzi to Anthony Manheim and Tom Fox, March 11, 1990.

5   Anthony Manheim to the Brooklyn Bridge Park Coalition Working Group, October 14, 1990.

6   Ibid.

7   Brooklyn Chamber of Commerce, Waterfront Development Committee, meeting minutes, March 25, 1991.

8   Michael Clark, "Piers Study Says Park Plan Too Costly," *Brooklyn Paper*, January 18–24, 1991.

9   Quoted in ibid.

10   Anthony Manheim to John Watts, Tony Schnadelbach, et al., January 22, 1991.

11   Alan Breznick, "Golden Pushes Plan for Brooklyn Piers," *Crain's New York Business*, April 22, 1991.

12   Quoted in ibid.

13   Quoted in ibid.

14   Quoted in Joanne Nicolas, "Elected Officials Close to a Deal on Piers 1–5," *Brooklyn Heights Press & Cobble Hill News*, April 1, 1991.

15   Quoted in Anne-Marie Otey, "Borough Hall Likes 'Reuse' Option, Wants Authority to Pursue Plan: Golden to Meet with Officials on Piers Proposal," *Phoenix*, April 4, 1991.

16   Quoted in Breznick, "Golden Pushes Plan for Brooklyn Piers."

17   Howard Golden to Anthony Manheim, April 16, 1991.

18   Quoted in Michael A. Armstrong, "Reject Piers 1–5 Options; Review Proposals from Boro Prez," *Phoenix*, April 25–May 2, 1991.

19   Anthony Manheim and Tom Fox to Howard Golden, May 21, 1991.

20   Armstrong, "Reject Piers 1–5 Options."

21 Marilyn Gelber, interview by David Shirley and Nancy Webster, August 25, 2014.

22 Ibid.

23 Quoted in Michael Clark, "Piers Players Bicker over Stalled Project," *Brooklyn Paper*, April 26–May 2, 1991.

24 Ken Fisher, interview by David Shirley and Nancy Webster, August 25, 2014.

25 Quoted in Clark, "Piers Players Bicker."

26 Quoted in ibid.

27 Ibid.

28 Anthony Manheim to John Watts, Ted Liebman, et al., memorandum, July 1991.

29 Gelber, interview.

30 Michael Clark, "Cuomo Plan Uplifts Piers Buffs," *Brooklyn Paper*, October 4, 1991.

31 Ibid.

32 Quoted in ibid.

33 Quoted in Mary B. W. Tabor, "Despite Opposition, Agency Plans to Sell Brooklyn Piers to Private Developer," *New York Times*, April 3, 1992.

34 Quoted in ibid.

35 Quoted in ibid.

36 Quoted in Mary B. W. Tabor, "Port Authority Pulls Back from Sale of Waterfront," *New York Times*, April 8, 1992.

37 Anthony Manheim to the members of the Brooklyn Bridge Park Coalition, February 4, 1993.

38 Anthony Manheim to Martin Connor and Eileen Dugan, February 19, 1993.

39 Anthony Manheim to the members of the Brooklyn Bridge Coalition, "Summary Progress Report," February 23, 1993.

40 Ibid.

FIVE. BANGING THEIR CUPS ON THE HIGH CHAIR

1 Anthony Manheim, notice of General Meeting of the Brooklyn Bridge Park Coalition, July 9, 1993.

2 Quoted in Anne-Marie Otey, "New Threat on Piers," *Phoenix*, April 16, 1992.

3 Anthony Manheim, interview by David Shirley, February 25, 2014.

4 Mark Baker, interview by David Shirley, February 26, 2014.

5 John Watts, interview by David Shirley, February 28, 2014.

6 Ibid.

7 Dennis Holt, "Brooklyn Broadside: New Park Board's Creation Stirs Historic Memories," *Brooklyn Daily Eagle*, August 1, 2010.

8 Quoted in Lynnette Holloway, "Neighborhood Report: Brooklyn Heights; Keeping a Vista View," *New York Times*, January 30, 1994.

9 Quoted in ibid.

10 Anthony Manheim to Mario Cuomo, January 7, 1994, quoted in "Residents Push State for Brooklyn Bridge Park Creation," *Brooklyn Heights Courier*, March 21–April 3, 1994.

11 "Residents Push State."

12 Quoted in ibid.

13 Watts, interview.

14 Andrew C. Revkin, "Pataki Lists Tracts to Protect," *New York Times*, November 22, 1995.

15 New York State Assembly, Office of Assemblywoman Eileen C. Dugan, "Assemblywoman Dugan and Senator Connor Secure a Half Million Dollar State Grant for the Brooklyn Bridge Park Coalition," press release, June 23, 1996.

16 David Rohde, "Neighborhood Report: Fulton Ferry; Fulton Landing Plan Rises from the Ashes for Another Try," *New York Times*, June 15, 1997.

17 Howard Golden, "Two Plans for Waterfront Are Not in Conflict" [editorial], *New York Times*, June 6, 1997.

18 Quoted in David Rohde, "It's a Park, It's a Lumberyard," *New York Times*, January 19, 1997.

19 *Brooklyn Bridge Park Coalition v. Port Authority of New York and New Jersey*, 951 F.Supp. 383 (E.D. N.Y. 1997).

20 David Rohde, "Neighborhood Report: Downtown Brooklyn/Brooklyn Heights—Update; Lumberyard Can Remain Park's Unlikely Center," *New York Times*, February 2, 1997.

21 Port Authority of New York and New Jersey, "Brooklyn—Port Authority Marine Terminal—Brooklyn Bridge Park Coalition—New Lease," board minutes, August 28, 1997.

22 Greg Brooks, interview by David Shirley and Nancy Webster, September 18, 2014.

23 Franklin Stone, interview by David Shirley and Nancy Webster, September 11, 2014.

24 Brooks, interview.

25 Brooklyn Bridge Park, Inc., "Eileen's Legacy," memorandum, April 3, 1997.

26 Anthony Manheim to Frank McNally, March 6, 1987.

27 Martin Connor, interview by David Shirley and Nancy Webster, April 24, 2015.

28 Gary VanderPutten, interview by David Shirley, April 30, 2014.

29 Amy Waldman, "Neighborhood Report: Brooklyn Waterfront; One Park, Many Squabbles," *New York Times*, January 25, 1998.

30 Ken Fisher, interview by David Shirley and Nancy Webster, August 25, 2014.

31 Baker, interview.

32 VanderPutten, interview.

33 Baker, interview.

34 Praedium Group, *Economic Viability Study: Piers Sector, Brooklyn Bridge Park* (New York: Praedium Group, February 1997), 3.

35 Brooklyn Bridge Park Coalition, "Gala 'Coming of Age' Benefit," March 29, 1997.

36 Baker, interview.

37 Ibid.

38 VanderPutten, interview.

39 Ibid.

40 Ibid.

41 Ibid.

SIX. CHANGING OF THE GUARD

1   Tensie Whelan, interview by David Shirley, February 25, 2014.

2   Fred Bland, interview by David Shirley, May 1, 2014.

3   Irene Janner, interview by David Shirley and Nancy Webster, August 26, 2014.

4   Bland, interview.

5   Whelan, interview.

6   Tom Fox, interview by David Shirley, February 27, 2014.

7   Bland, interview.

8   Henrik Krogius, "Waterfront Park: Getting Acts Together," *Brooklyn Heights Press & Cobble Hill News*, January 21, 1999.

9   Henrik Krogius, "Heights Association Questions LDC's Progress on Piers, Praises Manheim," *Brooklyn Daily Eagle*, February 1999.

10 Gary VanderPutten, interview by David Shirley, April 30, 2014.

11 Ibid.

12 Whelan, interview.

13 Ibid.

14 Ibid.

15 VanderPutten, interview.

16 Ibid.

17 Marianna Koval, interview by David Shirley, February 25, 2014.

18 VanderPutten, interview.

19 Koval, interview.

20 Brooklyn Bridge Park Conservancy [Coalition], *Waterfront Watch* 1, no. 1 (1999).

21 Brooklyn Bridge Park Conservancy, *Waterfront Watch* 1, no. 2 (1999).

22 Brooklyn Bridge Park Conservancy, *Waterfront Watch* 1, no. 3 (1999).

23 Ibid.

24 Tensie Whelan and John Watts, "Letter: Walentas' Plan 'Inappropriate,'" *Brooklyn Heights Press & Cobble Hill News*, June 17, 1999.

25 VanderPutten, interview.

26 Dennis Holt, "Fisher, Millman Join Opposition to DUMBO Plan," *Brooklyn Heights Press & Cobble Hill News*, June 3, 1999.

27 Quoted in Julian E. Barnes, "Neighborhood Report: Brooklyn Waterfront; Dueling over Dumbo: Commerce vs. Parks," *New York Times*, April 11, 1999.

28 Quoted in Thomas J. Lueck, "Unveiling a Bold Vision for Brooklyn's Waterfront," *New York Times*, May 24, 1999.

29 Tensie Whelan, "In Brooklyn, a Stunning Design That's All Wrong" [editorial], *New York Times*, May 31, 1999.

30 VanderPutten, interview.

31 Joshua Laird, interview by David Shirley and Nancy Webster, October 17, 2014.

32 Quoted in "Park Coalition Names Albert Butzel President; Changes Raise Question of Co-work with LDC," *Brooklyn Heights Press & Cobble Hill News*, October 13, 1999.

33 Koval, interview.

34 Albert Butzel, interview by David Shirley, September 12, 2014.

35 Brooklyn Bridge Park Coalition, "13 Guiding Principles to Govern Redevelopment on the Downtown Brooklyn Waterfront," June 29, 1992.

36 Joanne Witty, interview by David Shirley, October 1, 2014.

37 Ibid.

38 Quoted in "New Coalition Director Looks to Widen Piers Park Support," *Brooklyn Heights Press & Cobble Hill News*, October 20, 1999.

39 Koval, interview.

40 "New Coalition Director."

41 Witty, interview.

42 Franklin Stone, interview by David Shirley and Nancy Webster, September 11, 2014.

43 Josh Sirefman, interview by David Shirley and Nancy Webster, September 30, 2014.

44 Witty, interview.

45 Ibid.

46 Dick Dadey, interview by David Shirley and Nancy Webster, September 11, 2014.

47 Matt Urbanski, interview by David Shirley and Nancy Webster, October 15, 2014.

48 Michael Van Valkenburgh, interview by David Shirley and Nancy Webster, October 15, 2014.

49 Candace Damon, interview by David Shirley and Nancy Webster, April 17, 2015.

50 Ibid.

51 Dadey, interview.

52 Witty, interview.

SEVEN. TEARING DOWN THE BARBED WIRE

1 Mark Baker, interview by David Shirley, February 26, 2014.

2 Marianna Koval, interview by David Shirley, February 25, 2014.

3 Quoted in Brooklyn Bridge Park Conservancy, *Waterfront Matters* 2, no. 1 (2000): 1.

4 Marianna Koval, "Soapbox; An Opportunity to Seize," *New York Times*, July 2, 2000.

5 Koval, interview.

6 Dennis Holt, "Park Coalition Fundraiser Becomes a Victory Party," *Brooklyn Heights Press & Cobble Hill News*, June 15, 2000.

7 Brooklyn Bridge Park Conservancy [Coalition], *Waterfront Matters* 2, no. 2 (2000).

8 Holt, "Park Coalition Fundraiser."

9 Ken Fisher, interview by David Shirley and Nancy Webster, August 25, 2014.

10 Tom Montvel-Cohen, interview by David Shirley and Nancy Webster, October 26, 2014.

11 Koval, interview.

12 Albert Butzel, interview by David Shirley, September 12, 2014.

13 Greg Brooks, interview by David Shirley and Nancy Webster, September 18, 2014.

14 Quoted in Wendy Froede, "Let the Planning Begin! Planners, Public Draw Wish List for Heights, DUMBO Waterfront," *Park Slope Paper*, November 12, 1999.

15 Koval, interview.

16 Quoted in Julian E. Barnes, "As Some Fight a Park Plan, Its Supporters See Elitism," *New York Times*, August 16, 2000.

17 Dennis Holt, "*Times* Article Had Wrong Stress," *Brooklyn Heights Press & Cobble Hill News,* August 24, 2000.

18 Joanne Witty, interview by David Shirley, October 1, 2014.

19 Ibid.

20 Ibid.

21 Koval, interview.

22 Ibid.

23 Butzel, interview.

24 Quoted in Brooklyn Bridge Park Conservancy, *Waterfront Matters* 3, no. 1 (2001).

25 Gregg Birnbaum, "Pataki Boosts Park Plan in Slap at Giuliani," *New York Post*, January 6, 2001.

26 Martin Connor, interview with David Shirley and Nancy Webster, April 24, 2015.

27 Ibid.

28 Ibid.

29 Quoted in Nichole M. Christian, "Long a Dream, Brooklyn Park Nears Reality," *New York Times*, January 6, 2001.

30 Quoted in ibid.

31 "Mayor Giuliani Delivers Eighth and Final 'State of the City' Address," *New York Times*, January 9, 2001.

32 Koval, interview.

33 Ibid.

34 Baker, interview.

35 Quoted in Brooklyn Bridge Park Conservancy, *Waterfront Matters* 4, no. 1 (2002).

36 Joshua Laird, interview by David Shirley and Nancy Webster, October 17, 2014.

37 Brooklyn Bridge Park Conservancy, *Waterfront Matters* 4, no. 2 (2002): 11.

38 New York City, Office of the Mayor, "Mayor Michael R. Bloomberg and Governor George E. Pataki Announce Creation of Brooklyn Bridge Park," press release, May 2, 2002.

39 Dick Dadey, interview by David Shirley and Nancy Webster, September 11, 2014.

40 Koval, interview.

41 Quoted in Brooklyn Bridge Park Conservancy, *Waterfront Matters* 2, no. 3 (2002).

42 Quoted in Brooklyn Bridge Park Conservancy, *Waterfront Matters* 5, no. 2 (2002): 1.

43 Quoted in ibid.

44 Baker, interview.

45 Koval, interview.

46 Ibid.

47 Montvel-Cohen, interview.

EIGHT. THE PERFECT IS THE ENEMY OF THE GOOD

1 Brooklyn Bridge Park Development Corporation, *Brooklyn Bridge Park Civic and Land Use Improvement Project: Modified General Project Plan* (New York: Brooklyn Bridge Park Development Corporation, December 18, 2006).

2 Michael Van Valkenburgh, interview by David Shirley and Nancy Webster, October 15, 2014.

3 Henrik Krogius, "What Happened to Brooklyn Bridge Park?" *Brooklyn Daily Eagle*, September 20, 2004.

4 Dick Dadey, interview by David Shirley and Nancy Webster, September 11, 2014.

5 Quoted in "Selling Brooklyn Bridge Park" [editorial], *New York Times*, February 13, 2005.

6 Quoted in Brooklyn Bridge Park Conservancy, *Waterfront Matters* 7, no. 1 (2005).

7 Daniel Doctoroff, interview by David Shirley, May 18, 2014.

8 John Alschuler, interview by David Shirley and Nancy Webster, July 2, 2014.

9 Gary VanderPutten, interview by David Shirley, April 30, 2014.

10 Quoted in Lisa Selin Davis, "The War for Brooklyn," *TimeOut*, July 27–August 2, 2006.

11 Quoted in Elizabeth Stull, "Foes Sue to Stop the Park," *Brooklyn Heights Press & Cobble Hill News*, May 25, 2006.

12 "Judge Dismisses Brooklyn Bridge Lawsuit," *New York Sun*, November 29, 2006.

13 Adrian Benepe, interview by David Shirley and Nancy Webster, August 22, 2014.

14 Quoted in "Judge Dismisses Brooklyn Bridge Lawsuit."

15 Quoted in Davis, "War for Brooklyn."

16 Brooklyn Bridge Park Conservancy, *Waterfront Matters* 7, no. 1 (2005).

17 Koval, interview.

18 Ibid.

19 Nancy Bowe, interview by David Shirley, September 30, 2014.

20 Josh Sirefman, interview by David Shirley and Nancy Webster, September 30, 2014.

21 "Selling Brooklyn Bridge Park."

22 Brooklyn Bridge Park Conservancy, *Waterfront Matters* 9, no. 1 (2007).

23 Ibid.

24 Koval, interview.

25 David Kramer, interview by David Shirley, September 10, 2014.

26 Koval interview.

27 Quoted in "Port Authority Transfers Piers to Brooklyn Bridge Park," *Brooklyn Progress*, June–July 2006.

28 Quoted in Charles Hack, "Waterfront Park Clears Another Hurdle," *Brooklyn Daily Eagle*, June 1, 2006.

29 Benepe, interview.

30 Sirefman, interview.

31 Brooklyn Bridge Park Conservancy, *Waterfront Matters* 10, no. 1 (2008).

32 Dennis Holt, "Landmarks Commission OK's Purchase Building's Demolition," *Brooklyn Daily Eagle*, February 23, 2006.

33 Quoted in "Purchase Building Demise Angers Many," *Brooklyn Heights Courier*, February 27, 2006.

34 Joanne Witty, interview by David Shirley, October 1, 2014.

35 Van Valkenburgh, interview.

36 Matt Urbanski, interview by David Shirley and Nancy Webster, October 15, 2014.

37 "Brooklyn Bridge Park Gets New President," *Brooklyn Daily Eagle*, November 27, 2007.

38 Patricia Harris, interview by Nancy Webster, June 30, 2015.

39 Regina Myer, interview by David Shirley and Nancy Webster, August 29, 2014.

40 Ibid.

41 Ibid.

42 Quoted in Brooklyn Bridge Park Conservancy, *Waterfront Matters* 10, no. 1 (2008).

43 Sarah Portlock, "'Pop' Over," *Brooklyn Paper*, October 2, 2008.

44 Nancy Webster, interview by David Shirley, September 24, 2014.

45 Ibid.

NINE. A PARK AT LAST

1   Quoted in Stephen Witt, "New Governor Mum on Brooklyn Bridge Park—Spitzer Slaps Gag on ESDC," *Times Ledger*, January 12, 2007.

2   Charles V. Bagli, "A Warning on Governor's Island Funds," *New York Times*, March 12, 2009.

3   Quoted in Dennis Holt, "Paterson Comes to Brooklyn to Show Support for the Park," *Brooklyn Daily Eagle*, June 4, 2008.

4   Quoted in Bagli, "Warning on Governor's Island Funds."

5   Diane Cardwell, "When Parks Rely on Private Money," *New York Times*, February 5, 2010.

6   Robert Lieber, interview by David Shirley and Nancy Webster, April 27, 2015.

7   Peter Davidson, interview by David Shirley and Nancy Webster, April 27, 2015.

8   Daniel Doctoroff, interview by David Shirley, May 15, 2015.

9   Davidson, interview.

10 Ibid.

11 Lieber, interview.

12 Diane Cardwell, "State Agrees to Let the City Finish Brooklyn Bridge Park," *New York Times*, March 9, 2010.

13 New York City, Office of the Mayor, "Mayor Bloomberg, Governor Paterson, Senator Squadron and Assembly Member Millman Announce Agreement on Funding and Governance of Brooklyn Bridge Park," press release, March 10, 2010.

14 Quoted in ibid.

15 Regina Myer, interview by David Shirley and Nancy Webster, August 29, 2014.

16 Lieber, interview.

17 Quoted in "Mayor Bloomberg, Governor Paterson and Local Officials Open First Section of Brooklyn Bridge Park," State News Service, March 21, 2010.

18 Quoted in Andy Newman, "Brooklyn Bridge Park Opens, Slightly," *New York Times*, March 22, 2010.

19 Jennifer Klein, interview by David Shirley and Nancy Webster, September 17, 2014.

20 Adrian Benepe, interview by David Shirley and Nancy Webster, September 22, 2014.

21 "Brooklyn Bridge Park Financing Alternatives Studies," CityRealty: New York City Real Estate, CityRealty.com.

22 Brooklyn Bridge Park, Committee on Alternatives to Housing, Memorandum of Understanding, August 1, 2011.

23 Quoted in Lisa W. Foderaro, "Housing Deal Ensures Park in Brooklyn Will Expand," *New York Times,* August 1, 2011.

24 Quoted in ibid.

25 Quoted in Mary Frost, "Opposition Coalition Split on Housing Deal," *Brooklyn Daily Eagle*, August 4, 2011.

26 Quoted in ibid.

27 Claude Scales, "Tobacco Warehouse Meeting Marked by Controversy," *Brooklyn Heights Blog*, November 16, 2010.

28 Rich Calder, "Judge Rips Bldgs. Boot," *New York Post*, July 13, 2011.

29 Myer, interview.

30 Quoted in Lisa W. Foderaro, "Deal Allows Development in Brooklyn Bridge Park," *New York Times*, May 22, 2012.

31 Myer, interview.

32 New York State, Office of the Governor, "Governor Paterson Announces Major Step for Brooklyn Bridge Park," press release, June 20, 2009.

33 Myer, interview.

34 Ibid.

35 Ibid.

36 New York City, Office of the Mayor, "Mayor Bloomberg Announces Approval of Development That Will Allow for Expansion and Funding of Brooklyn Bridge Park," press release, July 21, 2013.

37 Myer, interview.

38 Ibid.

39 Matthew Parker, "Brooklyn Bridge Park Post-Hurricane Update from Regina Myer," *Brooklyn Heights Blog*, November 3, 2012.

40 Quoted in Matthew DeLuca, "Jane's Carousel Survives a Very Close Call with Hurricane Sandy," *Daily Beast*, November 1, 2012.

41 Sasha Goldstein, "Jane's Carousel in Brooklyn Bridge Park Made Safe from Another Hurricane Sandy," *Daily News,* September 18, 2013.

42 Michael Van Valkenburgh, interview by David Shirley and Nancy Webster, October 15, 2014.

43 Michael Van Valkenburgh, "Perspective: How My Firm Saved Brooklyn Bridge Park from Sandy's Fury," *Innovation by Design*, October 25, 2013.

44 Quoted in Brooklyn Bridge Park Corporation, "BBP Releases RFP for Residential Development at BBP That Will Provide Affordable Housing and Funding for Park," press release, May 13, 2014.

45 Josh Barbanel, "For Brooklyn Park, an Agreement That's a Bridge Too Far," *Wall Street Journal*, February 26, 2016.

46 Benjamin Crane, interview by David Shirley, February 28, 2014.

47 Morrison Hecksher, *Creating Central Park* (New York: Metropolitan Museum of Art, 2008); Anthony Manheim, interview by David Shirley, February 25, 2015.

48 Manheim, interview.

49 Tom Fox, interview by David Shirley, February 27, 2014.

50 Benepe, interview.

51 Michael R. Bloomberg, written interview by David Shirley and Nancy Webster, July 2015.

52 Candace Damon, interview by David Shirley and Nancy Webster, April 17, 2015.

53 John Alschuler, interview by David Shirley and Nancy Webster, July 2, 2015.

54 David Offensend, interview by David Shirley, May 2, 2014.

55 Marianna Koval, interview by David A. Shirley, February 25, 2014.

BIBLIOGRAPHY

ARTICLES AND BOOKS

Allen, Oliver E. *The Tiger: The Rise and Fall of Tammany Hall*. Boston: Da Capo Press, 1993.

Armstrong, Michael A. "Reject Piers 1–5; Review Proposals from Boro Prez." *Phoenix*, April 25–May 2, 1991.

Bagli, Charles V. "A Warning on Governor's Island Funds." *New York Times*, March 12, 2009.

Bahrampour, Tara. "Metro Briefing." *New York Times*, November 1, 2000.

Barbanel, Josh. "For Brooklyn Park, an Agreement That's a Bridge Too Far." *Wall Street Journal*, February 26, 2016.

Barnes, Julian E. "As Some Fight a Park Plan, Its Supporters See Elitism." *New York Times*, August 16, 2000.

——. "Neighborhood Report: Brooklyn Waterfront; Dueling over Dumbo: Commerce vs. Parks." *New York Times*, April 11, 1999.

Birnbaum, Gregg. "Pataki Boosts Park Plan in Slap at Giuliani." *New York Post*, January 6, 2001.

Blair, William G. "Brooklyn Heights Plan Is Disputed." *New York Times*, July 9, 1984.

——. "No. 1 No More, New York Port Seeks to Strengthen Its Role." *New York Times*, September 24, 1982.

Breznick, Alan. "Golden Pushes Plan for Brooklyn Bridge Piers." *Crain's New York Business*, April 22, 1991.

Brooklyn Bridge Park Conservancy [Coalition]. *Waterfront Matters* 1, no. 1 (1999).

——. *Waterfront Matters* 1, no. 2 (1999).

——. *Waterfront Matters* 1, no. 3 (1999).

——. *Waterfront Matters* 2, no. 1 (2000).

——. *Waterfront Matters* 2, no. 2 (2000).

——. *Waterfront Matters* 2, no. 3 (2000).

——. *Waterfront Matters* 3, no. 1 (2001).

——. *Waterfront Matters* 4, no. 1 (2002).

——. *Waterfront Matters* 4, no. 2 (2002).

——. *Waterfront Matters* 5, no. 2 (2002).

——. *Waterfront Matters* 7, no. 1 (2005).

——. *Waterfront Matters* 9, no. 1 (2007).

——. *Waterfront Matters* 10, no. 1 (2008).

"Brooklyn Bridge Park Financing Alternatives Studies." CityRealty: New York City Real Estate, December 2, 2010. CityRealty.com.

"Brooklyn Bridge Park Gets New President." *Brooklyn Daily Eagle*, November 27, 2007.

Brooklyn Historical Society. "Brooklyn Heights Association Pier Study Revealed Before Audience of 400." *Brooklyn Heights Press & Cobble Hill News*, February 26, 1987.

Calder, Rich. "Judge Rips Bldgs. Boot." *New York Post*, July 13, 2011.

Capote, Truman. *A House on the Heights*. New York: Little Bookroom, 2001.

Cardwell, Diane. "State Agrees to Let the City Finish Brooklyn Bridge Park." *New York Times*, March 9, 2010.

——. "When Parks Rely on Private Money." *New York Times*, February 5, 2010.

Caro, Robert. *The Power Broker: Robert Moses and the Fall of New York*. New York: Vintage, 1974.

Christian, Nichole M. "Long a Dream, Brooklyn Park Nears Reality." *New York Times*, January 6, 2001.

Clark, Michael. "Cuomo Plan Uplifts Piers Buffs." *Brooklyn Paper*, October 4, 1991.

——. "Piers Players Bicker over Stalled Project." *Brooklyn Paper*, April 26–May 2, 1991.

——. "Piers Study Says Park Plan Too Costly." *Brooklyn Paper*, January 18–24, 1991.

Craft, Herbert C. *The Lenape or Delaware Indians: The Original People of New Jersey, Southeastern New York State, Eastern Pennsylvania, Northern Delaware and Parts of Western Connecticut*. South Orange, N.J.: Seton Hall University Museum, 1996.

Crane, Hart. *The Letters of Hart Crane, 1916–1932*. Edited by Brom Weber. Berkeley: University of California Press, 1965.

——. "Proem to the Bridge." In *The Collected Poems*, edited by Waldo Frank, 46. New York: Liveright, 1966.

Davis, Lisa Selin. "The War for Brooklyn." *TimeOut*, July 27–August 2, 2006.

DeLuca, Matthew. "Jane's Carousel Survives a Very Close Call with Hurricane Sandy." *Daily Beast*, November 1, 2012.

Dunlap, David W. "Brooklyn's Waterfront: Two Visions of a Compelling Vista." *New York Times*, August 19, 1988.

——. "Port Authority Endorses Plan for Pier." *New York Times*, December 4, 1989.

Everdell, William. *Rowboats to Rapid Transit: A History of Brooklyn Heights*. New York: Brooklyn Heights Association, 1973.

Foderaro, Lisa W. "Deal Allows Development in Brooklyn Bridge Park." *New York Times*, May 22, 2012.

——. "Housing Deal Ensures Park in Brooklyn Will Expand." *New York Times,* August 1, 2011.

Frankel, Max. "Moses Fences Off Park Area at Night." *New York Times*, April 24, 1956.

Froede, Wendy. "Let the Planning Begin! Planners, Public Draw Wish List for Heights, DUMBO Waterfront." *Park Slope Paper*, November 12, 1999.

Frost, Mary. "Opposition Coalition Split on Housing Deal." *Brooklyn Daily Eagle*, August 4, 2011.

Gargan, Edward A. "City Will Revamp Ports Department." *New York Times*, July 9, 1981.

Garrity, Tracy. "Piers Panel Throws Cold Water on Halcyon Port Authority Study, and Opts for Housing." *Phoenix*, February 25, 1986.

Golden, Howard. "Two Plans for Waterfront Are Not in Conflict" [editorial]. *New York Times*, June 6, 1997.

Goldstein, Sasha. "Jane's Carousel in Brooklyn Bridge Park Made Safe from Another Hurricane Sandy." *Daily News,* September 18, 2013.

Gottlieb, Martin. "City's First Major Fish Plant Set for Brooklyn Waterfront." *New York Times*, December 10, 1983.

Hack, Charles. "Waterfront Park Clears Another Hurdle." *Brooklyn Daily Eagle*, June 1, 2006.

Hall, Peter. *Cities of Tomorrow: An Intellectual History of Urban Planning and Design Since 1880*. Hoboken, N.J.: Wiley, 2014.

Hand, Scott M., and Otis Pratt Pearsall. "The Origins of Brooklyn Bridge Park, 1986–1988." 2014. Published on the Brooklyn Historical Society catablog. http://brooklynhistory.org/docs/OriginsBrooklynBridgePark.pdf.

"Hearing Debates Waterfront Planning." *Brooklyn Publication*, October 3–9, 1987.

"Heights Demand Rights: Dr. Hillis Speaks Plainly Before New Association for Transit Benefits." *New York Times*, February 6, 1910.

Holloway, Lynette. "Neighborhood Report: Brooklyn Heights; Keeping a Vista View." *New York Times*, January 30, 1994.

Holt, Dennis. "Brooklyn Broadside: New Park Board's Creation Stirs Historic Memories." *Brooklyn Daily Eagle*, August 1, 2010.

——. "Fisher, Millman Join Opposition to DUMBO Plan." *Brooklyn Heights Press & Cobble Hill News*, June 3, 1999.

——. "Landmarks Commission OK's Purchase Building's Demolition." *Brooklyn Daily Eagle*, February 23, 2006.

——. "Park Coalition Fundraiser Becomes a Victory Party." *Brooklyn Heights Press & Cobble Hill News*, June 15, 2000.

——. "Paterson Comes to Brooklyn to Show Support for the Park." *Brooklyn Daily Eagle*, June 4, 2008.

——. "*Times* Article Had Wrong Stress." *Brooklyn Heights Press & Cobble Hill News*, August 24, 2000.

"A Hotel on the Piers? Not a Good Idea; Access to the Piers: The Next Controversy." *Brooklyn Heights Press & Cobble Hill News*, October 31, 1985.

"Judge Dismisses Brooklyn Bridge Lawsuit." *New York Sun*, November 29, 2006.

Koval, Marianna. "Soapbox: An Opportunity to Seize." *New York Times*, July 2, 2000.

Kozinn, Allan. "Bargemusic: Brooklyn's Floating Concert Site." *New York Times,* August 31, 1990.

Krogius, Henrik. "Heights Association Questions LDC's Progress on Piers, Praises Manheim." *Brooklyn Daily Eagle*, February 1999.

——. "Port Authority Plan Would Turn Heights into 'Thoroughfare'; No Vision, Only Profit Motive; Port Authority Severs Its Ledgers More Faithfully Than It Serves the Public." *City Express*, July 28, 1988.

——. "Review and Comment: Waterfronts." *Brooklyn Heights Press & Cobble Hill News*, June 17, 1999.

——. "Waterfront Park: Getting Acts Together." *Brooklyn Heights Press & Cobble Hill News*, January 21, 1999.

——. "What Happened to Brooklyn Bridge Park?" *Brooklyn Daily Eagle*, September 20, 2004.

——. "Will Brooklyn Heights Lose Sight of Manhattan's Skyline?" [editorial]. *New York Times*, August 30, 1986.

Lipton, Eric. "New York Port Hums Again, with Asian Trade." *New York Times*, November 22, 2004.

Lueck, Thomas J. "Office Growth Slows in Boroughs Outside of Manhattan." *New York Times*, February 15, 1988.

——. "Unveiling a Bold Vision for Brooklyn's Waterfront." *New York Times*, May 24, 1999.

Lyons, Richard D. "Fair Winds Building for East River Plans." *New York Times*, August 8, 1987.

——. "In Brooklyn Heights, a Spotlight on 87 Neglected Acres." *New York Times*, October 27, 1985.

"Mammoth Waterfront Development Might Connect Montague St. with the Piers." *Brooklyn Heights Paper*, October 19–25, 1985.

"Mayor Bloomberg, Governor Paterson and Local Officials Open First Section of Brooklyn Bridge Park." State News Service, March 21, 2010.

"Mayor Giuliani Delivers Eighth and Final 'State of the City' Address." *New York Times*, January 9, 2001.

Moore, Marianne. "The Camperdown Elm." In *The Poems of Marianne Moore*, edited by Grace Shulman, 354. New York: Penguin, 2005.

"Moses Yields to Mothers; Drops Tavern Parking Lot." *New York Times*, July 18, 1956.

"New Coalition Director Looks to Widen Piers Park Support." *Brooklyn Heights Press & Cobble Hill News*, October 20, 1999.

Newman, Andy. "Brooklyn Bridge Park Opens, Slightly." *New York Times*, March 22, 2010.

Nicolas, Joanne. "Elected Officials Close to a Deal on Piers 1–5." *Brooklyn Heights Press & Cobble Hill News*, April 1, 1991.

Nolan, James. "New York Legislators Charge Agency Is Partial to New Jersey Piers." *Journal of Commerce*, September 21, 1987.

Oser, Alan S. "Perspectives: Downtown Brooklyn; Coming Attractions for Office Tenants." *New York Times*, June 28, 1987.

Otey, Anne-Marie. "Borough Hall Likes 'Reuse' Option, Wants Authority to Pursue Plan: Golden to Meet with Officials on Piers Proposal." *Phoenix*, April 4, 1991.

——. "New Threat on Piers." *Phoenix*, April 16, 1992.

"Park Coalition Names Albert Butzel President; Changes Raise Question of Co-work with LDC." *Brooklyn Heights Press & Cobble Hill News*, October 13, 1999.

Parker, Matthew. "Brooklyn Bridge Park Post-Hurricane Update from Regina Myer." *Brooklyn Heights Blog*, November 3, 2012.

Pineda Revilla, Beatrice. "History of the Fulton Ferry Landing." The Sixth Borough: Redefining Brooklyn's Waterfront: Brooklyn Heights. http://thesixthborough .weebly.com/history-of-fulton-ferry-landing.html.

Polsky, Carol. "Battle over City's Waterfront." *Newsday*, July 1986.

"Port Authority in Port Biz for Bucks, Pier Panel Quizzes Agency Reps on 'Profit' Motive." *Brooklyn Paper*, January 23–29, 1988.

"Port Authority Moves to Open Pier Area for Development." *Phoenix*, January 11, 1988.

"Port Authority Pier Planning Action Angers Heights Group." *Brooklyn Paper*, October 24–30, 1987.

"Port Authority Transfers Piers to Brooklyn Bridge Park." *Brooklyn Progress*, June–July 2006.

Portlock, Sarah. "'Pop' Over." *Brooklyn Paper*, October 2, 2008.

"Purchase Building Demise Angers Many." *Brooklyn Heights Courier*, February 27, 2006.

"Residents Push State for Brooklyn Bridge Park Creation." *Brooklyn Heights Courier*, March 21–April 3, 1994.

Revkin, Andrew C. "Pataki Lists Tracts to Protect." *New York Times*, November 22, 1995.

"The River Café Celebrates Its 30th Birthday." *Brooklyn Daily Eagle*, July 5, 2006.

Rogoznica, June. "Power Players of the Waterfront." *Round-Up*, May 1987.

Rohde, David. "It's a Park, It's a Lumberyard." *New York Times*, January 19, 1997.

——. "Neighborhood Report: Downtown Brooklyn/Brooklyn Heights—Update; Lumberyard Can Remain Park's Unlikely Center." *New York Times*, February 2, 1997.

——. "Neighborhood Report: Fulton Ferry; Fulton Landing Plan Rises from the Ashes for Another Try." *New York Times*, June 15, 1997.

Scales, Claude. "Tobacco Warehouse Meeting Marked by Controversy." *Brooklyn Heights Blog*, November 16, 2010.

Schneider, Martin L. *Battling for Brooklyn Heights: The Fight for New York's First Historic District*. New York: Brooklyn Heights Association, 2009.

"Selling Brooklyn Bridge Park." *New York Times,* February 13, 2005.

Shorto, Russell. *The Island at the Center of the World: The Epic Story of Dutch Manhattan and the Forgotten Colony That Shaped America*. New York: Vintage, 2004.

Stull, Elizabeth. "Foes Sue to Stop the Park." *Brooklyn Heights Press & Cobble Hill News*, May 25, 2006.

Tabor, Mary B. W. "Despite Opposition, Agency Plans to Sell Brooklyn Piers to Private Developer." *New York Times*, April 3, 1992.

——. "Port Authority Pulls Back from Sale of Waterfront." *New York Times*, April 8, 1992.

Tippins, Sherill. *The February House: The Story of W. H. Auden, Carson McCullers, Paul and Jane Bowles, Benjamin Britten and Gypsy Rose Lee, Under One Roof in Wartime America*. New York: Houghton Mifflin, 2005.

"To Extend the Piers: New York Dock Company Begins Work in the East River." *Brooklyn Eagle*, June 15, 1902.

"Tracks, Piers, Factories and Warehouses Make the Wheels of Industry Go 'Round." *Brooklyn Eagle*, May 30, 1936.

Van Valkenburgh, Michael. "Perspective: How My Firm Saved Brooklyn Bridge Park from Sandy's Fury." *Innovation by Design*, October 25, 2013.

Wagner, Robert F., Jr. "New York City Waterfront: Changing Land Use and Prospects for Urban Development." In *Urban Waterfront Lands*, edited by Committee on Urban Waterfront Lands, 78–99. Washington, D.C.: National Academy of Sciences, 1980.

Waite, Thomas L. "Pier Redevelopment Plans Stir Concern." *New York Times*, May 1, 1998.

Waldman, Amy. "Neighborhood Report: Brooklyn Waterfront; One Park, Many Squabbles." *New York Times*, January 25, 1998.

Whelan, Tensie. "In Brooklyn, a Stunning Design That's All Wrong" [editorial]. *New York Times*, May 31, 1999.

Whelan, Tensie, and John Watts. "Letter: Walentas' Plan 'Inappropriate.'" *Brooklyn Heights Press & Cobble Hill News*, June 17, 1999.

Whitman, Walt. "Crossing Brooklyn Ferry." In *The Complete Poems*, edited by Francis Murphy, 189–95. New York: Penguin, 1986.

Winslow, George. "Will Watchtower Development Block Our Promenade View?" *Brooklyn Heights Press & Cobble Hill News*, October 31, 1985.

Witt, Stephen. "New Governor Mum on Brooklyn Bridge Park—Spitzer Slaps Gag on ESDC." *Times Ledger*, January 12, 2007.

PLANS AND REPORTS

Brooklyn Bridge Park Development Corporation. *Brooklyn Bridge Park Civic and Land Use Improvement Project: Modified General Project Plan*. New York: Brooklyn Bridge Park Development Corporation, December 18, 2006.

Buckhurst Fish Hutton Katz. *The Future of the Piers: Planning and Design Criteria for Brooklyn Piers 1–6*. New York: Buckhurst Fish Hutton Katz, 1987.

Dongan, Thomas. The Dongan Charter of the City of New York. April 27, 1686. University of California Digital Library.

Empire State Development Corporation. "Historical Resources." In *Final Environmental Impact Statement*. New York: Empire State Development Corporation, December 9, 2010.

Halcyon Ltd. *Development Concepts for the Brooklyn Piers* [Halcyon Report]. Hartford, Conn.: Halcyon, 1985.

Hoffman, Deborah. "The Revitalization of Fulton Ferry: A Prototype of Waterfront Development in New York City." New York University, Graduate School of Public Administration, July 1979.

Landmarks Preservation Commission. *Dumbo Historic District Designation Report*. New York: Landmarks Preservation Commission, December 18, 2007.

—. *Fulton Ferry Historic District Designation Report*. New York: Landmarks Preservation Commission, 1977.

New York City, Office of Downtown Brooklyn Development. *Fulton Ferry*. New York, April 1972.

New York City Charter. "City Planning." Section 197-c: Uniform Land Use Review Procedure. New York, July 2004.

New York City Public Development Corporation. *New York City's Waterfront: A Plan for Development: A Report to the Mayor by the New York City Public Development Corporation*. New York: Public Development Corporation, July 1986.

Praedium Group. *Economic Viability Study: Piers Sector, Brooklyn Bridge Park*. New York: Praedium Group, February 1997.

Schnadelbach Partnership. "Harbor Park: A Maritime and Public Use Development on the Brooklyn Piers." May 1988.

INTERVIEWS

Alschuler, John. Interview by David Shirley and Nancy Webster, July 2, 2015.

Baker, Mark. Interview by David Shirley, February 26, 2014.

Benepe, Adrian. Interview by David Shirley and Nancy Webster, September 12, 2014.

Bland, Fred. Interview by David Shirley, May 1, 2014.

Bloomberg, Michael R. Written interview by David Shirley and Nancy Webster, July 2015.

Bowe, Nancy. Interview by David Shirley, September 30, 2014.

Brooks, Greg. Interview by David Shirley and Nancy Webster, September 18, 2014.

Butzel, Albert. Interview by David Shirley, September 12, 2014.

Connor, Martin. Interview by David Shirley and Nancy Webster, April 24, 2015.

Crane, Benjamin. Interview by David Shirley, February 28, 2014.

Dadey, Dick. Interview by David Shirley and Nancy Webster, September 11, 2014.

Damon, Candace. Interview by David Shirley and Nancy Webster, April 17, 2014.

Davidson, Peter. Interview by David Shirley and Nancy Webster, April 27, 2015.

Doctoroff, Daniel. Interview by David Shirley, May 18, 2015.

Favuzzi, Maria. Interview by David Shirley, February 25, 2014.

Fisher, Ken. Interview by David Shirley and Nancy Webster, August 25, 2014.

Fox, Tom. Interview by David Shirley, February 27, 2014.

Gelber, Marilyn. Interview by David Shirley and Nancy Webster, August 25, 2014.

Goulder, Cindy. Interview by Nancy Webster, May 12, 2015.

Harris, Patricia. Interview by Nancy Webster, June 30, 2015.

Janner, Irene. Interview by David Shirley and Nancy Webster, August 26, 2014.

Klein, Jennifer. Interview by David Shirley and Nancy Webster, September 17, 2014.

Koval, Marianna. Interview by David Shirley, February 25, 2014.

Kramer, David. Interview by David Shirley and Nancy Webster, September 10, 2014.

Laird, Joshua. Interview by David Shirley and Nancy Webster, October 17, 2014.

Lieber, Robert. Interview by David Shirley and Nancy Webster, April 27, 2015.

Manheim, Anthony. Interview by David Shirley, February 25, 2014.

Montvel-Cohen, Tom. Interview by David Shirley and Nancy Webster, October 26, 2014.

Myer, Regina. Interview by David Shirley and Nancy Webster, August 29, 2014.

Offensend, David. Interview by David Shirley, May 2, 2014.

Parsekian, Robert. Interview by David Shirley and Nancy Webster, September 17, 2014.

Sirefman, Josh. Interview by David Shirley and Nancy Webster, September 30, 2014.

Stone, Franklin. Interview by David Shirley and Nancy Webster, September 11, 2014.

Urbanski, Matt. Interview by David Shirley and Nancy Webster, October 15, 2014.

VanderPutten, Gary. Interview by David Shirley, April 30, 2014.

Van Valkenburgh, Michael. Interview by David Shirley and Nancy Webster, October 15, 2014.

Watts, John. Interview by David Shirley, February 28, 2014.

Webster, Nancy. Interview by David Shirley, September 24, 2014.

Whelan, Tensie. Interview by David Shirley, February 25, 2014.

Witty, Joanne. Interview by David Shirley, October 1, 2014.

LETTERS, MEMOS, MINUTES, AND PRESS RELEASES

Brooklyn Bridge Park, Inc. "Eileen's Legacy." Memorandum, April 3, 1997.

Brooklyn Bridge Park, Committee on Alternatives to Housing. Memorandum of Understanding, August 1, 2011.

Brooklyn Bridge Park Coalition. "Gala 'Coming of Age' Benefit." March 29, 1997.

——. "13 Guiding Principles to Govern Redevelopment on the Downtown Brooklyn Waterfront." June 29, 1992.

Brooklyn Bridge Park Corporation. "BBP Releases RFP for Residential Development at BBP That Will Provide Affordable Housing and Funding for Park." Press release, May 13, 2014.

Brooklyn Chamber of Commerce, Waterfront Development Committee. Meeting minutes, March 25, 1991.

Brooklyn Heights Association. Newsletter, Spring 1986.

——. Newsletter, Fall 1986.

——. Newsletter, Winter 1989.

Brooklyn Heights Association, Board of Governors. Annual Meeting minutes, May 10, 1984.

——. Annual Meeting minutes, February 5, 1985.

——. Annual Meeting minutes, Spring 1985.

——. Annual Meeting minutes, February 25, 1986.

——. Annual Meeting minutes, February 24, 1987.

——. Annual Meeting minutes, February 9, 1988.

Brooklyn Heights Coalition. Meeting minutes, April 8, 1990.

Community Board 2, Planning and District Development Committee. Meeting minutes, November 11 and 28, 1988. In Scott M. Hand and Otis Pratt Pearsall, "The Origins of Brooklyn Bridge Park, 1986–1988." 2014. Published on the Brooklyn Historical Society catablog. http://brooklynhistory.org/docs/OriginsBrooklyn BridgePark.pdf.

Favuzzi, Maria. Maria Favuzzi to Anthony Manheim and Tom Fox, March 11, 1990.

Golden, Howard. Howard Golden to Anthony Manheim, April 16, 1991.

——. Howard Golden to Mario Cuomo, December 4, 1989.

Hand, Scott. Scott Hand to Earl Weiner, May 16, 1986.

——. Scott Hand to Philip LaRocco, August 25, 1986.

LaRocco, Philip, and Alair Townsend. Press release, February 18, 1986.

Manheim, Anthony. Anthony Manheim to the Brooklyn Bridge Park Coalition Working Group, October 14, 1990.

——. Anthony Manheim to Frank McNally, March 6, 1987.

——. Anthony Manheim to John Watts, Ted Liebman, et al. Memorandum, July 1991.

——. Anthony Manheim to John Watts, Terry Schnadelbach, et al., January 22, 1991.

——. Anthony Manheim to Mario Cuomo, January 7, 1994.

——. Anthony Manheim to Martin Connor and Eileen Dugan, February 19, 1993.

——. Anthony Manheim to the members of the Brooklyn Bridge Park Coalition. "Summary Progress Report," February 4, 1993.

——. Anthony Manheim to the members of the Brooklyn Bridge Park Coalition. "Summary Progress Report," February 23, 1993.

——. Anthony Manheim to Scott Hand, Otis Pratt Pearsall, et al., November 10, 1986.

——. Anthony Manheim to Scott Hand and Otis Pearsall, July 22, 1986.

——. Anthony Manheim to Scott Hand and Otis Pearsall, July 28, 1986.

——. Notice of General Meeting of the Brooklyn Bridge Park Coalition, July 9, 1993.

Manheim, Anthony, and Tom Fox. Anthony Manheim and Tom Fox to Howard Golden, May 21, 1991.

New York City, Office of the Mayor. "Mayor Bloomberg, Governor Paterson, Senator Squadron and Assembly Member Millman Announce Agreement on Development, Funding and Governance of Brooklyn Bridge Park." Press release, March 10, 2010.

——. "Mayor Bloomberg Announces Approval of Development That Will Allow for Expansion and Funding of Brooklyn Bridge Park." Press release, July 21, 2013.

——. "Mayor Michael R. Bloomberg and Governor George E. Pataki Announce Creation of Brooklyn Bridge Park." Press release, May 2, 2002.

New York State, Office of the Governor. "Governor Paterson Announces Major Step for Brooklyn Bridge Park." Press release, June 20, 2009.

New York State Assembly, Office of Assemblywoman Eileen C. Dugan. "Assemblywoman Dugan and Senator Connor Secure a Half Million Dollar State Grant for the Brooklyn Bridge Park Coalition." Press release, June 23, 1996.

Pearsall, Otis. Memorandum, July 14, 1986.

——. Memorandum, November 28, 1988.

Port Authority of New York and New Jersey. "Brooklyn—Port Authority Marine Terminal—Brooklyn Bridge Park Coalition—New Lease." Board minutes, August 28, 1997.

——. "Port Authority Marks 50th Anniversary of Containerization at Port of New York and New Jersey." Press release, April 25, 2006.

Stanton, Judy. Judy Stanton to Scott Hand, February 6, 1987.

INDEX